Penguin Education

Teaching and Learning in Higher Education
Second Edition

Ruth Beard

D1426803

Teaching and Learning in Higher Education

Second Edition

Ruth Beard

Penguin Books

Penguin Books Ltd, Harmondsworth,
Middlesex, England
Penguin Books Inc, 7110 Ambassador Road,
Baltimore, Md 21207, USA
Penguin Books Australia Ltd,
Ringwood, Victoria, Australia

First published 1970
Second edition 1972
Copyright © Ruth Beard, 1970, 1972

Made and printed in Great Britain by
Hazell Watson & Viney Ltd, Aylesbury, Bucks
Set in Linotype Baskerville

Contents

Preface

It is pleasant to be asked to prepare the second edition of a book less than two years old in a field which until recently commanded few readers. The last few years have seen a rapid growth of interest in teaching and learning in higher education and in the development of organizations designed to foster their improvement. This is due partly to pressures on university and college teachers to increase their effectiveness, but partly also to the collective efforts of enthusiastic teachers with concern for their subjects and for the welfare of their students. For instance, the Education Division of the Chemical Society contains over fifteen hundred teachers from universities and colleges. During the last two years the majority of universities have made arrangements for at least an initial training of new teachers. Some have given responsibility for this to a working party of senior teachers, others have invited an existing body, such as a Department of Education, to organize suitable activities, and a growing number is setting up a unit having the specific purpose of providing courses for their teachers and of engaging in educational research. In London the small unit which was originally financed by the Leverhulme Trust in 1965 has four additional staff since the University voted a grant to the Institute of Education for this purpose in 1969.

The augmented text of the second edition of *Teaching and Learning in Higher Education* includes the work of some of these units in addition to a growing number of teaching innovations introduced by enterprising individuals or departments. In addition, I have made a number of references to the very interesting work of the Open University and to research at one of the numerous units which have been set up in

Europe to develop new teaching methods. However, there are few references to the considerable volume of publications from the United States where there is growing concern with the purpose of higher education, causes of student discontent, programmes for disadvantaged students, interpersonal relations in the classroom and other questions which are raised in moving towards universal higher education. In Britain, smaller numbers of more highly selected students, and our better staff–student ratio, protect us from the more acute manifestations of problems experienced in the States; and it is to be hoped that our growing interest in teaching and learning may enable us to evolve solutions to our problems as they arise.

Although fundamental and complex problems must necessarily be mentioned, I hope that this book will provide sufficient guidance to indicate a variety of ways in which teaching can be improved immediately – by eradication of errors, the use of new methods or through modification of courses. Despite the hopes of a few teachers that all the answers will be supplied in one course, or one book, it is no more possible to train a teacher by simply making him read a book than it is to train a physicist, engineer or historian in this way. A text can provide a coherent background of concepts and principles where these exist (and so far they do not for teaching and learning), or supply knowledge about techniques, but to teach successfully each individual must practise the skill, receiving feedback on his performance, in order to discover his own particular abilities and failings. Yet, however great his skill becomes, if he is teaching a curriculum which is ill-suited to present needs, his students may remain apathetic; and if he uses methods at variance with the ways in which his students learn, no amount of practice or use of technical aids is likely to add greatly to his success. He should, therefore, be aware of modern developments and understand how students learn in order to adapt his curriculum and teaching methods accordingly.

For these reasons this book is concerned with much more than teaching techniques or 'teaching tips'. It stresses, in the first place, the need to redefine the purposes of higher education and course objectives and to relate these with methods in teaching and assessment. Secondly, the kinds of learning which occur in higher education are discussed at some length for, despite the paucity of research, existing evidence should at least convince teachers of the need to vary their methods. Thirdly, teaching techniques are discussed, drawing on findings from inquiries and researches as well as innovations in teaching which have proved successful; and, finally, the limitations of methods of assessment are considered at some length and their value is discussed in relation to various objectives in teaching and learning. In these ways it is hoped that the reader will not only discover new teaching techniques to improve his students' learning, and ways of evaluating their performance and his own, but will also become more sensitive to deficiencies in the organization of courses which give rise to discontent by reducing the experience of learning from one which is exciting, illuminating and a sound preparation for living to one of cramming facts and figures for examinations.

In conclusion, I should like to thank those who helped in the preparation of this volume and to acknowledge illustrative material which I have been allowed to use in the text and short sections from articles which I have published elsewhere. In writing the first edition I was indebted particularly to my niece Sarah Davies for numerous suggestions as to how to improve its clarity and style, and to her husband D. K. Davies, my colleagues Derek May and Kay Pole, and Elizabeth Oliver, secretary to the Unit 1965-9, for reading and commenting on some parts of the text. I am grateful also to secretaries Angela Gannicott, Judy Hallows and Gwen Heath who have each assisted in typing or carefully checking parts of the text and references.

In Chapter 2, Drs E. R. Williams and E. R. Wooding have permitted me to reproduce a diagram from their article in *Physics Education*; there is also an outline of the objectives of Mr M. Holland's course in French language which appeared in the Unit's fourth conference report, and illustrative items from complete schemes of objectives prepared by staff of this Unit: by David Warren Piper for a course in design education and, with Mrs Dallas of King's College, for the training of biology teachers, and by Kay Pole, our Research Officer financed by the Leverhulme Trust, with a working party of university teachers, for undergraduate physics. In addition Arthur Marwick and The Open University Press have kindly permitted me to quote Aims and Objectives from pages 5 and 6 of the Correspondence Course *What History is and Why it is Important*.

I have also referred a number of times to objectives in the teaching of history suggested by Professor Maxwell and her colleagues in discussion at Rhodes University. I am indebted to Dr M. L. J. Abercrombie for the use of a negative of the ships' boiler illustrated in Chapter 3. Dr Crombag and his colleagues at the University of Leyden have permitted me to reproduce in Chapter 7 a network which they devised as part of a method to guide students of law in problem solving. *Points to aid essay writers* quoted in Chapter 8, were issued at a course for new lecturers by Dr Leba Goldstein. In Chapter 7 I have used again the description of programmed texts which were originally written for the *Physiotherapist*, while in Chapter 9 I have drawn on the material and repeated some sections of the paper I read at the Universities Conference in Spring 1969 on Assessment of Undergraduate Performance, convened by the Committee of the Vice-Chancellors and Principals of the Universities of the United Kingdom and the Association of University Teachers. At intervals throughout the text I have inserted paragraphs already published by the Society for Research into Higher Education Ltd in two monographs.

I am most grateful to all of these bodies or individuals for their kindness in allowing me to do this.

Chapter 1
Planning Courses and Curricula

The changing situation

The clamour of complaint about teaching in higher education and, more especially, about teaching methods in universities and technical colleges, serves to direct attention away from the important reorientation which has recently begun. The complaints, of course, are not unjustified. In dealing piecemeal with problems arising from rapidly developing subject matter, many teachers have allowed courses to become overcrowded, or too specialized, or they have presented students with a number of apparently unrelated courses failing to stress common principles. Many, again, have not developed new teaching methods to deal adequately with larger numbers of students, and the new audio-visual techniques tend to remain in the province of relatively few enthusiasts despite their great potential for class and individual teaching.

However, this is hardly surprising, for until recently, the majority of teachers in higher education have not been offered any courses on teaching methods and those they now have are usually too brief to be really effective. Moreover, it is well known that in universities, prowess in teaching contributes little towards promotion in comparison with that in research. Development of new teaching techniques is therefore a spare time occupation even when interest and the potential value of a new method would seem to justify intensive work during a term or a longer period.

In the absence of provision for discussion of teaching methods, past attitudes persist. Some teachers still subscribe to the view, more commonly held in the last century by those who catered for the leisured classes, that a university education should not be concerned in any sense with vocational training; to these teachers education consists in 'enlargement of the mind' which comes about through contact with scholarly and cultured companions. This has been termed the 'philosophical view' in an interesting article by Hunter (1971) concerning law teaching and features as the 'country-house-party model' in Becher's discussion of the effectiveness of higher education (1971). There is, of course, some merit in this approach for very able students who can direct their own studies independently and who have acquired standards of criticism to apply to their work. But as a method it is inefficient in transmitting these skills to less able, or less well-prepared, students even if a high staff–student ratio and concern for students' welfare results in ample tutorial supervision. Moreover, it seems reasonable to question the value of an enlargement of the mind which leads to uncongenial limitations of prospects for the rest of life, as it does for many young women who must accept teaching or secretarial posts unless they have resources to undertake further extensive training. Nevertheless this view met with little criticism so long as the majority of students were either clever or affluent and not too seriously occupied with preparation for a career. Today, however, pressure of numbers tends to make tutoring more difficult; competitive selection, together with public financing of the colleges, combine to exclude affluent dilettantes; and the serious students who remain no longer regard higher education as a privilege but as a social right and expect correspondingly more of their teachers. Thus in an increasingly professional world amateurism in teaching is no longer acceptable.

An attitude of an opposite kind, more common among teachers in vocational schools, and of the applied sciences, who were probably themselves taught in such schools before related theoretical studies had greatly expanded, leads them to concentrate on drilling students in information and practical skills. They see no need to provoke students into thinking about the subject but tend to maintain, on the contrary, that acquisition of 'a body of knowledge' is essential before any genuine thinking is possible. This, too, is an attitude which students accept with resignation at best, for increasingly they are coming to believe that higher studies should not be narrowly useful but should also be educational in a wide sense. Other university teachers still expect to be offered as students only potential scholars who will devote themselves exclusively to acquisition of knowledge and development of prowess in research. They tend to neglect students who seek a higher education with other kinds of advancement in mind or who take their subject as a subsidiary study. Although Hunter calls this the 'scientific view' it is commonly seen in arts departments also. Even where attitudes are less extreme there is often the same tendency to repeat uncritically teaching methods which the teachers themselves experienced as students. Little thought is given to the purposes of higher education in its social context, nor is an analysis made in any detail of the requirements of the professions in which the students will serve. Yet there are many developments which indicate a need for new approaches towards teaching and learning. The chief areas of change derive from professional demands, particularly in the sciences, for more broadly based knowledge, or knowledge from several fields, and a greatly increased need for skill in communication and ability to cooperate effectively in teams. To cite a few examples – some areas now develop so rapidly that knowledge is out of date in as little as two years so that the preparation of textbooks is impossible; the National Register of Scientific and Technical Personnel in the United States lists nearly a thousand distinct specializations in the natural sciences alone, whereas twenty years earlier there were about fifty. So vast is the increase in available information and the rapidity with which it becomes out of date that a new emphasis in students' learning of skill is required; such as how to obtain information and to apply it to new situations, instead of the acquisition of a 'body of knowledge' which was formerly considered essential and has sometimes been accepted as sufficient. In addition it demands training for flexibility as new specializations develop; in industry, for example, rapid changes in techniques and developments in knowledge result in demands for scientists with a broad background in science and the capacity to respond flexibly to new materials or methods.

The need to prepare students to cooperate with specialists

in other fields has also grown considerably during the last twenty years. For example, architects in planning a new town or even a single school or hospital must cooperate not only with colleagues but also with officials of local authorities, engineers or borough surveyors, builders and their clients; industrial designers and commercial artists have similar problems and doctors in large town practices need to cooperate with personnel in a number of ancillary services. Indeed, in almost all professions, individuals are called on to cooperate to an increasing extent, perhaps by working in teams or in communicating information to committees consisting of specialists in other fields who make different assumptions, employ different vocabularies and concepts and have somewhat different modes of thinking. Moreover, the widespread use of new techniques, especially television, has led to a demand for a high standard in oral reporting. It is therefore of some considerable importance that communication skills should be fostered in the majority of courses in higher education and it would undoubtedly be beneficial for students and their teachers to have some knowledge of group dynamics.

These considerations point to a reorientation in higher education, in particular in the education of average and less able students. Where formerly the progress of many of them was deemed satisfactory if they could reproduce a body of knowledge or acquire skills with minimal understanding, increasingly more is expected of them. One might say that we formerly trained guides who, as teachers, could direct their pupils along the same paths as those they themselves took or, in industry, used their knowledge to solve familiar kinds of problems, whereas today we need to explore. An explorer must be more resourceful than a guide, capable of working effectively in different conditions from those in which he was trained, learning rapidly from his own experience or that of others and taking responsibility when he has the greatest skill, but accepting other people's leadership if a different expertise is needed. This requires that he should be skilful in communication and have insight into personal relationships. It does not imply, of course, that every student will have to work continuously in cooperation with others, indeed, the value of individual resourcefulness is greater even than it formerly was, but additional skills and qualities are needed.

Moreover, these requirements of students involve new ways of assessing performance. A guide is performing adequately if he reproduces his information correctly and shows how to apply it – if this is needed – in known situations. Many examinations for honours degrees still require little more than this. The value of an explorer, however, lies only partly in his information as such but more in his ingenuity in dealing with the unexpected, flexibility in facing new circumstances, ability to obtain relevant information, capacity to inspire confidence and to promote cooperation, and so on. Thus in evaluating his prowess, skills and attitudes will be given as much, or more, credit than the amount of his information.

In teaching for adaptation to continuous change, therefore, students need to be given a considerable measure of responsibility and to experience situations and problems, individually or in groups, to which they have not been told the solutions; discussion on a basis of equality with fellow students and teachers (so far as possible) should also play a greater part in their education for they must learn to depend less on figures of authority and to profit from criticism from equals or even inferiors. Thus we may expect that in most areas less time will be given to lecturing whilst more will be assigned to group methods and individual work, teachers being viewed less as distant authorities but rather as leaders of teams in which students are junior partners.

At this point it may be pertinent to consider whether the best kind of university education already meets these requirements, for it was developed to train an élite capable of advancing knowledge and administrators skilled in the art of communication and government. Its broad purposes, as usually accepted, could hardly be better expressed than by Sir James Mountford in *British Universities* (1966):

This brings us to what is the most important point about the nature of teaching and education at a university level. It must necessarily provide the student with a body of positive knowledge which enhances his store of learning and in part equips him for his career in later life. But it also has another and more notable attribute. It inculcates in the student an attitude of mind which regards the critical assessment of facts and values as more important than dogmas, and which holds that a grasp of underlying principles is more valuable than the accumulation of information or the acquisition of skills and techniques. A university expects that at the end of their courses its students will not merely be able to comprehend the extent and significance of what is already known within their own field, but will be receptive to what is new, eager to explore it, show the ability to cope with it and – above all – be able to work confidently on their own. By entering a university a student has undertaken to accept a rigorous intellectual discipline and to be more than a passive receptacle for information, much of which in many subjects may be out of date within twenty years. To the limit of his capacity he is trained to collect evidence for himself and form a balanced judgement about it. He fortifies his ability to think for himself; he refuses to accept orthodoxies simply because they are orthodox; and when he dissents, he does so on the basis not of prejudice but of reason. This is what good teaching achieves in a university.

Thus he enumerates many of the intellectual qualities required in dealing with rapid developments in knowledge. Moreover it seems reasonable to assume, although he does not explicitly say so, that the qualities he describes here should result in good understanding of personal interactions, interest in applying knowledge or in employing new techniques and capacity for innovation. Nevertheless there is an assumption here which is not borne out by research; that information about a subject suffices to enable the learner to apply his knowledge. In fact, evidence suggests that individuals may be able to recite extensive information but fail to apply it or, as is more commonly recognized, may learn how to behave in practical situations but lack the skill to explain their behaviour verbally. Even where theoretical or practical work is integrated, as in teacher training, extreme instances of both kinds still exist. For intelligent application of pertinent research a grasp of both aspects is essential. Yet too often in social sciences emasculated courses are devised which offer information without practice, so providing opportunity to discuss or to write about a subject while neglecting the skills which contribute to its growth. Thus we may find a department of archaeology which offers no field work and no study of human groups, departments of political science and local government which offer three years' theoretical studies without requirement of any relevant experience, and so on. Perhaps this would not be a matter for serious complaint if practical courses followed theoretical training, as clinical medical training follows the Second M.B. course or a graduate course in sciences; but, where it is possible for a teacher to lack a basis of experience in his subject, it is hardly surprising if students – and especially mature ones – complain of dull, unrealistic courses and invite the writer to suggest how they should be redesigned.

The development of thinking in students

Accumulating evidence suggests that some of the students' difficulties arise from characteristics in thinking which are common to many first-year students, if not to the majority of undergraduates, whatever their field of study. An investigation made among sociology students identified a number of these characteristics (Gibson, 1970). Students had a notion that theories and hypotheses were falsified when they had been shown not to apply in certain circumstances, they over-generalized experimental results, failed to recognize particular experiments as building blocks in a wider theory, failed through lack of knowledge to give precise meanings to terms such as 'balance', 'attitude' and 'prejudice', rejected quantitative data so regressing large tracts of social psychology back into philosophy, and were confused as to what constituted evidence. Gibson notes a corroborative observation by Peters (1958) concerning students' tendency to seek highly general theories which are logically impossible, and quotes Veness (1968) who spoke of 'concepts so lacking in form and content that they can be conveniently squeezed from the tube in any shape required.'

These observations together with those of teachers in other fields indicate four main kinds of limitation. First, students are very commonly said to have a poor understanding of concepts. In an inquiry at Surrey into students' mathematical and scientific knowledge on entry to university, O'Connell, Wilson and Elton (1969) found that although students had a knowledge of facts and formulae sufficient to form a good basis for university work, they were weak in concepts and ideas. The majority of the students were unclear about the concepts 'vector' and 'scalar', they had hazy ideas about exponentials and wave motion and showed some confusion of thought about 'diffraction' and 'interference'. The authors attributed these deficiencies to failure on the part of school teachers to discuss concepts. Physicists in London discussing their objectives in teaching also commented on students' weaknesses in comprehending some concepts, citing 'inertia' and 'entropy' as often poorly understood. A group of historians attempting to make a similiar outline of objects spoke of the need to assist students in understanding the basic concepts of the subject, giving 'civilization' as an instance.

Secondly, many students expect a greater degree of accuracy than is reasonably attainable; for instance, they believe that it is possible to make a 'correct' translation from one language to another, exactly conveying the original meaning; or, if disabused of this belief, they hope at least to attain the 'best' translation. Students of science and mathematics expect to obtain 'the right answer' and continue calculations or experiments in order to obtain an unrealistic degree of precision.

A third prevalent characteristic is seen in the belief that theories are 'true' or that authorities are above criticism. The historians I have just mentioned try to wean their students from a belief that authorities are infallible by showing that even great scholars may disagree, or by drawing attention to errors, through study, for instance, of Pirenne's thesis on the dating of the collapse of the classical world. Physicists comment on the distress caused to some students when well-established theories are questioned; like the students of sociology studied by Gibson they feel that a theory which has an exception can no longer be trusted. A desire for certainty or for something 'absolute' and definitive to hold on to may be seen even amongst mature students when they find their beliefs and assumptions effectively challenged. As one mature student of education said despairingly after taking part in a philosophical discussion 'If everything is relative, nothing is true, nothing matters!' Her difficulty seemed to arise from an unquestioning dependence on authority, in this instance vested in 'absolute truths', to which everything could be conveniently referred, and her assumption that, in their absence, no meaningful judgements could be made. Where students of sociology are reported to be confused and frustrated early in their university studies, it may be that they have suffered similar disillusionment on finding that their chosen subject offers no panacea to solve the world's problems but is full of uncertainties.

Fourthly, many students have difficulties in handling evidence. Gibson's findings are mainly concerned with this. The historians, too, when discussing their objectives, spoke of the students' need to learn how to consider evidence in order to arrive at a relatively unbiased opinion, resisting the temptation to manipulate evidence to predetermined ends or to reach premature conclusions on some aspects of it. Abercrombie had noted limitations of similar kinds in first-year students of biological sciences in 1948 (1966). Like Elton and his colleagues she attributed this to the teaching they received in their schools or at college:

As a teacher of zoology I had been disappointed in the effects that learning about science seemed to have on habits of thinking. It was found that students who had satisfied the examiners for the Higher School Certificate and were well grounded in the facts of biology, physics and chemistry, did not necessarily use scientific ways of thinking to solve problems presented in a slightly new way. They might be able, for instance, to recite all the lines of evidence for the theory of evolution but yet be unable to use this material to defend the theory in argument with an anti-evolutionist. They might know what the function of a certain organ is believed to be, but did not always know why, nor did they clearly understand on what kind of evidence a belief of that sort is based. When asked to describe what they saw in dissecting an animal, or in looking through a microscope, they often did not distinguish sufficiently sharply between what was there and what they had been taught 'ought' to be there. The effect on students of two or three years' teaching at the university was no more encouraging. It seemed that scientific ways of thinking did not automatically result from learning the facts of science and that a more radical approach to training was necessary.

Thus, although psychologists who devised intelligence tests in the earlier part of the century believed that intelligence reached its full development at sixteen years, and Piaget's investigations into children's thinking cease at this age, possibly because he shares this belief, there is evidence from a number of sources that further developments in thinking occur during early maturity at least among students engaged in higher studies. Whether these developments result from the greater demands made on individuals as they approach maturity, from a process of physical and intellectual maturation relatively independent of schooling and social demands, as a result of higher education, or a combination of these, is perhaps a matter for investigation. It certainly seems probable that an education which demands mature modes of thinking will hasten the process although, as we shall see in Chapter 3, tolerance of uncertainty is closely related with personality characteristics. Where students are required to do little more than to learn 'a body of knowledge' or to quote the opinions of authorities or information dictated by teachers, it seems probable that their development in thinking will be inhibited. And, in common with children who are given work unsuited to their growing capacities, they may become apathetic or work only for extraneous rewards such as good examination results.

Those who are acquainted with the work of Piaget concerning the development of children's thinking from infancy to adolescence (Inhelder and Piaget, 1959, or see Beard, 1969 for a simple outline), may be interested to consider the students' thinking in relation to the development he describes in adolescence. His 'period of formal operations' begins at about twelve years and is concluded at about sixteen. He believes that it is initiated by increasing collaboration which involves exchange of viewpoints and discussion of their merits before joint control of a group is possible. In this way children develop a habit of considering points of view previously alien to them and thus progress to making use of assumptions simply for the sake of argument. This leads to ability to make hypotheses and to go beyond the tangible, finite and familiar to conceive the infinitely large or infinitely small, or to invent imaginary systems. Exchange of viewpoints also leads adolescents to mentally survey many possibilities, to give full definition, to look for general laws, or to form theories, and to recognize that rules and conventions may differ among different groups of people. To attain mature modes of thinking, they need to extend this range of achievements. Where as adolescents they are content to give good definitions, as students they must learn to appreciate the difficulties inherent in defining some abstract concepts. The abilities adolescents attain, to see many viewpoints and to solve problems systematically, must be fused and extended in interpreting or criticizing experimental data. And the realization which comes in early adolescence that rules are made by adults and so may be discarded must develop into a greater detachment from authority figures, or of theories, into recognition of their essential fallibility.

Piaget's view that higher levels of thinking are initiated by discussion is borne out by two experiments in the teaching of sciences, but the methods might be applied in other fields. Abercrombie (1960) used discussion methods in which she withdrew from the role of authority figure to that of observer and occasional commentator. In this way she left the students to educate each other through argument with their peers. Subject matter for discussion was provided by an activity in which each student committed his thoughts to paper. Epstein (1970) developed his method initially to interest a group of intelligent seventeen-year-old non-scientists in the advances of modern biology. The students learned about a subject, for example photosynthetic organisms, through discussion of recent research papers with teachers working in the field. They discussed how a biologist went about solving a problem, considered definitions of words and concepts which they then classified – thirty terms being clarified in this way on the first day of the course, since the original terms chosen required classification of other terms. Each concept was explained in fairly simple experimental terms whenever possible. If that took too long, it was explained superficially but with as little misleading information as possible. By the end of one week Epstein could comment 'As I pondered the events of the first week . . . it occurred to me that the students had gone through the definitions and explanations of perhaps fifteen terms. This began to look like a considerable accomplishment . . .' During successive discussions an increasing number of students 'caught on' and became 'enthralled with both the science and their ability to understand it'. A later course of a similar kind with science specialists took longer as they were so eager to obtain detailed information. Some of these students were able to follow graduate colloquia after only seven weeks in college, having reached the frontiers of insight and knowledge as well as the ability to read journals. Few courses lead to so much initial enthusiasm or to such considerable advances in understanding. The method has now had some successful trials in economics, chemistry and philosophy (Epstein, 1972).

Criticisms of higher education

In fact, the volume of criticism from teachers, their students and future employers suggests a need to re-examine higher education in all its aspects. Scientists in industry comment that many young scientists and engineers are unsuitably trained, lacking both broadly based scientific knowledge to enable them to transfer from one field to another, and the capacity to solve problems systematically while keeping records of their findings. Managers employing young scientists as their juniors complain that they often prove incapable of making decisions on incomplete evidence but desire certainty – which is unattainable – before they take action. Poor ability to cooperate in teams, or to communicate effectively with colleagues, is frequently mentioned by junior staff or those in ancillary services who find themselves inadequately or inappropriately used by their seniors; and it is seen also in the discontent of those who must work in cooperation but who have become habituated in school and college to working in isolation for their own advantage. Many teachers in universities and technical colleges complain that students are not interested in the work as such but come to college because it is the accepted thing to do; they also find that the majority of students are interested only in passing examinations in the hope of obtaining lucrative posts. The students' lack of direction perhaps suggests a need for more effective careers guidance, but in the matter of examinations the power for change is in the hands of the teachers. For, if they assess everything of importance in the course, students' concern to gain a qualification will assure that they give due weight to every aspect of their studies. It is the narrowly conceived examination, perhaps demanding little more than memorization from lecture notes and books, which concentrates students' attention within a limited range and frustrates attempts to interest them in more enlightened courses and teaching methods.

Criticisms by students have recently become more far ranging and more vociferous. In their views, although most teachers would probably subscribe to the aims outlined by Sir James Mountford, not only is teaching often poor but courses are sometimes designed in a manner antagonistic to the development of understanding.

The students' complaints

Whereas the teachers point to the problem of students who are vocationally orientated with no wish to broaden their studies, Marris (1964) in his inquiry among students of three universities and a technical college found rather the reverse:

. . . you want to do so much, and you're only given the chance to do so little – for instance attending lectures in the evenings by other societies, reading more widely. I can remember when I first came up, the Vice Chancellor said that the essence of university was that you should be intellectually excited. But if you are, there is very little chance of fulfilling or satisfying that excitement (Southampton lawyer).

The complaints of those who cover too wide a field in the time available show that some students have little time to think or to grasp essentials:

Part one irritated me a lot, we were doing something of every subject, not getting any interest out of it – just tricks and dodges. If you could set a twenty-minute question on it in an examination, it was in (Cambridge engineer).

The trouble is, there are so many branches of civil engineering and you do need an understanding of the whole field: it would be difficult to specialize any more. But you need a bit more time to think about the basic principles. There's a fantastic amount of course work – lab.

reports, writing up experiments, questions, drawing work you have to do – and it takes up two-thirds of your time, and leaves you very little time for revision or trying to understand the lecture . . . . It doesn't train you to think, it's just mechanical, it's trotted out to you all the time, as though you were machines (Northampton).

The latter complaint is one of the many which arises from over-loaded syllabuses. In view of the rapidity with which knowledge grows in most fields this is a problem which might be universal but for the determination of some departments to revise syllabuses regularly, casting out less valuable content, reorganizing what remains to give a better understanding, or offering choices between the ever-increasing number of topics. However the introduction of more efficient teaching techniques may make it possible to cover more ground – and with greater interest – in the time available.

Nor is it only lecturers who speak of spoon-feeding with disfavour; students also complain of it:

It would be better for us if we did more for ourselves. In practical work, for instance, we're given a chart showing us exactly what we're to do. You could take a chap off Trumpington St and give him the sheet, and he'd be able to do it (Cambridge engineer).

What I'd like to get out of a lecture is basic principles and enough information for me to go to the library and work up something myself (Northampton).

The attitudes reflected in these comments no doubt account for the quite general preference for projects among students and, in particular, research projects; for these give them an opportunity to study a subject in depth, the excitement of searching for relevant information and evidence, or the satisfaction of exploring a problem, deciding what questions should be answered and setting up experiments accordingly. Well-chosen projects have a coherence that courses containing many subjects tend to lack; they can lead to more profound study of a problem than the superficial, broad coverage of many fields allows, and they may also have more relevance to existing problems in other fields than the intensely specialized courses which some students deplore:

It's bad to become narrower and narrower. I'd prefer a much broader outlook. I've done science all my life, and my knowledge of history and things like that is very limited (Southampton).

I think really I'd prefer it less specialized. As it is, the course deals only with the theoretical branches of maths. I think you should include the ideas of how maths can be applied to science and, at the other extreme, philosophy to the social sciences. I think there is a lack of demonstration of how maths does, in fact, fit in with other subjects — we can't draw barriers around our subjects and put them in little boxes (Leeds).

In some universities, of course, students of mathematics already have opportunities to develop applications in other fields, as mathematics students in colleges of education do, although these are frequently offered only to less able students. There seems to be a case here for providing options allowing the future pure mathematician to study further abstractions while the potential applied mathematician employs his mathematics to solve problems in other areas; this would go some way to meeting the diversity of interest and ability which is found in any large department.

To these criticisms by students must be added the very general one of those in large departments that contact with members of staff is insufficient. In some departments increasing numbers have led teaching staff to feel this themselves and to institute group discussion to supplement lectures, thus giving students the opportunity to discuss problems. The advantages that almost all teaching staff mention in group discussions are that they get to know the students and they obtain feedback on their teaching. One may question, however, whether it is desirable to double the work of staff and students in this way, especially if during the lecture students spend the time writing down subject matter which they have no time to take in. It would be better to devise methods where both objectives are achieved simultaneously wherever this is possible. For example, a shortened lecture followed by questions to which students write answers, and discuss briefly with their neighbours, before putting any outstanding questions to the lecturers, gives the student an opportunity to use, and so better understand, the subject matter. It also allows the lecturer to circulate round the class (if it does not exceed about fifty members) listening to discussion and thereby discovering difficulties and any points which he failed to make clear.

Reports prepared by the students themselves (see British Medical Students Association, 1965; National Union of Students, 1969a, 1969b) and inquiries into teaching (see Australian Vice-Chancellors Committee 1963; P. Marris, 1965; University Grants Committee, 1964) suggest that these discrepancies between intention and achievement in teaching arise from lack of expertise on the part of a substantial proportion of the teachers, from courses which, for various reasons, are not adequately suited to the students' needs, and from examinations which concentrate the students' efforts into a narrow range of skills. The seriousness of the problem varies considerably between subject fields and departments, depending on the rate of development of the subject, the skill of teachers and their awareness of the need for change, and with the numbers and abilities of the students who enter the courses. But the main criticisms are that some courses give students insufficient preparation to meet the demands that will be made of them in their future professions, that many are overcrowded due to the addition of further compulsory topics and that examination systems are often ill-suited to the assessment of students' abilities in the skills and knowledge taught in the courses. In addition, some students wish for more choice as to the content of their studies. In criticizing teaching, both students and investigators point to obvious failures in communication as well as to poor teaching methods arising from lack of knowledge of how students learn.

Some attempts are being made to modify courses comprehensively, taking into account the different aims and objectives appropriate to the field, students' capacities and the effects of methods of assessment on their interest and the direction of their studies. As yet, however, the majority of new courses incorporate modifications of a less ambitious nature.

Courses and curricula

The solution most commonly favoured when subject matter increases is simply to lengthen the corresponding courses. In pure sciences, for example, those who wish to teach in universities or to qualify for higher posts in industry or the Civil Service normally stay to obtain higher degrees before taking up their careers. In the applied sciences a vast increase in relevant theory has led to demands for longer theoretical courses prior to vocational training, or in combination with it. Thus, in medicine there is a growing demand for a three-year course such as the new human biology degree prior to clinical studies. Non-graduate teachers now spend three years in training largely because they can give greater attention to psychology, sociology and the philosophy of education and, since 1968, some students have been able to spend a further year in theoretical studies to obtain the degree of Bachelor of Education. In engineering, a more economical solution – sandwich courses which alternate six-month periods of practical experience in industry with six months of theoretical studies during four years – extends the degree course by a year but produces students already vocationally trained and able to apply theory. Even the relatively new professions such as physiotherapy and social work are demanding longer training not only, as is sometimes supposed, because this will give them higher status, but rather because of the development of the social sciences and the consequent greater demands on their services.

As shown by students' complaints, a danger which too often materializes as courses are extended, is that they become overloaded, leaving the students too little time to think and burdening them with excessive detail; they therefore fail to obtain an over-all grasp of the structure which is needed to give clarity to their learning. Partly for this reason possibilities other than extending courses have been proposed. It has been suggested, for example – and in this instance partly for economy – that students might undertake either two-year degree courses in which they would gain sufficient knowledge of the modes of thinking appropriate in their field, or four-year courses allowing for a greater degree of specialization.

Since the *Swann Report* (1968) and *McCarthy Report* (1968) conclude that, in future, only 40 per cent of students and technologists will require highly specialized knowledge, it is proposed that the majority of science students might take broadly based courses and qualify in the shorter period. However, it would need to be demonstrated that they could attain the requisite scientific skills and attitudes and the ability to educate themselves in this time; for they, no less than the most able students, will need to keep pace with considerable, and in the long term, unpredictable, developments.

Fragmentation of knowledge could also become a major problem when teachers reconsider the structure of the curricula and teaching methods in *toto*; for, in an increasing number of fields, specialists require additional subjects – such as physics for medicine, or statistics and computing for designers – and need to extend their studies to communicate with clients or specialists who provide inter-related services. Students of law now study aspects of sociology; student engineers attend lectures in law, management, administration, etc., while some medical schools have recently established departments of epidemiology and social medicine which are engaged in studying the lives and problems of local people. These demands can result in a proliferation of courses unless fundamental re-thinking is undertaken. It seems essential, therefore, to develop courses and methods in teaching which will provide a common ground-work so far as possible, stressing common principles, so enabling students to integrate knowledge from various sources. In addition to attending a number of apparently unrelated courses, for example, most student engineers undertake projects in which they become aware of interconnexions of technical questions with social, political and economic ones.

A well-established trend in higher education is the development of broader courses with opportunity to specialize in one of two different directions, as in combined honours courses. Another way to achieve flexibility is obtained by the new B.Sc. courses which permit students to select 'units' for study (see Burge, 1968). In one such course, a unit is defined as one-third of the amount of work which any adequately prepared student can reasonably be expected to complete in a year; that is to say, one-third of the total work which every student who is capable of obtaining a degree at all should be able to manage. In order to obtain a degree, students must complete at least nine course units and must satisfy the examiners in a minimum of eight. But able students take as many as twelve units. They therefore have flexibility both as to content and extent of their studies; for example, they may combine the study of chemistry with that of textiles, or physics with biology or biochemistry, dividing the units as they wish. This seems to be generally a desirable development, but some university teachers are beginning to express concern that students sometimes combine easy, and unrelated, options or that they choose unrealistic combinations that may make it difficult for them to obtain posts after graduating. Nevertheless, there is talk of extending this system to arts subjects also on the grounds that it would promote greater breadth of studies as well as allowing for diversity in interest and ability. Thus even within a traditional pattern of teaching an increasing degree of choice will be permitted.

Some teachers are now suggesting that where cooperation between specialists from different fields is ultimately required, there should be a measure of common training for students. Possibly a more realistic and flexible approach in most cases would take the form of work on a problem by students from a number of different departments. In this way they would inevitably discuss their different specialities and experience some of the difficulties which occur as individuals vie for their group interests. Alternatively, cooperation may sometimes be learned by role playing which takes place in the course of simulated exercises. In either case a major advantage lies in the discussion provoked between the students themselves for, if they are to work well in teams, they must be prepared to learn from their equals or even those inferior in status.

Breadth of content is achieved in a B.Sc. degree at Manchester which is designed to give insight into the role of science in relation to politics, economics, industry and philosophy while offering a broad coverage of physics with some engineering and computer programming (Jevons, 1970). A new M.Sc. in the same department requires more extended studies of social issues relating to the sciences.

A method of studying intensively in a single field is described by Parlett and King (1971) who introduced 'concentrated study', i.e. full-time study of a single subject for a short period, in this instance physics, at MIT. It provided an opportunity to rethink, from first principles, how the subject should be taught and enabled instruction to be organized in such a way that it permitted close supervision and intellectual contact between instructor and students. This rearrangement of the course gave time for movies, lectures by visitors, visits to scientific installations when and where appropriate; the students were expected to work in the library and to look at a variety of texts and original literature.

A course of a different kind, concentrating on development of appropriate skills rather than breadth, is beginning at Sussex University School of Molecular Sciences where students can now take a B.Sc. by thesis. It is commonly known as the Eaborn degree after the chairman of science who introduced it.

Of special interest in view of the desire of many students for a greater say in the content of their studies is a course of an unusual kind in an independent school of architecture in London. In this school great importance is attached to the development of individual students. It is a major concern of the staff, in particular of unit masters who are in charge of groups of students drawn from the second, third and fourth years, to help each individual to develop in his own way, leading him to an appreciation of his own values and enabling him to see what is his own line in practice. They are concerned that students should both feel, and be, free to develop in any direction they wish. Students may, therefore, exercise a large influence on the structuring of their own curriculum and may determine the nature and sequence of the problems they study as studio programmes. Nevertheless it is the responsibility of the unit master to see that each student follows a programme during the three-year period which develops his design ability in the broadest and most balanced way possible. He must also ensure that the student is exercised in all the strategies and techniques of design.

Even this 'student-centred' curriculum does not go to the extremes of self-direction and freedom from evaluation which some of the most radical students elsewhere seem to wish for. It is recognized that anyone learning in a new field requires to develop a basic command of information and skills and that some assessment is essential to inform him as to his success. Information is stressed initially during the foundation, first-year, course. This includes, along with intensive work in design, an introduction to the study of physiology, sociology, anthropology, corporative philosophy and logic. It begins with introductory projects relating to spatial and visual perception and concludes with the first major design project of the course. Moreover, the first year is probationary; it is used among other things to determine whether or not each student has the potential to continue with the study of architecture. Thus students are assessed from their course work and not from a single examination which is sometimes so much resented by students of other subjects. Indeed, assessment in this school tends to be more continuous and, perhaps, more informative than it is in traditional courses.

Varied attempts are also made to ensure that students learn to evaluate their own progress with increasing skill. On entry to the second year, they are required to prepare personal statements of intent to cover the three-year period in their unit; they make similar statements for individual programmes. At various stages in each programme and at periodic intervals, students evaluate their own progress in the light of these statements. But of most value in learning is the evaluation provided in the course by frequent 'juries' in which students present their designs to the unit master, tutors and other members of the unit, discussing them at length with everyone present and answering their criticisms.

More revolutionary, in Britain, is that students have some influence on staff appointments and that staff are appointed for a period of one year. Heads of servicing departments have an expression of intent for three years, and the principal for five years. Thus there is a similarity with some Canadian universities where all staff are appointed for two years in the first place and where senior posts are awarded for a period of five years. In both cases this is prompted by the belief that less permanence makes for flexibility and helps to keep teachers up to date by giving them a diversity of employment.

An answer to the charge that courses are too narrowly specialized has been attempted in designing new courses at Sussex (see Daiches, 1964), where links between subjects are stressed. Thus in arts, the three fields of European, English and social studies begin with a common first year which allows some choice of subjects, and proportions of subjects from the chosen field may vary. The tutorial system which operates in arts and social sciences also provides opportunities for integrating knowledge from different areas. In physical sciences the undergraduate majors in one subject, spending two-thirds of his time on mathematics, physics or chemistry, but sharing the remaining third between three subsidiary subjects; the latter are chosen from mathematics relevant to the field of study, related sciences or a study of the role of the specialism within the whole structure of scientific knowledge including the human, industrial, political or sociological fronts. During two preliminary terms the unifying aspects of all sciences are stressed, i.e. their common language, mathematics and their substance which consists of matter in all its forms. Throughout the courses all undergraduates attend lectures, seminars and discussions in such subjects as science and industry, science and government, the moral responsibility of the scientist, etc. In these ways it is hoped to avoid the extremes of specialization and, at the same time, the superficiality of a typical general degree course. By the end of this course the student should have a deep understanding of the fundamentals of his main subject, a knowledge of its relation with other scientific fields and an awareness of his role as a scientist and of the role of science in the world today.

The Open University is committed to experimental courses of an entirely new kind. It is the first full-scale multi-media system of higher education (Lewis, 1971a) employing correspondence materials, radio and television broadcasts, home experimental kits and the like. By these means it provides courses in their own homes for large numbers of adult, part-time students who are not required to have the usual entry qualifications. Work in two hundred study centres supplements the correspondence and television courses, enabling students to obtain help from tutors or counsellors, and to meet each other for discussion. Short residential courses, such as summer schools, provide further opportunities for discussion, practical work and so on.

In different ways all of the new universities have given thought to the problem of a broadly based education and to the possibilities of widening the students' outlook on the world and its problems, while providing sufficient specialized study to equip them for their future professions. The most notable result of such considerations is the Foundation Year at Keele, known popularly as 'From Plato to Nato' (despite a greater range at either extreme) in which all students study short courses extending over the whole field of human knowledge. The intention in these courses is to avoid the excessive specialization which is often deplored in sixth forms. Subsequently students take two principal subjects and two subsidiary ones, selecting at least one from each of the two complexes of sciences and mathematics, on the one hand, and social sciences and humanities, on the other. A disadvantage from the point of view of the students is that the course takes an additional year; but it also allows them to change their speciality, and a sizeable number does so. Perhaps it is for this reason that the rate of application remains high.

An extra year to allow for a change in direction is, of course, provided in some other universities; for instance, there is a first-year course for arts students to study medicine at one of London's medical schools and for arts students wishing to specialize in physics at the University of Surrey. The technical colleges and polytechnics also offer opportunities to students to re-direct their studies.

It is probably still too early to assess the effectiveness of these courses. They are undoubtedly popular; but there is evidence of some prejudice against them. In discussing a junior post in one college in London University a member of staff said, 'We had some applicants from new universities but we didn't interview them of course!' It is possible that his department constitutes a local pocket of resistance to change, but lecturers from other departments who were listening did not comment adversely. There is certainly a fear among some specialist students in traditional departments that the introduction of compulsory 'broader courses' would distract them and make it impossible for them to attain their present high standard.

Since the content and organization of courses are matters to be decided by university and college administrations, by specialist professional bodies and by the staff of departments concerned, it is not possible here to do more than raise problems which they must consider. We have mentioned two attempts, at Keele and Sussex, to re-examine the purposes of university teaching and to devise curricula in accordance with them. The satisfaction of students and staff is a guide to the evaluation of these courses but it will take time to assess their value in terms of professional competence. Whatever their degree of success, radical re-planning will increasingly be needed to meet the many problems which a rapidly changing situation produces. Although this book is concerned primarily with teaching methods, these cannot be considered in isolation from the curricula which students follow. Poorly conceived curricula provide little opportunity for genuinely effective learning; fragmented courses make it difficult for students to integrate their knowledge; those which are overfull leave too little time to develop understanding of the field; and students whose time is occupied in writing notes which are not understood at the time, will feel, with some justice, that they are not being educated but are simply being crammed to pass examinations. In such circumstances improved techniques in teaching may still be met by student opposition or, at best, will achieve more effectively ends which are educationally questionable. For these reasons it is essential that teachers should define long-term aims in courses which are relevant to the field of study, and ensure that their curricula are designed to achieve them. Moreover, they need some knowledge of the psychology of learning in order to devise teaching methods which will enable students to learn most effectively.

Reorientating teaching

Since trained teachers are rare in universities and unusual in technical colleges, it is hardly surprising that teaching staffs sometimes have difficulty in devising good courses or carrying them through effectively. Thus if curricula are to be restructured and constantly modified as knowledge grows and professional requirements change, experiments will be needed in supplying information to teachers and in providing continuous feedback as to the success of entire programmes, individual courses or of teaching and learning.

In my view the function of planning curricula and courses should remain firmly in the hands of the subject specialists and should not be relinquished to psychologists or specialists in education, as sometimes seems to be the case in training courses in the forces, in industry and even in some schools and college courses in the United States. What is needed is a way of co-operating with the psychologist, or educationist, to use his expertise for the benefit of both staff and students. The teachers in the field have the basis of experience in their subject. Cooperation of this kind is an essential feature in designing and preparing courses at the Open University; a team of educational technologists is available to offer guidance to each group of specialists in setting up clear objectives and in timing preparation of correspondence courses and homework assignments (Lewis 1971b). What the educational psychologist can offer is knowledge about the process of learning, individual differences, methods of evaluation, application of new techniques, etc. More successful courses will be devised by combining knowledge from both areas. In the ensuing chapters, therefore, there are few directives for teachers to follow but information is provided, together with examples of innovations and experiments, to enable them to draw their own conclusions and to modify their teaching more knowledgeably.

Different ways of using psychologists or education specialists need to be tried out on an experimental basis. In the first place, experiments might be carried out in the supply of training for lecturers in universities and colleges. Most of the existing courses are either very brief, intended only to orientate new lecturers, or consist of a sporadic series of lectures, often on unrelated topics, organized by enthusiasts in a school or department. More systematic training is being considered but, since we have no basis of experience other than for school teachers – and this seems largely irrelevant – we could profitably experiment with different kinds of training. For example, we might study the effect in some colleges of appointing a permanent research officer to be responsible for advising teachers and to help in directing experiments in teaching. This is already done in colleges of London University and is becoming common in medical schools in North America. Most of these officers cooperate with the teachers in planning courses, set up experiments in teaching, evaluate learning and teaching and recommend modifications in the course, or in teaching methods, as these are seen to be desirable. In other schools and departments a tutor has been appointed to take responsibility for the training of new lecturers, by organizing an initial course and, perhaps, one day per week throughout the year for the study of different aspects of teaching. As in one Australian university, an initial course for new lecturers lasting a fortnight or so might be followed by observation, with some criticism, of their teaching; a further block course could be organized later. From such experiments it should be possible to suggest how best to deploy specialists in education, how full courses should be and what further aid is desirable.

In order to provide more detailed guidance which lecturers require in teaching their own subjects, professional bodies might be asked to prepare reports such as those produced during the last forty years by the Mathematical Association for teachers mainly in secondary schools. In these reports highly competent teachers describe methods which they have found most effective in teaching specific topics and discuss, in appendices, alternative methods favoured by minorities. *The Report on the Teaching of Geometry*, for example, describes methods suited to pupils of different age groups and levels of sophistication in addition to outlining methods appropriate to the usual topics in O- and A-level syllabuses. In universities similar reports might be in pamphlet form for easy replacement as subjects and techniques develop and should be based on findings of educational research so far as this is possible.

In addition, professional bodies could contribute to the study of curricula in the light of professional demands and of modern developments, and in laying down guide lines concerning objectives, teaching techniques and methods of assessing learning. Our experience suggests that this is a more difficult task in fields such as clinical medicine or teaching in which interactions between people play an important part, and where choice among a variety of procedures arises partly from personal biases. But, both in these subjects and in those where the definition of objectives is easier, it is wise to begin from the widest possible basis of experience and by studying the results of inquiries in similar fields from the United States, industry, the forces, and so on.

Finally, extensive and well-planned programmes of research are needed both to determine the effectiveness of different teaching methods over a period of time and to evaluate courses. Innovations tend to arouse enthusiasm temporarily improving performance, due simply to the stimulus of novelty; improvement may occur because the method suits a teacher or his students better. It can be misleading to suppose that they will succeed equally well elsewhere and over a longer period of time unless they are tried out in a number of different colleges with students of varying abilities and teachers of different kinds. In this way it is possible to discover whether a method has universal applicability or under what circumstances it proves effective. Moreover, some improvements in learning are achieved at a considerable cost in teaching time and effort. If this effort results in a book to guide other teachers, or audio-visual materials for independent use by students, the effort seems justified; but, in general, increased teaching time must be balanced with increased effectiveness in learning. Thus the evidence gained from research should enable teachers not only to ensure that they achieve their objectives but that, in doing so, they make the best use of their resources.

Chapter 2
Objectives in Specific Fields

Why specify objectives?

When long-term objectives have been decided on, it remains for teachers in each field to plan their own courses and intermediate and short-term objectives which will bring about the desired kinds of behavioural changes in their students. The traditional kind of syllabus which consists of a list of topics, or books to be read, does not suffice for this purpose for it fails to specify just what it is that students will learn to do. No doubt teachers have this in mind, but there is some evidence that unless objectives are both stated and deliberately catered for they tend to be neglected. As an instance, in the medical field where many of the experimental inquiries into teaching have been made, Miller (1962) found that an aim high in the prospectus at the Medical School at the University of Illinois was 'critical thinking'; but in observing teaching in the school he found that students had little opportunity to ask questions or to take part in discussion. When students' grades were compared with scores in a standardized test of critical thinking, it proved that the least critical twenty-five obtained high grades whereas the most critical twenty-five had low ones.

In Britain, critical inquiries into examinations and courses show similar discrepancies with stated aims. Although teachers of sciences commonly say that studying their subjects should teach pupils to think as scientists, an investigation into A-level papers by the Institute of Physics in 1966 (see Spurgin, 1967) showed that 85 per cent of questions could be answered by recalling information alone. Thus these examinations were encouraging memorization rather than thinking. Even at university level the state of affairs seems little better. For example, a young lecturer in biology told the writer in 1967 that he had gained a first-class degree because of his excellent memory, adding that he knew he had no aptitude for research. Inquiry into final assessments suggests that they are rarely based on capacity to think out new problems *ab initio*, and that there are few opportunities for students to show originality. Where discussion takes place prior to the planning of scientific courses it is found that skills such as the ability to evaluate data and experimental reports, the solving of open-ended experiments or unfamiliar problems and, perhaps, the successful following through of a research project are likely to be required as evidence that a student deserves a degree enabling him to take up a scientific career. In the arts similar considerations have led some teachers of language to discard what they regard as second-hand learning, such as translations, and to turn to active command of the language and to what students can learn by their own observations.

In addition, of course, the system of assessment should reinforce the intentions of those who plan courses and curricula. Objectives, teaching methods and evaluation – whether in the form of feedback to the student or of tests and examinations – need to be considered as a nexus. Different examination systems therefore match different objectives. For instance, in an investigation into biochemistry examinations in 1969 (Beard and Pole, 1971), we found that some teachers gave as their major objective that students should acquire 'a body of knowledge'. Investigation showed that these teachers set examination questions which could be answered almost exclusively from knowledge of lecture notes and books. In contrast, in one school where the staff are concerned that students should learn to obtain and to use information for themselves and to gain skill in interpreting experimental data reported in journals, the examination consists of four distinct sections. Two of these test acquisition of the body of knowledge, i.e. (1) multiple-choice items test factual recall (2) five traditional essay questions require recall of facts and principles or selection of generalizations. The other two correspond with the newly defined objectives: (3) a prepared essay question on a nucleic

Table 1 **Objectives in university education** (for consideration and comment)

Objectives	Teaching method or student activity	Evaluation or feedback
Knowledge		
At the end of a university career, a student should:		
know the basic terminology of his subject	lectures; assigned reading; practicals; demonstration, etc.	multiple-choice-question examinations; correct use of forms in essays, discussion, etc.
know the principles (basic laws and concepts) of his subject understand some of the uses to which his subject is put	lectures; assigned reading; practicals; demonstration, etc. contact with research, industry, professionals in own field; experiments, projects, where appropriate	correct reference to laws, etc. arguments; essay writing, etc. informative assessment of project essays, etc.
be acquainted with principles and applications of related subjects	general studies; background reading	synthesis of data from various sources
Skills		
University teaching in general should enable the student:		
to write coherently	essays; laboratory reports; dissertations; papers to be given in tutorials	informative assessment of those
to be verbally articulate	giving papers; effective argument in discussion groups; tutorials, etc.	criticism by other students and tutors
to make his own independent judgements	meets contradictions; contrasting points of view; use of discussion to expose student's assumptions, etc.	e.g. 'compare and contrast' questions in examinations; evaluation of arguments, etc.

to obtain information efficiently	use of library, abstracts, etc.; preparation for essays, projects; open-ended experiments	informative comment on performance; open-book examinations
to think creatively, imaginatively and in abstract terms	research projects; tackling unsolved problems; use of concepts in arguments, discussion	quality of writing (publications?); assessment of method in tackling problems; credit for originality
to cooperate with colleagues and other professionals in future career	joint projects; role playing; group discussion to give insight into group interactions	evaluation of student's behaviour in a group by tutors and other students
to develop adaptability, i.e. to cope with changing patterns of knowledge (both general technological advance and new ideas in own subject)	exposure to new ideas (not accepting everything given as 'facts')	follow up after graduation

Attitudes
An aim in university teaching is to foster in the student:

enthusiasm for learning	non-assigned reading; extracurricular meetings (e.g. science clubs)	extent of extracurricular activity; posing new problems for own investigation
scholarly concern for accuracy	contact with teachers and researchers displaying such accuracy; continuous checking of own results	assign marks for accuracy in examinations
awareness of moral, social, economic, political and scientific problems of society	general studies; some projects; modern history, literature, sociology	impressionistically, from student's writing and discussion

acid or protein of the student's own choosing, allows students six weeks for reading, discussion and, possibly, experimental work; (4) a set of three 'situations' is presented which purports to be the results of the sort of investigation carried out by biochemists. Students are asked to 'explain as fully as you can what you consider is happening and try to account for all the results recorded. Give some brief theoretical background against which the problem and your solution can be set. Indicate what further investigation would help test the correctness of your explanation.' In these ways higher levels of thinking and evidence of ability to set up experimental investigations are required from every student.

The scheme in Table 1 was drawn up for use during a course for new lecturers in 1970, to draw attention to the close relationship between objectives, teaching method or students' activities, and the system of evaluation.

Objectives as incentives

Objectives are also needed as goals in learning. Where goals are too remote there is a tendency to let work slide in the belief that it can be made good later; if they are not clearly defined, the result may well be apathy and inactivity. A few years ago it was fairly commonly reported of students in clinical courses in medical schools that they did little work and spent too much time in social activities or in playing games. Inquiries showed, however, that students who behaved in this way had practically no responsibility in their activities and little guidance as to what forms the activities should take. In all the schools, of course, students are taught by consultants during ward rounds and are allowed to examine a few patients and to make some tests, but there may be no well-defined duties to fill the day and, moreover, in some medical schools consultants advise their students not to read! In contrast, in the best American schools (and in some British schools) where students are a few years older and are given considerable responsibility, students are enthusiastic and hardworking.

It hardly requires the investigations of psychologists to appreciate that some kind of feedback is needed to enable anyone engaged in learning to find out whether he is doing what is required of him. If he is not told whether he succeeds and has no means to judge for himself there is little point in making further efforts. Until the learner has established standards by which to assess his own performance he needs detailed and prompt criticism to redirect his learning – unless the task is of a kind which automatically demonstrates his errors, such as typewriting. This criticism usually comes from the teacher but may be provided by programmes which contain answers, or by a computer which works on the same principle or possibly via tape or video-tape of the learner's performances. Even when the student has developed standards of his own an expert skilled in teaching can point out refinements in style and technique and it is at this stage that study of an expert's work is most profitable. If, in addition, it is possible to add some test enabling the student to assess how he is progressing, or to view his performance against an expert one, then he is likely to become intensely interested and to progress rapidly with a minimum of assistance.

One of the main objections by teachers to the recent proposal by students that they should study projects of their own choosing is that the goal would be too remote, at least for weaker students or those with powerful motivations in other directions, and that teaching staff would not all prove capable of setting up intermediate goals or providing sufficient feedback to a large number of students. This might well be a genuine problem if students spent their time exclusively in these ways; but the evidence is that working on projects is usually highly motivating. No doubt, this is partly due to the intrinsic interest of a topic which the student has chosen for himself but, in discussion with his tutor, he will have set up intermediate goals, such as subsidiary questions to consider or problems to solve and will have been directed to some references. Provided that the topic is at a suitable level most students then apply themselves vigorously to it, sometimes at the expense of other work, for as initial goals are realized there is a likelihood that new ones will be framed and pursued.

Various ways of providing students with an outline, or even a detailed statement, of objectives have been developed during the last few years. In physics (Wooding and Williams,

1967, 1968) and in architecture (Darke, 1968) decisions relating to post-graduate studies or to the making of designs have been outlined in sequences of network analyses. A basic network shows major decisions and their inter-relationships against a time scale, and each step is analysed further in additional networks. This is to ensure that no essential steps are omitted and that preparations are made in good time for subsequent steps. Thus in preparing a post-graduate thesis successive networks show: (a) overall plan of research project; (b) activities involved in learning the background of a subject; (c) production of research proposal; (d) experimental and theoretical investigation; (e) evaluation of results; and (f) reporting the investigation. Figure 1 outlines (c).

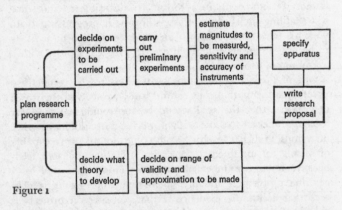

Figure 1

This method has also been used at the Open University in an attempt to guide teachers during planning and preparation of courses. As Brian Lewis points out (1971b), a thorough-going systems approach to planning seems to be necessary;

different parts of the university system tend to be richly and subtly interconnected. Decisions and actions that are taken in one part of the system can therefore have quite unforeseen consequences – ripple effects, in fact – across the system as a whole. . . . The sequencing of the various activities has been thought out with some care. Any member of staff who adopts the sequencing suggested is therefore likely to reap a number of benefits. At the very least, he may avoid some of the hidden pitfalls.

The network in question which is designed to guide teams in preparing a single course, comprises more than one hundred and thirty boxes, many of them multiple, and occupies a length of four-and-a half feet when printed in a journal. Lewis claims that the effect of studying this particular network has been salutary enough to convert quite a few academic members of staff to the systems-thinking approach.

However, in a third article he comments on the limitations of networks for this purpose (Lewis, 1972). He notes that the three requirements for their successful use are not met, i.e. that it is possible to break tasks into subtasks for which accurate time estimates can be made, that relationships and dependencies among subtasks can be specified in advance, and that rethinking or revision of a subtask is unnecessary. In Open University courses there is no unique way of breaking down the overall course production task, it is impossible to assign meaningful time estimates, some subtasks may ultimately be omitted or they may be altered if students complain or an irreplaceable contributor is sick, and, above all, valid differences of opinion as to order and content are inevitable. Nevertheless, he concludes that, against a background of ignorance, 'even the weakest attempt to construct a network and a scheduling scheme can be salutary and rewarding'.

In an alternative method used in an industrial design course, objectives showing expectations of students in successive years have been set out in general terms covering the very different projects which students undertake. These goals include such skills as problem solving, designer-client relationships, and so on. The objectives are available both to staff and students and thus serve as a reminder of the standards required throughout the course. More detailed sequences of objectives either exist or can readily be provided for subjects suitable for learning by teaching machines and programmed books. In one engineering department, for example, students have a list of objectives showing what formulae and principles they will learn during the course (Hill, 1969). Thus, in each of these ways, the majority of students are spurred on by knowing what is expected of them and by being able to assess the extent to which their tasks have been completed.

Problems raised in defining objectives

The degree of precision with which it is possible to specify behavioural objectives inevitably differs for different subjects and activities. It is easy, for instance, to be fairly precise about behavioural changes which will result from learning descriptive aspects of organic chemistry: in the first place students should be able to quote them. But we cannot say exactly what they will gain from undertaking research projects of their own choosing. It is true that there are certain aims in introducing projects which are the same for all students, for instance, that they should learn to find and to use information from a wide range of sources, tackle a genuine problem, or keep good experimental records, yet the range in performance may be enormous. Whilst one student achieves highly original work, the main achievement of another may be a competent survey of relevant literature. The more 'open-ended' the activity the more difficult it is to state exactly what purpose it serves. In such instances, therefore, definition of objectives is likely to stop at the point where the main course objectives have been outlined. Yet even this activity is considered valueless by some teachers of arts subjects who claim that it is impossible or misleading to spell out aims in their subjects. One young lecturer who attended a course commented subsequently that the possibilities and limits of educational objectives were a problem to her, and cited subjects in which the desired skills were invisible mental skills involving creative thinking. Where this is the case it may be hard for teachers to say what they are looking for even if they can recognize evidence that it has been attained.

Conceivably there is a difference not only between 'open-ended' activities and those directed to known ends but also between advanced and elementary studies. The advanced student's own objectives tend to play an increasing role and may take unexpected directions as his abilities, or new interests, develop. It is perhaps not without significance that at the Open University no aims are listed in the study of English literature, which is, or can be, one of the most 'open-ended' studies, in addition to being an advanced study for native-born subjects. In history, however, objectives are stated for the Foundation Course (Table 2), despite indignant protests by some teachers in history departments elsewhere that this is a meaningless exercise. Conceivably their courses are advanced and allow maximum choice to individuals. But where students report that the subject is tested entirely through three-hour essay papers, in which success depends to a substantial extent on knowledge of lecture notes, it seems probable that stating objectives is uncongenial rather than impossible.

Table 2 **Humanities Foundation Course Unit 5**
What history is and why it is important (Marwick, 1970)

The overall aims of the 'Introduction to History' block are:

1. To justify the study of history as a *relevant* subject and as a valuable introduction to the *varieties* of human experience.

2. In general to steer you to a balanced position from which you can appreciate, on the one hand, that history is a serious discipline, not mere speculation as the older universities have too often suggested, while, on the other hand, it is not a mere matter of 'ascertaining the facts', but involves a high degree of creative imagination.

3. To awaken you to the richness and complexity of primary source material.

4. To introduce you to some of the fundamental problems involved in the handling of source material.

5. To make you aware of how history is written.

6. To provide the basic criteria upon which you can assess the relative merits of different secondary authorities.

7. By explaining basic principles and exposing the more obvious pitfalls, (periodization, semantics, imprecision) to guide you towards intelligent historical composition of your own.

8. To discuss, how far, and in what senses, history can set the temporal and social context for the case studies which make up the rest of the course.

Objectives
Para. 2. Here now is a complete plan of the four units and the objectives within these units. The table of the section is given first, followed by the objective. The idea of listing objectives in this way is so that you should be able to see for yourself what it is you are

expected to be able to do at the end of each section. Once you have completed the entire four weeks you should then be in a position to achieve the eight general *aims* listed above.

Part I What History is and why it is important

1. Definitions

You should understand that the word 'history' is used in various different ways: the 'history' we are mainly concerned with is 'the historian's attempt to reconstruct and interpret the past', not 'the past' itself. You should be able to distinguish between the different uses of the word 'history'.

2. Justifications for the study of history

You should be able to list the various justifications which can be given for studying history. Beyond that you should familiarize yourself with the idea that history is a *social necessity* – the idea that history is as necessary to man and society as memory is to the individual, that without history man and society would be totally disorientated, would have no real sense of identity. You do not have to agree with this justification, but you should be able to argue about it.

3. The basic concerns of the historian

You should be aware of the three basic concerns of the historian, which are:

(i) Man in society.

(ii) Change through time (a vital ingredient in history, and one which distinguishes it from the more static studies of the social scientist).

(iii) Particular unique events (as opposed, again, to the abstract conceptualizations of the social scientist).

You should also understand that history involves *explanation* and the study of the *interconnection* between events: *history* should be distinguished from *chronicle* – mere narration of events without explanation or interpretation. You should therefore be able to distinguish history from other types of writing which occasionally bring in the past, such as sociology, political science, biology, astronomy, etc.

4. The subjective element in history

You should understand why it is that although the historian should try to be as objective as he can, it is never completely possible to suppress the personal and subjective element in history. You should understand why it is that history must always in some sense be, as E. H. Carr has said, 'a dialogue between the present and the past': that is, in reconstructing and interpreting the past the historian is always influenced by the attitudes and prejudices of the age and society in which he lives.

5. The development of the modern discipline of history

It is not necessary for you to have a complete knowledge of the history of history, but you should know the names of, and the main achievements associated with, some of the really outstanding historians in the last two hundred years. You should understand how in the twentieth century there has emerged the concept of 'total history' – that is, history which looks at man's past in all its aspects, cultural and social, as well as economic and political.

6. History as science, history as art, history as art and science

You should understand the various basic arguments which are put forward on the different sides of this quite difficult problem. You should be able to reach some conclusions of your own about how far history is scientific, how far it is an art.

The earliest attempt to categorize objectives was made in the United States by Bloom and his associates (1956) who wished to facilitate exchange of information between educators about curricula developments and methods of evaluation. They began by collecting educational objectives from institutions and from literature, classifying them initially under the headings of knowledge, intellectual abilities and intellectual skills. Next they proceeded to make further subdivisions, arranging cognitive objectives in order from the simplest to the most complex, attempting to make these subdivisions in such a way that all those using their material could communicate with each other about the specific objectives as well as the testing procedures by which their achievement could be evaluated. At this stage their main headings were:

1. Knowledge, including knowledge of terminology, specific facts, conventions, methods, methodology, principles, etc.

2. Comprehension, shown in ability to translate from verbal to symbolic statements, to interpret by recording or rearranging material, or to extrapolate, determining implications, consequences, effects, etc.

3. Application, meaning the use of abstractions – such as general ideas, rules of procedures, technical principles, ideas, etc. – in particular and concrete situations.

4. Analysis, implying skill in breaking down a communication into its constituent elements or parts such that the relative hierarchy of ideas is made clear and/or the relations

between the ideas expressed are made explicit; this also includes ability to recognize unstated assumptions, and skill in distinguishing fact from hypotheses and in recognizing form and pattern in literary or artistic works as a means to understanding them.

5. Synthesis, i.e. the putting together of elements and parts so as to form a new whole. This may take the form of a communication in which the writer seeks to convey ideas, feelings and/or experiences to others or the development of a plan of work; or it may be seen in ability to propose ways of testing hypotheses or in deduction of propositions and relations from a set of basic proportions or symbolic representations.

6. Evaluation, implying the making of judgements about the value of material and methods for given purposes, for example, evaluation of the accuracy of a communication for such evidence as logical accuracy, consistency and other internal criteria, or ability to compare a work with other works of recognized excellence.

It will be appreciated that complete and sharp distinctions are not possible since each category includes the preceding ones and because the experiential backgrounds of students influence the level at which they think. Thus what is a genuine problem to one student may be familiar and simply a matter for recall to another. However, in common with other classificatory systems this has the advantages of facilitating communications and drawing attention to omissions or to failure in relating what is taught with what is evaluated in examinations.

Our impression in using McGuire's (1963) modification of these categories in the investigation of biochemistry examinations (Beard and Pole, 1971) was that many of them are too broad. In particular, the first category includes too wide a range of capabilities, from restatement of isolated facts to knowledge of concepts and principles. We would have preferred the classification Nedelsky used in discussing the teaching of physics (1949) for this seems more readily applicable to acquisition of a 'body of knowledge'. Within his first level 'knowledge', i.e. 'remembering what was taught in the course', he suggests three subdivisions: subject-matter knowledge, analytical knowledge and knowledge of methodology. The first of these seems to be roughly equivalent to McGuire's 'recall of specific facts'; the second is described as 'knowledge of relations or patterns' in which the ability to organize materials of the course should help the student to retain these relations. The third is also concerned with the apprehension of relationships, in particular the interrelation of different areas of physics, and between physics and other sciences. Whether these should be distinguished as though they are separate abilities is questionable, however. Factorial studies in the Department of Chemistry at East Anglia suggest the existence of three distinct factors relating to multiple discrimination, concept learning and problem-solving items, but the results do not support the cumulative property of this taxonomy or that of Gagné (Stolz, 1970).

Not only have these classifications been questioned by psychologists but they have also been attacked on theoretical grounds by philosophers. Sockett (1971) comments on the inadequacy of educational objectives such as 'remembering', 'reasoning' or 'concept formation' which are too broad to be meaningful. Everything we do can be seen as an instance of 'remembering'; terms such as these derive a meaning only in relation to content. He also finds a category unacceptable if it covers different behaviours for different individuals, e.g. 'problem solving', where one student remembers a solution whilst another works out a method of his own. He points out the difficulty Bloom and his associates ran into through failure to consider general as well as specific objectives; they therefore have no place for an objective such as 'getting children to understand society'. He comments, too, on the 'breath-taking naïvety' of the knowledge category which brings together knowledge of such a diversity of kinds; and he suggests that the taxonomy might be seen as a taxonomy of educational processes rather than objectives.

Pring (1971) criticizes the divisions of the taxonomy – between cognitive and affective objectives – and, in the cognitive objectives, between knowledge and intellectual abilities. 'To know that something is the case entails understanding what it *means* to say that something is the case and this in turn entails being able to apply this knowledge to particular situations.' Thus he might find more acceptable a category corresponding with the psychologist's first factor relating to 'a body of knowledge'. His comment that 'to think scientifically entails a concern – a feeling, if you like – for the standards of scientific truth', agrees with the conclusion of some physicists working with a psychologist (Pole, 1972) that most effective objectives were incorporated in the specification of 'skills', i.e. in the student's ability to employ his knowledge in various ways.

When a satisfactory classification is found, a different but very real problem is that the nature of the objectives themselves may not be agreed by colleagues in a single department. In the first place, of course, some fundamental rethinking will probably be required and not everyone is prepared to undertake it, but analysis of objectives may also serve to highlight genuine disagreement. In a department of psychiatry, an inquiry into the aims of twenty-one teachers showed that their aims fell into four distinct groups (Walton and Drewery, 1964). All groups wished to provide systematic information, but this was the sole aim of three teachers, six others taught with a psycho-dynamic orientation, seven shared these objectives but aimed to teach behavioural science also, while the remaining five, in addition to these three objectives, wished to modify the behaviour of their students.

Defining objectives in specific fields
Attempts by university teachers to analyse their curricula systematically suggest that three or four main categories usually suffice. Thus, in physics, in the skeleton plan (Table 3) the headings 'Knowledge' and 'Skills' are used. This scheme relates objectives with both teaching methods (or student activities) and assessment (or feedback on performance). In French language (Table 4) 'practical command' is substituted for 'skill', 'theoretical grasp' for 'knowledge' and 'aesthetic perception' for 'attitudes' but in this first-year scheme there is an additional category of 'general reorientation away from second-hand learning'. This scheme reveals some gaps where objectives do not correspond exactly with learning activities

and neither relates with assessment nor learning nor evaluation by examinations. The majority of teachers do not yet attempt to distinguish current assessment from end-of-year tests or qualifying examinations, so tending to obscure omissions in each; while few appreciate the need to establish a close correspondence between objectives and final assessments.

A more complex scheme has proved necessary for a course in the training of biology teachers (Dallas and Piper, 1972). Each of six main headings has been considered from seven aspects, resulting in a matrix comprising forty-two categories. The main headings used are:

1. Philosophy of the curriculum and role of the teacher.
2. Content of courses taught.
3. Classroom techniques.
4. Integration of content and techniques.
5. Organization and administration.
6. Insight on own performance.

The seven aspects from which each is considered are:

1. Premises.
2. Changes desired in attitudes and values.
3. Knowledge to be gained.
4. Skills required.
5. Methods of teaching and learning.
6. What should be assessed.
7. Method of assessment.

Thus in the matrix under 23 (combining main heading 2 with aspect 3) the following subheadings appear:

1(a). Of conceptual hierarchies proposed by others.
1(b). Of normal range of mental and social skills.
2(a). Of as much of the whole range of biological knowledge as possible and of lower-school science.
2(b). Of the case for biology as an integrated science and of its interdisciplinary role.
3. Of the methodological and conceptual basis of curriculum reform projects.

These are further elaborated and discussed. The book will be the first of a series 'Case Studies in Course Design' edited by Piper.

Table 3 Objectives in teaching physics at university level (main headings with illustrative sub-headings)

Knowledge

Objectives	Activities	Evaluation
1. Knowledge of the language of physics, e.g. 1.1.1. scientific vocabulary, etc.	1. Lectures. Practicals. Use of technical terms, formulae, etc. in problem solving, lab reports.	1. Traditional written examinations multiple choice exams. 'Points' tests. Correct use of technical terms in writing and discussion.
2. Knowledge of the major concepts, principles and laws of physics. 1.2.1. Concepts, e.g.: dimensions and units, etc. to 1.2.7. Maxwell's equation	2. Lectures. Basic reading. [. .] Active discussion of concepts Use questions as means of learning as well as of assessment e.g. 'instant feedback' in lectures.	2. Traditional written examinations multiple choice exams. Intelligent use of concepts, principles and laws in problem solving, project work, discussion, etc.
3. Knowledge of a representative sample of the basic body of knowledge in physics, etc. 1.3.1. Classical mechanics, etc. to 1.3.9. Some topics from contemporary physics.	3. Lectures. Basic reading. Other presentation methods, e.g. audio tapes, closed circuit TV demonstration. Practical classes. Students should have an outline.	3. Traditional written (and practical) examinations; multiple-choice exams. Informative assessment of essays, examination answers, laboratory work, projects, etc.
4. Knowledge of mathematical techniques of importance to the understanding of physical theory.	. Mathematics courses. Continuous use of mathematical skills. [. .] Handouts to illustrate model problems.	4. Assessment of work in problem classes. Correct and intelligent use of mathematical techniques.

5. Knowledge of experimental techniques and methods in the design and analysis of experiments.	5. Formal laboratory work, Open-ended experiments. Preparation for projects, Work on projects.	5. Assessment of laboratory reports. Open-book order. Performance in discussion of project with supervisor. Assessment of project.
6. Knowledge of the applications of physics in science, technology and industry.		
7. Knowledge of the inter-relatedness of science, e.g. 7.1 Interrelations of different aspects of physics, etc.		
8. Knowledge of the philosophy of physics, e.g. 8.1. the methods of science, etc.		

Skills

1. Collection of information	1. (a) on teacher's part Give sources of information in reading lists and bibliographies, etc. (b) on students' part Expand lecture notes, e.g. to include information obtained from reading.	1. Are these followed up? etc. Indirect evidence from essays and essay-type examination answers, etc.

Table 3 – continued

2. Application of principles of physics (examples of which are given under 2).	2. (a) on teachers' part. (b) on students' part.	
3. Application of mathematical techniques (examples of which are given under 4). [..]	3. Continuous exposure to *use* of mathematics in all aspects of physics.	3. Generally, responses and suggestions in tutorials, classes, etc. [..]
4. Application of experimental techniques. [..]	4.1. First-year practical work of a traditional kind (set experiment with notes)	4.1. Traditional practical examinations – are given techniques successfully applied? [..]
4.6. Designing experiments, taking account of practical and economic constraints.	4.6. Third-year project work in consultation with demonstrators. Hypothetical design exercises in tutorials.	4.6. Give all students same design problem as part of project – assess quality of designs suggested.
5. Flexibility in solving problems 5.1	5. (a) on teachers' part. Give alternative proofs, etc. in lectures, etc.	5. Specific examination questions, e.g. 'Indicate two or more solutions for the following problem, ... etc.
6. Evaluation in solving problems. 6.1. Recognizing when an adequate result has been obtained, in terms of time available, levels of accuracy, etc. [..]	6. Presentation of information on scientific method as part of practical course.	6.1. Assessment of laboratory performance; did student stop at a suitable point? [..]

6.4. Assessing the reliability of others' work.	6.4. Discussion in class of other students' experimental work.	6.4. Standard of discussion; were relevant criticisms made?
7. Interpretation and explanation.	7. Project work, open-ended experiments.	7. Assessment of project reports, laboratory notes, essays.
8. Communication.		
8.1. Taking intelligible notes. [··]	8.1. Expand lecture notes, etc.	
8.5. Arguing effectively and relevantly in discussion.	8.5. Tutorials . . . Extra-curricular speaking and discussion.	8.5. Tutors' impressions oral examinations, etc.
9. Judgement.		
9.1. Recognizing the explicit assumptions in a piece of written work and understanding their consequences. [··]	9.1. –	9.1. and
	9.4. Lectures in history and philosophy of science. Exposure to philosophical arguments and discussion. [··]	9.2. Given a piece of written work at an appropriate level, be able to pick out, and state, the basic assumptions, explicit and implicit [··]
9.5. Judging the validity of a hypothesis (bearing in mind the frequent need to advance theory on existing evidence).	9.5. Teachers' encouragement of intelligent guesses.	9.5. Performance in projects and open-ended experiments. Relation of a hypothesis to research conclusion.

Table 4 Learning by doing: French language studies (University of Reading)

Year 1: General re-orientation away from second-hand learning, non-practical performance in inappropriate registers, with maximum attention given to small-unit accuracy.

To: active command for students' own purposes, in appropriate register, and following on learning from own observation, aiming at large-scale competence (the paragraph is more important than the sentence) in abstract but non-figurative language, as well as in ego-centric concrete language which is all he can handle now. (learning by using = learning to use)

(a) Objectives: practical command	Related activity	Evaluation
1. Raise speed of aural comprehension, of large units of meaning.	1–5. The paraphrase exercise. Listens to uninterrupted, deliberate reading of a coherent, self-contained passage (c. 300 words) of original French writing. Follows second reading *visually*, interrupted by comments and questions. *Listens* to third, faster reading. May take notes at any stage to assist reformulation, but influence of note-taking on reformulation closely watched by tutors to redirect the slavish penpushers to a more intelligent method. Recomposes the text in writing (c. 35–40 minutes).	The correction of the paraphrase exercise. Entails reorientation of tutor, who must:
2. Raise speed of visual comprehension of large units of meaning, within a time limit, at expense of *total* small-unit comprehension.		(i) recognize the nature of the student's reformulation, so that he can be guided towards *independent*, *conscious* expression of ideas and away from slavish regurgitation of words and phrases (however correct);
3. Develop observation and short-term retention of new or unfamiliar items of lexis and structure.		(ii) recognize what are the most urgent needs of each student, and present him with what he evidently lacks:
4. Develop observation and elucidation of meaning by *context*.		

5. Develop capacity for individual reformation of predetermined *content*, in preparation for writing of dissertations in French.
6. Develop capacity for spontaneous speech.

6. Weekly hour in groups of 12+. From games ('20 questions') to short prepared talks on topics of current study.

(iii) correct the student's work in the general direction of the student's attempt, not to any absolute standard. There can be no *comparative* evaluation of first-year independent writing, except in very broad limits; standards vary enormously because all writing done under translation conditions has been totally unreal. The effort of evaluation must first be directed towards the *nature* of the performance, the *degree* of independence acquired; only when the student is functioning under his own steam can the tutor see what his standard in fact *is*; that includes not only what he knows and can *do* with the language, but also what he can learn from observation himself. There *are* students who can learn Greek in two terms flat, but can't improve their French from merely *hearing* and *reading*. Such students have probably been so badly taught that they cannot

Table 4 – continued

Objectives: theoretical grasp	Related activity	Evaluation
		conceive of any except the classical methods of learning dead languages (or they may have a special cast of mind). They should be directed away from modern languages. The year abroad will do nothing for them.
(b) *Objectives: theoretical grasp*	*Related activity*	*Evaluation*
1. Reorientation: the student will come to understand what is meant by:	1. The paraphrase exercise.	
(i) active command of language,		
(ii) independent reformulation of a given content,		
(iii) learning from first-hand observation instead of from second-hand instruction.		
2. Remedial tasks: he will begin to eliminate commonest first-year errors (identified over past five years). He will observe the structural analysis *implied* in the remedial tapes, in their organization. This structural analysis not presented until year 2.	2. Fortnightly laboratory taped exercises on selected grammatical structures (pronouns, infinitives, articles).	2. Undergoes multiple-item test related exactly to content of tape, before and after performance. Statistical analysis of results shows overall measure of improvement, individual variation, weak areas of the tape.

Objectives	Related activity	Evaluation
3. Constructive tasks: he will acquire elementary vocabulary for presentation of ideas, processes of thought, argument (abstract vocabulary).	3. Attends expository lecture, with examples and discussion. Observes the corrections made in this field to his own writing.	
(c) Objectives: aesthetic perception		*Evaluation*
1. Reorientation: he will begin to distinguish:	1. The commentary accompanying the paraphrase exercise.	No method of evaluating student's performance yet devised. Evaluation mostly directed towards the *materials* being used: how good are they?
(i) spoken and written registers,		
(ii) concrete, abstract and figurative language,		
(iii) archaic and modern usage.		
2. Constructive tasks: developing speed and suppleness of the ear, so as to catch all kinds of non-academic language (song, cabaret, parody, theatre, interview, formal discourse not previously written).	2. Attends language laboratory, weekly one hour, listening, transcribing, responding to short questions, under guidance of monitor.	

A different vocabulary from that of Bloom is used in the Joint Board's notes for the guidance of schools which set out the aims in the A-level engineering course relating these with learning activities and evaluation techniques (Joint Matriculation Board, 1968). The fourteen aims in practical work appear under four main headings: (a) technique, (b) originality, (c) analysis, (d) synthesis. Technique, for example, includes the development of the facility for making accurate observations and the ability to make reasonable estimates of the errors incurred in making such observations, and familiarization with and facility in the use of scientific apparatus and equipment. Practical work is to be taught, firstly, by 'controlled assignments' which are of short duration and resemble traditional experimental work in schools and, secondly, by 'experimental investigations' which pose an engineering or scientific problem. The latter involves the student in an analysis of the situation and an appropriate selection of procedures and techniques for solution and will take some six to twelve hours to complete. In addition to practical work, major 'projects' are employed which require a pupil to design a device, or design and conduct an investigation to fulfil a specification, and to evaluate the degree of fulfilment achieved. Projects are set since they call for 'mental connective abilities rather than for craft skills . . . the emphasis being on design of formulation problems, literature search in its widest sense and evaluation'. Evidence of having achieved all these aims, to a satisfactory standard, is required for the final assessment. Thus there is evidence here that examination of objectives has resulted in substantial change in the course and to a lesser degree in the ways in which the pupil's learning is evaluated.

In case it should be supposed that objectives cannot be specified in courses where students are pursuing different projects, or in which their progress is seen not so much in realization of a succession of skills and abilities as in a gradual increase of expertise in the same skills, or deepening in understanding, we will look briefly at objectives in the previously mentioned industrial design coures (Burke, 1968; Piper, 1967). In analysing the skills required by industrial designers, the psychologists and teaching staff who specified objectives for this course saw it in terms of problems to be solved rather than products to be designed and thus were able to specify general objectives relevant to any kind of industrial design. A small part of a very large table of objectives is reproduced. The larger table, some ten feet by twelve when typewritten, is available in a reduced form on the wall of a room for reference by both staff and students. This provides a constant reminder of standards required at each stage, and links objectives with the activities the student should undertake. Thus under 'Solution' are listed the steps in solving the problem, i.e. deciding what information is required, collection of data, recording the data, processing it, formulating a solution and finally evaluating it (see Table 5).

Defining short-term objectives

The next step in analysing objectives is to specify changes in behaviour in more detail under each of the major headings. This is, of course, an essential step in preparation of programmes for teaching machines or programmed texts and, if subject matter has already been analysed for this purpose, detailed objectives already exist. This is most likely to be the case in quantitative topics and in those with relatively unchanging subject matter such as anatomy; but programmes have been written in less structured fields such as clinical medicine. These will be discussed further in Chapter 7.

At this level terms such as 'understanding' and 'knowing' which do not describe clearly specifiable behaviours are avoided as far as possible. In programming a civil-engineering course in Birmingham (Croxton and Martin, 1965), short-term objectives describe exactly what the student should be able to do at the end of the course.

Introduction to shear stress

1. To understand the action of shearing forces and to show how these are resisted by shear stresses within the material.

2. To define average shear stress and to consider examples of its application in practical engineering situations; e.g. riveted joints.

3. To understand the necessity for considering the shear stresses on an infinitely small element when the distribution of shear stress is non-uniform.

4. To prove the existence of complementary shear stress on a two-dimensional element.

5. To solve problems involving complementary shear stresses in two dimensions and to extend the idea to three dimensions.

6. To define shear strain.

7. To define modulus of rigidity, and explain its meaning in engineering terms.

8. To solve general problems involving axial forces, shear forces, shear stress, average shear stress, shear strain and modulus of rigidity with applications to engineering structures.

In a department of mechanical engineering objectives have also been worked out in this way, and are available to staff and students (although for the 50 per cent of the work which is covered by projects this is not feasible). One lecturer who defined objectives for an entire course commented:

> This is what has been done. The question we must ask ourselves is whether it is worth while to analyse objectives. The only expenditure in analysing objectives is the time involved but this need not be very great. In the first example, the analysis of the 2M Fluid Mechanics Course took altogether less than twenty hours of my time. This is to be compared with 2,000 hours or so of staff time connected with the course during the five-year period in which I give the lectures.
>
> The advantages of analysing objectives are not readily quantified. In my own experience this type of analysis leads to better teaching; it ensures that the lecture material is appropriate and that correct emphasis is given to it in the lectures. Having analysed one's objectives in this way, in behavioural terms, it is natural to reconsider the assessment procedures and to make them appropriate to the objectives (Hill, 1969).

Preliminary analyses

When teachers object that it is not possible to specify objectives in their fields it may be because the needs of specialists have not been adequately investigated or because the subject matter has not been analysed for difficulties nor sequenced in a logical order (if this is appropriate). In such cases preliminary analyses may be needed before an attempt is made to define teaching objectives.

Table 5 Design education

The fundamental aims of the course and their related performance requirements (charts 1 and 2) were derived from the initial statement concering the nature of the course. Aims 1 and 2 (chart 1) embody the context in which the design takes place. Aims 3 to 7 (chart 2) cover the cycle of operations which is the *design process*. The *design cycle* is then further developed on the next page (chart 3) and shows the constraints or steps taken (shown above the rule) and the areas of study which are fed to the students in relation to each of these steps (shown below the rule).

The context Chart 1

Aim	Required performance	Statement
		Chart 3
1. To enable the student to have a defensible concept of the designer's responsibilities.	The student will be systematic in his professional decisions (systematically evaluating his decisions against general social criteria).	
2. That the student will be successful in establishing a relationship between the designer and managers, acceptable to both.	The student will be able to: (a) recognize and fit in with those managers' norms which are not critical to the solution of design problems, (b) be successful in changing those managers' norms which are critical to the solution of design problems.	Locating the problem area. Reaching agreement with managers on the exact nature of the problem. Stating the problem.

Table 5 – continued
The design cycle Chart 2

		A systematic method for the identification of problems in a face-to-face situation. Fact gathering in a face-to-face situation. Consulting techniques. Industrial organization.
3. That the student will state design problems in manageable terms.	The student will ensure that a comprehensive brief is produced. (This means a systematical appraisal of the problem area.)	
4. That the student will solve design problems well and economically.	The student will be able to: (a) discover and evaluate existing solutions, (b) reach the best solution via the best method (both sets of values measured against explicit criteria).	
5. That the student will communicate the solution of a design problem in a way most likely to ensure its acceptance.	The student will be able to: (a) effectively present the solution of a design problem, (b) overcome irrational resistance to its acceptance.	
6. That the student will implement the solution of a design problem successfully.	The student will be able to ensure that the process of good decision making are continued through the development of the production process.	
7. That the student will secure maximum improvement in the quality of his future performance.	The student will be able to validate the accepted solution of a design problem.	

Chart 3

Deciding what information is required	Determine what is to be communicated to whom	Determining the method of production	Collecting information on performance of product
Collection of data	Deciding on a method of presentation.	Collecting information about the method of production	Recording information
Recording of data	Execution of presentation	(Adapting solution in the light of production methods)	Treating data
Processing of data		Execution	Drawing conclusions
Formulating solution	*Communication*	*Implementation*	*Validation*
Evaluating solution	Communications theory	Industrial organization	Statistics
Solution	Theory of perception	Human relations	Product testing
A systematic method for the solution of problems	Human relations	Consulting techniques	
Location of data	*Methods of communication*		
Use of library	Freehand drawing		
Information services	Engineering drawing		
Sources of information	Perspective drawing		
Engineering materials	Photography		
Techniques of production	Model-making		
Economics of production	Typography		
Human engineering – anthropometrics	Production of portfolio		
Human engineering – organization and methods			

Table 5 – continued

Solution	Communication
	English
	Workshop practice
Work study	
Human engineering – man/machine systems	
Human engineering – displays and controls	
Operations research market research	
Ordinary National Certificate in Mechanical Engineering	
Typing and brief writing	
Design methodology	
Systems analysis	
Psychology of problem solving	
Aesthetics	
Selection and design of filing systems	
Statistical concepts	
Application of computers	

Chart 4

Statement	Required performance—year 1	Required performance—year 2	Required performance—year 3	Required performance—year 4
A systematic method for the identification of problems	The student will have undertaken projects in which the nature of the problem will have been demonstrated to him. How these problems were identified will have been explained.	The student will identify problems according to a specified procedure. The student will have an appreciation of the psychology of problem solving.	The student will demonstrate ability in using systems for the identification of problems The student will demonstrate a knowledge of the application of computers to the identification of problems.	The student will demonstrate an ability to use the best system to meet a given situation.
Fact-gathering in a face-to-face situation			The student will demonstrate his competence in the collection of unbiased information.	
Consulting techniques				The student will demonstrate competence in consulting techniques. (Competence in guiding other people into making rational decisions.)
Industrial organization			The student will demonstrate a knowledge of the usual structure of business	The student will demonstrate that in any organization he will go to the appropriate

Table 5 – continued

			organizations (functions of the production, sales, design managers, etc.).	person/s to collect or give information.
Solution *A systematic method for the solution of problems*	The student will be familiar with writing up his project work according to the 5 stage Design Cycle (state, solve, communicate, implement, validate) even though knowledge of some of the stages is only rudimentary.	The student will demonstrate an ability to produce written reports, giving an analysis of all decisions taken and possibilities explored, though still working from a given brief (there will be increasing emphasis upon group working).	The student will demonstrate an ability, in specific projects, to isolate problems when only the context in which they exist is given.	The student will demonstrate competence in looking at real-life situations, locating and solving problems in realistic terms.
Location of data – *use of library* The student will have a knowledge of how Hornsey College and Hornsey Public Libraries are catalogued. The student will have undertaken a course of guided reading. The student will have adopted a standard method for referring to *all* sources of information.	The student will demonstrate skill in obtaining and collating data which may be spread over a wide range of sources. He will know how to use bibliographies, etc., and be competent at locating data not held by the College and Public Libraries. The student will demonstrate a knowledge of sources of information.			

Psychologists studying industrial learning, and more recently, learning in other fields, have developed a number of different kinds of analyses to provide them with information as to ultimate requirements, difficulties encountered in learning or ways in which learning is achieved.

In the first case, study of a master performance may suffice in industry to show the degree of skill and speed attainable and the organization of the task in the hands of an expert. This provides the goal for other learners of the same skill. However, where a complex cognitive skill is to be acquired instead of a manual one other considerations need to be taken into account. In the first place professional requirements may be changing so that the expertise of today is soon outdated. In the second, it may not be possible for less gifted learners to acquire the same skills as the most able, nor to learn effectively by the same methods. Among school children, for example, bright and dull children may all find answers to simple mathematical problems but the methods favoured by children of different abilities differ widely if they are left to their own devices; where they are shown which methods to use there is the usual disadvantage that the able do not work at full stretch while the 'dull' pupils never really understand what they are doing. Thus analyses suited to intellectual skills include those of professional requirements, and in particular how they are changing, as well as of performances of experts and of students of different capacities. Together they provide long-term objectives of educational programmes and indicate the varieties of programmes which may be needed to teach students of differing abilities.

In a second kind of analysis the subject matter itself is studied. Thus Gagné (1965) has suggested that such an analysis may take the form of a hierarchy. At higher levels of learning this is typically a hierarchy of principles. The formation of such a hierarchy in a logical order is one of the first steps in writing a programmed text for teaching machines or programmed books. In the case of a branching programme, where students' errors are corrected, it may involve returning to lower levels of learning such as classification, simple relationships or basic concepts which some students have missed or failed to learn at an earlier stage.

A different approach suggested by Gilbert (1962) involved analysis of subject matter in terms of stimuli and responses. These are related in three different ways: in the case of a generalization several different stimuli result in the same response; in a chain, the response to one stimulus is, in its turn, the stimulus to the next response, and so on; while in discrimination, which is said to be most difficult to learn, different responses must be made to alternative stimuli. As yet there are few applications of such analyses in higher learning, but the construction of algorithms to aid the making of decisions and diagnoses reduces difficult sequences of discriminations to simply replying 'yes' or 'no' to successive straightforward questions (see Gane, Horrabin and Lewis, 1966). They are described in more detail in Chapter 7.

Further analyses to aid in setting up short-term goals or in devising teaching methods are mainly concerned with the learner. These consist in studies of errors, of what may be termed consumer analyses in relation to learning, that is, a study of the learner's interests and goals. The former has received most consideration at lower levels of learning in order to set up remedial programmes for backward pupils, but there are too few studies produced to help teachers to present difficult topics and, at the same time, to avoid common errors among average pupils and students.

Interests of children are considered in primary-school programmes and in the new science programmes in secondary schools, etc. With students, however, it is still generally assumed that they ought to be interested in what is offered to them rather than that the presentation of programmes of work should be modified as far as possible in the direction of students' interests or to meet their different levels of attainment. Yet if the goal is effective learning, increasing provision for individual differences must be made in higher education also.

Chapter 3
The Psychology of Learning

To provide for effective learning the teacher needs some knowledge of the psychological factors which operate in stimulating a desire to learn and of those which interfere with the process. He needs to know how best to help students to memorize subject matter, or in what ways to present concepts, principles and their applications so that they will be understood and used intelligently, and so on. An inexperienced or unthinking teacher tends to give his students information in the expectation that it will be mentally filed away as neatly as it is in his own store of knowledge; he is unaware of prior learning which may make the new information appear meaningless, of assumptions which change its nature, or of gaps in knowledge so great that the new information is either wholly incomprehensible or cannot be accepted without distortion.

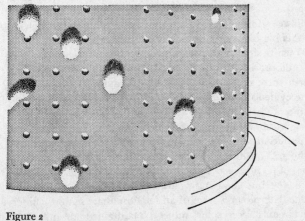

Figure 2

The existence of assumptions and a search for meaning are readily demonstrated. Figure 2 represents a section of a ship's boiler riveted in the usual way but also having indentations due to gun-fire. If the reader turns it upside down he will find that the rivets have now become indentations while the gun-fire indentations appear as protuberances. This is because he has been accustomed all his life to a world in which light comes from above. If he had been handed the picture upside down it would probably not have occurred to him to reverse it; he would simply have accepted his natural, but erroneous, interpretation of it. A doctor whose interpretation of X-rays would be seriously affected by an error, or a space traveller whose multi-directional movements extend his experience so that light may reach him from any direction, would probably display more caution in interpreting the picture. This tendency to interpret events in accordance with past experience is termed 'set'. In normal circumstances 'sets' of all kinds facilitate effective action since the individual need not then waste time considering what a perceived image implies or pause to decide what action he will take. In fact, there is evidence that most individuals desire constancy and tend to establish and maintain a world which deviates as little as possible from that which they have experienced in the past. This results in resistance to interference from competing systems as may be observed in the rejection of extremely unfamiliar art forms or in discussion between individuals with different biases. In the latter case individuals tend to protect their own position unconsciously – giving their own meanings to significant words used by participants with a different bias who, in turn, misunderstand their communications.

The evidence is that people differ in their capacity to relinquish 'sets', some doing so fairly readily, whereas others will distort information they receive, forcing it to fit familiar interpretation until the weight of contradictions obliges them to change. Thus in an experiment by Frenkel-Brunswik (1949) a series of pictures was shown to children and adults beginning with a dog but changing gradually from dog to cat so that intermediate pictures were of an indeterminate nature. Under these circumstances some subjects maintained an inflexible attitude, asserting that the creature was a dog until forced by contradictory evidence to relinquish this 'set', whereas others could tolerate a creature which had a nebulous character and described each picture on its merits.

That this is no simple matter of 'flexibility' or 'inflexibility' is shown by a further experiment by Festinger and Carlsmith (1959), who offered two groups of students rewards of one or twenty dollars to describe dull tasks as 'a lot of fun' to students about to undertake them. They found that those paid little subsequently voted the tasks more interesting than they had done previously, as though it was cognitively necessary to eliminate the lie by changing their attitude to fit the statement. Those who were well paid, however, changed their attitudes very little for the sum received seemed adequate to account for an action dissonant with their beliefs. Similarly, perhaps, students who expend a great deal of effort in courses which they do not find worthwhile at the time may praise them subsequently to justify their labours.

Figure 3

Figures 3 (a) and (b) pose a different problem. They are two of the incomplete pictures from the Gestalt Completion Test (see Thurstone, 1944). In trying to make sense of these pictures we do not begin with an assumption or 'set' but search our repertoire of perceptual memories to match them. Most people have a feeling of turning over possibilities in their minds until they find one which 'fits' or until they realize what the figure is in a 'flash of insight'. Once it is recognized it tends to seem so obvious that they are surprised that they did not 'see' it before. Figure 3 (a) represents a couple waltzing and is fairly easily recognized. Figure 3 (b) however, is often not seen as the head of a man and few people in England have sufficient knowledge to identify it as General Grant. Some people still have difficulty in making sense of either picture even when they are told in detail what to look for. Showing them an outline may help, but even this does not guarantee that sense will be made of the incomplete pictures when the outline is removed.

Very similar difficulties may be experienced by students in understanding a text, a proof or the significance of an experimental result. In these cases, however, the gaps are in their own information and understanding. While the teacher is there to draw in the outline it may be comprehensible but when they are once again on their own they may still not 'see' it. The remedy is to cover the argument step by step, finding out where the omissions are, and to repair them by additional explanations or subsidiary work. Discussions may fulfil this function if sufficiently pertinent questions are asked for the students to ascertain the nature of their difficulties.

These three tasks, therefore, serve to illustrate some of the conditions for understanding in learning: the student needs to have a knowledge of the goal, that is, he must know what he is required to do, he must be actively involved – telling him the answers does little to ensure that he will comprehend – he must be prepared to give up familiar interpretations if the data demand it and the goal must not be so unrelated to prior learning that it is impossible of achievement (such as identifying Figure 3 (b). A reader whose neighbour pointed out what the pictures represented before he saw it himself may wish to add that if the teacher concludes the search for his students they are likely to lose interest. Satisfaction in understanding information or solving a problem arises from the learner's own activity and from ultimate success in meeting the challenge it presents. Lack of interest tends to follow passive listening to an explanation as well as from past or present failure, from discovery that other people do better, or simply from not being so good in this kind of task as in others which are consequently found more rewarding. Thus teachers who solve all the problems, displaying their own superior skills, tend to depress interest in all but their most able students.

In studying learning the main questions to be answered are how people's perceptions and assumptions are built up, how they memorize information or learn concepts and principles and why some are more inventive or creative than others. Many people suppose that differences in these capacities are inborn; for example, it is quite commonly said that 'You have to be born with the ability to do mathematics.' But psychologists who study learning have usually given more weight to experience. Indeed, Watson (1914), the behaviourist, who believed that the learner's behaviour could be entirely shaped by the educator, asserted that if he was given one dozen healthy infants, he could, by appropriate training, turn them into artist, lawyer, teacher, etc., at will. The experiment did not take place and, like most of the early views on learning, this one has also been modified.

The thinking of teachers is still influenced to some extent by early theories of learning as well as by theorists of the two main schools of recent times: the Gestalt-field psychologists and the stimulus-response (S–R) associationists. A further group of educators and psychologists have been termed the 'functionalists'. They prefer not to systematize or to invent new terms before knowledge justifies it, but accept information from any source, conducting their own investigations into learning and waiting for definitive experiments before taking sides.

Since much of the early work was with animals and young children it was questionable whether it could be applied unchanged to all human learning; certainly such forms of learning as concept formation, learning and applying principles, or creative thinking require separate investigation. This is beginning to be undertaken and the different kinds of learning which are required in higher education are now being identified and studied.

Theories of learning

Early theories which still have some influence on teachers' thinking are those of 'faculty psychology' and 'natural unfoldment'.

The faculty psychologists stressed the value of mental discipline. Their view was that appropriate exercises would develop the 'faculties' of the mind, for example, that classics or mathematics would promote the 'logical faculty'. Teachers influenced by this school tend to consider that work develops 'character' if it is distasteful, and so keep assignments difficult and dull. Investigation by later psychologists showed, however, that logical thinking displayed in Latin and mathematics courses did not, in general, transfer to other studies or other situations unless there was common content, or common principles could be recognized and applied; and dull assignments tended to diminish interest rather than to promote capacity for hard work. This system, was, therefore, responsible for large numbers of pupils who, on leaving school or college, never opened a book again.

Natural unfoldment is a theory of a very different kind. It was developed by educators who were influenced by the views of Rousseau. It is based on the idea that man is good and active in relation to his environment; thus it is sufficient for a teacher to provide the conditions for natural, active self-determination. Understandably this view gained most support from teachers in infants' schools where a large part of learning is more naturally conducted through play, but some of the activities which they developed although having the appearance of play materials were, in fact, carefully planned to develop skills which would later be needed in reading and writing or in understanding arithmetic. In a few experimental schools, older children were also given considerable freedom either, as in Dalton schools, to organize their studies or, in one or two boarding schools, to select the lessons they would attend. This view also has been almost wholly superseded; methods used with children nowadays are increasingly based on experimental inquiry into children's learning and study of structure in subject matter. It is of interest, however, that demands of some of the more radical students to choose their own topics for study, abandoning organized syllabuses of work, seem to reflect a similar view that the 'natural unfoldment' of the student is preferable to inculcation of knowledge; at least no other theoretical position is advanced. However, it could be defended on the grounds of rapidly changing content of subject matter and the need to develop abilities for self-direction and problem solving.

The Gestalt-field psychologists

The position of the Gestalt psychologists was first stated by Max Wertheimer (1912). His central ideas were that understanding developed through studying organized wholes rather than a collection of parts and that the learner tried to integrate or to organize what he perceived or studied. In the case of visual perception Wertheimer formulated five laws – of similarity, proximity, closure, good continuation and membership character – through which order was imposed by the observer. Similarity, for example, means that similar items tend to be perceived as groups; proximity, that perceptual groups are most readily formed from items close together, while, according to the law of membership character, a single part of a whole does not have fixed characteristics but gets its characteristics from the context in which it appears. Closure implies simply that the perceiver tends to complete incomplete outlines or pictures, while good continuation is shown in continuing straight lines, curves by a continuation smooth curve, and so on.

The best-known experiments of the Gestalt psychologists were those of animal problem solving. Köhler (1925), for example, suspended bananas from the top of a cage and left boxes and a pole in sections where chimpanzees could see and use them. Apes that had previously played with these objects quickly perceived how to solve the problem, or were able to do so after a further clue such as seeing parts of the pole in line, or two boxes stacked together, whereas those who had never played with them failed. The Gestalt psychologists deduced that it was possible to devise situations which would enable an animal to reorganize its knowledge and thus to solve problems.

The field psychologists of whom Lewin is the best known (1936) have extended these ideas emphasizing the importance of the individual learner's whole experience and thus of his environment, that is, his geographical and behavioural 'field'. If an experience causes a meaningful reorganization of the learner's 'field' it is said to result in 'insight'. Psychologists of this school consider motivation important in learning and stress the need for autonomous activity on the part of the learner; the way in which information, skills, etc., fit in with his objectives determines how he uses them and what he perceives in the 'field'. Thus there is a simultaneous and mutual interaction between a person and his environment.

Although past experiences influence learning, field psychologists place the emphasis on the present situation; they consider that the kind of organization of current experience has an important influence on learning which can give rise to sudden developments or delays in the learner's goals. Tolman (1951) speaks of a 'placing-need' in learning, of the value of 'sign-posts' in acquiring a pattern, and of following 'signals' to a goal. It is the teacher's task to set up these signals, creating a kind of map to enable his pupils to progress with understanding in a new field. Tolman also introduces the idea of 'latent learning' which takes place incidentally during reading, in conversation, or from observation but is applied effectively when it is required despite the absence of systematic study. Teachers may use this ability of their pupils by introducing early on ideas which will facilitate acquisition of more difficult concepts, principles and skills that come later in the course.

Since psychologists of these schools attach so much importance to organizing learning in a way which is meaningful to the learner, they advocate teaching by discovery methods – which require pupils to answer questions and to solve problems – and through open-ended experiments and projects.

The S–R associationists

In contrast with the view of learning which emphasizes the importance of the whole situation, associationists have concerned themselves with acquisitions of successive steps in learning. The first associationist, Thorndike, postulated that through conditioning, specific *responses* became linked with specific stimuli; these links, bonds or connexions were products of a biological change in a nervous system. Thorndike thought that the chief way in which S–R connexions were formed was through random trial and error. It is true that much of his experimental work and that of most associationists was done with animals, but he considered that there was an essential similarity in all animal learning.

The behaviourist, Watson (1914), felt, more strongly than Thorndike, the need to base psychology exclusively on concepts derived from observed events as in physics and chemistry; in his view, therefore, all kinds of 'introspective' views of learning were irrelevant in psychology; like Thorndike he accepted the idea of 'association' of stimuli with responses maintaining that the learner's purposes or thoughts had nothing to do with such learning. Thought itself he explained as implicit speech.

Associationists, therefore, see the learner as less 'active' than do the field psychologists; he responds to a stimulus from the environment, this alters him, he is capable of receiving new stimuli which again modify his behaviour, and so on. They consider that the learner's behaviour is explicable wholly in terms of past experience and that learning is under the control of its consequences.

Skinner (1953, 1958) has stressed the importance of reinforcement in learning. In classical conditioning, as is well known, Pavlov induced salivation in a dog when it heard a bell, by initially presenting the food and sound together. A stimulus that is not originally a reinforcing one becomes so by repeated association with one that is. The sound is then a secondary reinforcer such as praise, good marks, knowledge of correct results, but it must follow promptly to be effective in the early stages of learning. More generalized reinforcers such as money or promise of reward also become effective; but the response is extinguished if the reward ceases to materialize although, for some time, there is a tendency to spontaneous recovery. In experiments with different schedules of reinforcement, Skinner found that after establishment of a response by continuous reinforcement, intermittent reinforcement was more effective. A variable ratio reinforcement with a given ratio between responses and reinforcements resulted both in a high rate of response and one which was very resistant to extinction. With animals he could therefore 'edge' behaviour towards a goal by gradual change in the conditions of reinforcement. These findings have been applied in his method of programmed learning in which a complex task is broken down into a logical sequence of short steps to each of which the learner must make a response. The learner progresses through the sequence of steps at his own rate and is 'reinforced' by knowledge of the correct answer after each response.

It should be noted that in this view positive reinforcement is most effective in teaching. Competition is necessarily 'punishing' to those who do least well and like all punishment slows down the rate of response and so is less effective than reward. Skinner favours avoidance of errors, rather than allowing them to occur and 'punishing' them, since punishment does not extinguish a habit. However, it does provide an opportunity during the decreased rate of response which follows, to introduce and reinforce correct behaviours. Skinner lists some current weaknesses in educational practice:

1. Behaviour is dominated by aversion (escape) stimulation – to avoid punishment or poor grades, etc.

2. Too great a lapse of time exists between behaviour and its reinforcement.

3. Programmes of teaching lack the skilful reinforcement which moves forward through a succession of styles to the final complex behaviour desired.

4. Reinforcement of desired behaviour comes much too infrequently.

Teachers influenced by the associationists, therefore, give frequent opportunities to students to answer questions, thus providing them with feedback on their learning, and give prompt, detailed and informative corrections to prepared work. They may also prepare or employ programmed texts and teaching machines for students to use in individual study. However, the limitation of the associationists to the investigation of simpler kinds of learning limits the value of their findings at higher levels.

The 'functionalists'

The educator, Dewey, who was the founder of this movement, emphasized the value of interest and effort in learning and children's motivation to solve their own problems. Where psychologists of other schools considered that the primary drives to action were biological needs, the functionalists recognized purposeful activity as itself a drive – in the sense that there was a drive to solve a problem or to complete a task. Psychologists from this group also made the early investigations into memory. They showed that, to assist memorization, subject matter should be meaningful, interrelationships between topics should be stressed, and frequent short periods of study are normally preferable to a few long ones. The reason for this is that interference results, with consequent forgetting, if many unrelated details are presented together, when a new topic is introduced at the end of a period of study or if two closely similar topics are learned together. In rote learning recall from oral recitation is more effective than from silent study but, in learning meaningful material, it is the activity of the student and his understanding and organization of the material which contributes most to memorization. In rote learning errors should be avoided for once learned they are likely to be retained; but, in learning a coherent body of knowledge, errors tend to be eliminated and once the knowledge is understood it is readily recalled.

The functionalist, Woodworth (1922), gave more consideration to motivation, distinguishing 'situation-set' which determined adjustment to, and use of, the environment, from 'goal-set' which described the inner 'steer' giving unity to various goal-directed activities.

Psychologists who have developed mathematical and cybernetic models of learning also belong in this group but their theories and findings so far contain little of relevance to learning in higher education.

Principles of learning

The principles these findings embody should be borne in mind when teaching. As teachers are well aware it is of first importance that students should be motivated; but by no means all of them recognize the part they can play in this by providing appropriate reinforcements or conveying their own enthusiasm.

At the simplest level motivation is to want something, e.g. esteem, and reinforcement consists in getting it. The wish to obtain esteem is a primary drive. If a student's contributions in oral and written work lead to esteem they become secondary reinforcers. Need to contribute in either of these ways is then a secondary drive. Since secondary drives and reinforcements depend for their efficacy on continued association with primary ones, they may be readily extinguished if the primary drive is not satisfied. The need for stimulation, or satisfaction of curiosity, also seems to be a primary drive (Borger and Seabourne, 1966) which is not confined to human beings (Butler, 1953). Maslow (1954) has classified needs which may be used to motivate individuals as (i) physiological (ii) safety, or security (iii) belonging (iv) esteem (v) self actualization. Herzberg (1966) found that 'good feelings', reinforcing interest in a task, were generally associated with events which indicated that an individual was doing his work well. 'Bad feelings' were associated with unsatisfactory environmental factors and treatment by superiors. Motivations therefore derive from feelings of accomplishment, recognition, responsibility, personal growth, or from work offering sufficient challenge, scope and autonomy and in which people are pushed to the limits of their capabilities.

It follows that teachers should provide work for which students take responsibility and in which they satisfy their curiosity, for example research projects, field studies and open-ended experiments. They should ask questions which stimulate curiosity rather than tell facts, promote interaction in cooperative groups, help students to 'belong' and give recognition and opportunities for success. In addition they should show their enthusiasm. Nineteen out of twenty classes did better on multiple-choice tests after an 'enthusiastic' lesson than after an 'indifferent' one (Mastin, 1963).

It is conceivable that despite these provisions for motivation, some students may remain uninterested. If so, it is worthwhile to inquire whether their objectives differ from those of their teachers. Medical students, for instance, may consider that some pre-clinical courses are not sufficiently relevant to their interests, whereas their teachers' concern is to give them a grounding in basic sciences with little, if any, application to medicine. If there is a divergence of views, discussion and some compromise may be needed to get the students involved in their courses; and, as we have seen in Chapter 2, examinations which do not match objectives may limit students' apparent interests.

When the purpose is to give information and to assist students in understanding difficult subject matter, the ways in which knowledge is organized and stored in memory need to be taken into account. It is obvious that students are unlikely to remember what they cannot understand; a new topic is meaningful only if it fits in with what an individual already knows. Since this is not something a teacher can do for each student discussion plays an important part in meaningful learning.

Logical arrangement is, perhaps, more within the teacher's control. But he should remember the findings of Miller (1970) discussed in his essay 'The magical number seven, plus or minus two: some limits on our capacity for processing information' that the number of 'chunks' of information that people can immediately recall is about seven. These chunks may increase in complexity as an individual gains in knowledge; thus in learning radio telegraphy they could be successively dots and dashes, letters, words, phrases or whole sentences. Although as Miller shows there are ways of increasing this number by organizing simultaneously in several dimensions or by recoding, there is reason to think that students new to a subject find five to seven headings sufficient to recall in a single lecture or hand-out. Logical arrangement also assists 'memory' since the student may then work out what a missing heading should be, or complete an argument.

An additional reason for limiting the amount of material presented at any one time is that 'interference' is a very important cause of forgetting. During a lecture for instance, subject matter presented later may interfere with that which came before. This is called retroactive interference. Or less usually the earlier material may interfere with what follows; this is known as proactive interference. Since subject matter which comes in the middle may suffer from both kinds of interference, it is commonly least well remembered.

It is for these reasons, and because rehearsal and repetition aid memory, that some psychologists have advocated the use of questions, problems, tests or group discussion during a 'lecture' period. There is evidence too that the rehearsal should be prompt to gain maximum effect. In his book on memory Hunter (1957) quotes an experiment in which matched groups of children read an article and took a test subsequently, either immediately, a day later, after seven days, or so on. Those tested immediately scored 53 per cent, those tested after a day scored 38 per cent, and a group who were not tested until seven weeks later scored only 26 per cent. These results, together with those of repeated tests with the same groups, confirmed that forgetting is rapid initially and then proceeds less rapidly as time goes on. Thus teaching by lectures, with no rehearsal, which is still so common in universities, tends to be a wasteful method of imparting information.

Knowledge of results, or 'feedback', accompanying rehearsal is, of course, even more effective than immediate repetition for in this way errors can be eliminated promptly. This can be achieved by informative marking but is most commonly accomplished in tutorials or other discussion methods, or by new techniques such as those described in Chapter 7.

Varieties of learning

A trend during the last five to ten years has been to study the learning of higher skills and abilities and to attempt to identify distinct kinds of learning. Gagné (1965) identified eight kinds. His headings will be used here but the work of other psychologists will be discussed as it is relevant.

In each of these kinds of learning, except possibly signal learning, an essential characteristic is that some mental activity on the part of the learner must be inferred to account for his learning. Commonly we call this thinking. In studying the development of thinking from birth to adolescence, Piaget

(1950) talks of 'schemas' or 'schemata' which are organizations of thought arising from the activities of children. As a child learns, schemas are modified, combining with other schemas or extending owing to new experiences. This is a useful conception but during the last twenty years or so Hebb (1966) has attempted to devise more exact terminology to describe the mental processes of the learner as well as hypotheses as to the interlinking of cell assemblies in the brain to explain the mental organization (Hebb, 1949).

In order to avoid the diverse associations with the word 'thinking' he has coined the phrase 'mediating process'. He defines it as an activity of the brain which can hold the excitation delivered by a sensory event after the event has ceased, thus permitting a stimulus to have its effect at some later time. The simplest function of a mediating process is to connect a stimulus with a response, but it may be excited also by other mediating processes instead of its own sensory event; and when a number of mediating processes interact in this way – being excited by each other as well as by the sensory event – the result is thinking. Theoretically, Hebb suggests, a mediating process might also be defined as the unit of elementary component of thought, replacing the term 'idea'.

A simple illustration of the interaction of mediating processes is instanced when a child is told to 'add the following pairs of numbers'; the instruction elicits a 'set' so that when 4 and 7 is seen the child promptly responds 11 and so on. But, of course, he will only be able to do this if he is already acquainted with the term 'add' and has acquired some facility in performing additions. Learning increasingly complex mathematical tasks depends on thorough knowledge of contributory ones. Students who have not mastered subordinate tasks tend to be highly unsuccessful in learning more advanced ones.

Since, in general, the nature of the association of cell assemblies which takes place in learning is dependent upon characteristics of the learner's nervous system – whether these are inherited or derived entirely from earlier learning – learning is essentially an individual process. This means that learning can, and increasingly does, take place without a teacher,

but it may also account for the difficulties which teachers sometimes experience in communicating with their students, for,
if some students assimilate knowledge differently, or have a
different background of prior learning from most students,
the teacher must meet them on their terms.

In some of the eight kinds of learning which follow, the
ways in which mediating processes are linked are obvious;
but in problem solving, and much new learning comes in this
category, facility in forming links between cell assemblies is
probably more important than any particular established
links, and this so far is more difficult to teach. Hebb suggests
that a variety of activities likely to result in the recall of many
mediating processes followed by a rest from the problem
seems most likely to be productive of successful combinations.

Signal learning
Signal learning takes place when two forms of stimulation
occur simultaneously, the one acting as a signal – a command, for example – and the other typically a reflexive emotional response (such as fear of punishment) which precipi-
tates some kind of action. It is commonly used with animals,
or young children, when the command 'No!' is at first followed promptly by a slap, but soon the command itself suffices
to make the animal or infant desist from some dangerous or
undesirable action. Despite its non-intellectual character it
operates in higher education; for example a teacher's facial expression may act as a signal that a contribution made in discussion will receive approval or 'punishment'. Indeed such
signals, often unconsciously emitted by the teacher, may have
a pervasive influence on the responses of his students.

Stimulus–response learning
In place of the emotional response of signal learning, this
kind of learning involves simultaneous precise movements of
the muscles in response to very specific stimuli. Thus in elementary stages of learning Dutch, the learner may be required
to respond *tuin* to the picture of a town. By listening to the
correct pronunciation on tape, perhaps by study of phonetics,
and recording and criticizing his own efforts with the teacher's

aid, he gradually improves his performance on successive occasions. This kind of learning seems to be suitable and effective in teaching non-specialists who require command of a limited vocabulary in a foreign language in a few well-defined situations.

Chaining activities

Chains of actions may range from inserting and turning the ignition key to start a car to a highly skilled gymnastic performance, a complex dissection, or assembly of an electrical circuit. Whatever its length, the response to the initial stimulus, is, in its turn, the stimulus to the next response, and so on. In the initial stages, trial-and-error learning may suffice to learn short chains, while somewhat longer ones can often be broken into two or three short chains, but if the tasks involved are unfamiliar or difficult the learner needs assistance. A number of methods are in use. One advocated by Gilbert (1962) is to allow the learner to complete the last step, then the last two, and so on until he can perform the whole chain; this has the advantage that he sees the task in entirety on each occasion. It also raises the problem that someone else must begin the task on each occasion and is therefore a method suitable only for a single apprentice or where other students who have recently learned the task are available to teach it to the succeeding group. The alternative method is to build up the task step by step from the beginning, giving special practice to the most difficult activities. Little evidence exists, however, as to the relative efficacy of these methods. However, if the latter is used it is important that the successive steps should follow each other promptly in order to be associated together.

The use of verbal instructions in the establishment of chains is almost universal but, interestingly, once the skill is acquired, they are often totally forgotten. One has but to ask a number of friends how they change gear in their cars to discover that the majority must go through the motions before they can describe them. In learning, verbal cues may be particularly useful when stimuli at different points in the chain are rather similar; for there is a danger that these stimuli may trigger off any of the corresponding responses indiscriminately.

Verbal association

Verbal association is a kind of verbal chaining which may range in difficulty from learning a word pair or common short phrases to memorizing all the bones of the body or recalling a chapter of a book verbatim. Since subject matter is usually meaningful, the method advocated is learning by wholes. Skinner, for example, suggests writing out the whole (if not too long), erasing key words, recalling them in context, erasing more, recalling them while reading the whole, and so on, until the entire content can be wiped out and recalled. Alternatively a long poem or passage may be memorized by learning sections of it; but, if so, the connexion between successive sections requires special attention. Since errors due to interference are highly likely, constant practice is desirable for accurate memorization.

In the case of memorizing for oral presentation, whether in the native language or a foreign one, a chain of muscular skills of the kind described in S–R learning is involved in addition to the verbal one. For this reason the learner should hear his performance and, if the language is a foreign one in which he is not yet expert, he needs the criticism of a native speaker to correct accent, intonation, pacing, and so on.

Gagné (1965) suggests that in reacting against excessive rote learning in the past we now fail to appreciate the value of a repertoire of learned passages of prose and verse in expressing ideas orally. He points out that the majority of orators have been well acquainted with literature and could repeat whole passages verbatim. However, this might equally be explained by exceptional capacity to memorize. One reason sometimes given by students for choosing to specialize in sciences is that they have poor verbal memories and cannot write fluently.

Multiple discrimination

In most subjects in higher education numerous discriminations must be learned between, for example, similar organisms, words, classes, formulae, symptoms, etc. Since considerable interference is set up in learning them, and errors tend to extinguish the correct responses, constant use and re-learning are needed to retain them. Some assistance in making and recalling discriminations can be provided by studying groups of similar objects or instances together, as boys study pictures of cars, and by the use of mnemonics. But it is the constant need to make the relevant discriminations that stimulates their learning, as is evidenced by the existence in Arabic of an extensive vocabulary relating to camels:

The number of different words relating to 'camel' is said to be about six thousand. There are terms to refer to riding camels, milk camels and slaughter camels; other terms to indicate the pedigree and geographical origin of the camel; and still others to differentiate camels in different stages of pregnancy and to specify innumerable other characteristics important to a people so dependent upon camels in their daily life (Thomas, 1937).

Thus the teacher who wishes to ensure that students learn to make discriminations must give many opportunties for them to do so in their work.

Concept learning
Concepts consist in abstraction of properties – categories or relationships – between things and events. Each advanced subject involves learning many new concepts. Learning normally consists in acquiring a word, e.g. 'capital', considering instances, negative instances (e.g. accumulation of funds which do not constitute capital), being able to identify new instances and perhaps providing a definition, or definitions. Inevitably this involves making discriminations also. 'Capital', in economics and accountancy, for example, has ten distinct meanings (Garbutt, 1963) all of which must be learned and distinguished. And as we have seen in Chapter 2, some advanced concepts are intrinsically difficult since they cannot be exactly or uniquely defined.

Bruner, Goodnow and Austin (1956) identified a number of strategies in learning concepts and pointed out how their acquisition assists learning: an object can be classified as another 'X', classification provides the direction of an inquiry, for example, 'Is it alive?' and it also enables the learner to relate entire classes and events. Strategies in attaining concepts are rarely required in learning which is guided by teachers but may well be needed in a research project. Even the anthropologist who wishes to know, for example, what characteristics determine high status in a given society, can usually obtain information from the people themselves. But the research worker may need to consider the nature of the concepts he seeks. Bruner and his associates give the hypothetical example of a neuro-anatomist's attempt to discover which of six cyto-architectural areas of the cerebral cortex are necessary in order for an organism to show pattern vision. All that he knows initially is that when all six areas are intact the ability for pattern vision exists, but if none is intact the brain does not have this capacity. His strategy in setting up his experiments, and indeed the conclusions he draws, will be affected by his idea of the concept he seeks – is pattern vision due to one area, to a combination of areas, to either one area or another or to one combination of areas or another? The latter are disjunctive concepts which are more difficult to handle. If this possibility does not occur to him, he may write a paper claiming that area 1 is the essential one, whereas other writers who proceeded from similar assumptions, arrive at 'area 2' or 'area 1 and 2' theories, and the correct theory 'either area 1 or area 2' remains unconsidered.

Principle learning
Principles are relationships between classes ranging from simple statements such as 'glands secrete', which involves understanding two concepts, to complex hierarchies of principles themselves. When teachers speak of 'learning the basic information' or 'acquiring an essential body of knowledge' it is the concepts and principles of the subject, together with their interrelationships and some of their applications, which they have in mind. To learn principles it is essential to know the concepts on which they depend; and higher-order principles depend, in their turn, on mastery of the more elementary ones which precede them. Principles may be clarified through questioning and discussion from observation or through experiments. In the sciences, exponents of discovery methods may insist that students should discover principles for themselves, as far as possible, although in most university teaching

principles are expounded and discussed in lectures; but at present there is no evidence from which to determine whether one method is more effective than the other (Ausubel, 1967). In either case, once mastered, they are highly resistant to forgetting.

A way of recalling relevant concepts and principles and arousing 'set' in studying is illustrated by a method used in reading texts in French literature in one department in London University (Uren, 1968). A preliminary discussion takes place around the theme of the text to be studied, and students are asked to predict points that are likely to be made: it is not uncommon for students to bring up in this way all the points touched on in the text before they have even heard it. They find it encouraging to realize that they already knew so much about the subject and their listening to the text itself is much more active, since they are curious to hear how the text treats the same theme. Their tutor takes the opportunity to point out the value of their adopting a similar strategy in their personal reading. This is, of course, an excellent method of arousing relevant organization mediating processes, so that new information can be integrated with them.

The role of principles in 'transfer of training' appears to be an important one since common principles facilitate learning in related fields; but this implies, of course, that the principles should be understood sufficiently well for the learner to make new applications. Teaching which emphasizes common principles, for example, in introductory courses before the teaching of separate branches of a science or different, but related, languages, will therefore enable students to learn more rapidly and to obtain a coherent grasp of the subject or field. Where transfer fails, or where students insist on compartmentalizing their knowledge, probable explanations are that principles have been learned by rote without appreciation of their implications or how to apply or derive them, or that common principles have been disguised by use of different vocabularies in each branch of the subject or field.

Problem solving

Whether problems are of the kind that occur in daily life or those met with in advanced studies, they are all solved by the use of principles. The result of solving a problem is that a higher-order principle is learned and that the same situation should not again be a problem. Experiments show that instructing students in specific solutions is not the best way to teach problem solving; it is better to help them, through questioning, to recall for themselves the principles which will enable them to find the solution, but this will be discussed more fully in Chapter 5.

Creative thinking appears to be higher-order problem solving. The evidence is that it depends on acquisition of extensive knowledge and the coordination of ideas from widely differing areas of knowledge. A method of promoting creative solutions to problems has been suggested by Gordon (1961) in his book *Synectics* by bringing together experts from different fields who do not mind putting forward apparently absurd suggestions. After becoming familiar with the problem they try to conceive it in quite unfamiliar ways or unusual settings, often by the use of metaphor or simile. From ideas thrown up at this point successful solutions may be developed. Interestingly, Gordon also quotes the case of a group of scientists in industry who became more 'creative' because they found that it was expected of them. Where formerly they had failed to produce sufficient inventions for patent to justify their existence or to keep the firm flourishing, having been informed by the manager of this state of affairs a stream of inventions followed.

Incidental learning

Processes which occur in learning almost without the conscious volition of the learner include the development of schemas of perception and action, conditioning, latent learning and, usually during interactions with other people, suggestion, imitation and identification. Since each of the first three has been briefly mentioned we will concentrate here on the processes which usually occur during interaction within groups.

The three processes of suggestion, imitation and identification have in common that they all play an important part in learning but that it is a part which tends to decrease with age and maturity in the learner. Children, and to a lesser extent students, may quite consciously imitate the behaviour of their peers or identify with some admired person; but some imitation takes place at a less conscious level where, for example, a slow worker is influenced to work more rapidly in the company of a highly practised or quicker group. Identification appears to be a more wholesale imitation of an individual or the taking over of behaviour characteristics of a group. This process is encouraged in schools which foster an ideal type and is probably one factor in operation when a student doctor, for instance, acquires professional attitudes.

Some types of suggestibility appear to depend on the use of language for they develop after infancy to a maximum at about eight years but thereafter decline as capacity for critical thinking develops (Barber and Calverley, 1963). However, individuals differ in the extent to which their behaviour and mental processes can be influenced without their knowledge and volition. Susceptibility varies also with the situation or with the kind of personal interaction. Although people are likely to be suggestible in relation to others with prestige, this is not necessarily the case. There is some evidence that, in relation to prestige figures, people tend to extreme degrees of suggestibility, *pro et contra*, or none, whereas the majority of people are somewhat suggestible in situations where prestige plays no obvious part. Interestingly, suggestions which are usually verbal and spoken may be equally effective when recorded (Hull, 1933).

In the case of 'indirect suggestion', where the response is suggested in such a way that individuals are unaware of being directed to behave in a particular manner, up to 90 per cent of experimental subjects prove susceptible (Hull, 1933). When samples of students were asked to read a passage, either silently or aloud, or to prepare a talk on the same topic, those who prepared and delivered a talk were significantly more influenced by the passage than those who did not (King and Irving, 1956). This raises questions whether teachers may not suggest the acceptance of certain views merely by asking students to report on them, or to be otherwise involved in defending them, and stresses the need – where rational thinking is the objective – for presenting several views (if these exist) at one time. Perhaps the experiment 'succeeds' by the same mechanism as one of Festinger and Maccoby (1964) who distracted their audience while a message unwelcome to some of them was put over. They showed a persuasive film arguing strongly against fraternities, once with and once without the addition of highly distracting material. Results indicated that those who had no strong views were uninfluenced by either presentation but that those previously committed in favour of fraternities were influenced by the film with distracting material, but not by the other, presumably because the distracting material prevented them from formulating counter-arguments.

The importance of being able to formulate and present a contrary view in resisting suggestion is supported by findings which show that those who initially asserted their independence in face of views they found unpalatable tended to remain uninfluenced (Gerard, 1964), and by a study where an inverse relationship was found between suggestibility and conscious, verbalizable resistance to test suggestions (Barber and Calverley, 1963). In an experiment by Lorge (1936) students did not, in general, base their judgements about the validity of statements on the prestige of the writers to whom they were attributed, but considered the whole context for the determination of meaning.

In group situations among students, Asch (1956) has reported a 'predisposition to conform'; but independence of judgement had been established by about half the groups studied. He showed also that where standards of a congenial group differed sharply from those of an individual member, his standards were weakened as a basis for judgement, whereas those of an antagonistic group tended to be rejected – and more decisively so in contrast with that of the congenial group than in comparison with the ego-standard; individuals whose views differed considerably from those of the congenial group were more likely to change than those who diverged slightly (Asch, 1940, 1948, 1956).

A characteristic common to all of these learning processes is that each may have an effect either of directing or limiting learning – an individual's belief in his capacity to succeed may be undermined by indirect suggestion, he may imitate undisciplined behaviour from companions in a group or, in childhood, he may have identified with an immature or delinquent parent or companion and, through conditioning, he may acquire stereotyped responses. Suggestion is also one of the tools in deliberate indoctrination. Since such learning is non-verbal it is relatively inaccessible to persuasion and still less to reasoning. Experimental results show that the chief defence, or remedy, is that students should develop the capacity to express resistance in verbal form. To aid this process teachers should encourage discussion of a variety of viewpoints and help students to become more critical by being aware of their own assumptions and prejudices. In so far as more primitive learning processes are used, their function in higher education appears to be to foster confidence, to motivate students to learn, or to induce desirable professional attitudes; and, since group influences are bound to operate, the composition of groups in teaching would be likely to repay study.

Individual differences which influence learning

One of the differences between students which is most commonly remarked on by their teachers is that between the 'bright' and the 'less able'. If challenged to state what they mean by their distinction those without a training in psychology may have difficulty in describing just what kinds of behaviour characterize the one from the other; however, they will probably refer to the rate at which students learn, the extent of their knowledge and the capacity of the 'bright' to organize knowledge and to coordinate relationships.

Measures made by psychologists which most nearly correspond with these capacities are those of verbal and non-verbal reasoning. Taken together these were at one time used to measure 'general intelligence' or 'g', which was believed to be a measure of innate intelligence. It was further believed that an individual's intelligence tended to remain constant in relation to his age group, so that if he was in the top thousandth of the population at six years he could also be in the top thousandth at ten or sixteen years. Tests of this kind were consequently used as predictors of success in selecting children for grammar schools. However, studies during the last fifteen years or so have shown that scores in these tests are influenced considerably by experience; half the children brought up on canal boats gained scores so low that they corresponded with those of mentally defective children in normal environments: the 'intelligence' of the children of migrants from the United States rose or fell according to whether the education was better or poorer in the area they moved to (Klineberg, 1938); practice in the tests gave rise to gains in score, on the average of about fifteen points, but some considerably greater, and so on (P. E. Vernon, 1960). Thus although reasoning tests are still found useful, results are interpreted with more caution nowadays than was formerly the case.

Other ways in which mental capacities may differ are in respect of 'special abilities'. These include verbal fluency, speed and accuracy in calculating, spatial imagination, mechanical skill, musical ability, perceptual speed and accuracy, and some more highly specific abilities such as memory for certain kinds of material or speed in some situations. There is some evidence for innate differences in these respects, for certain mental defectives known as 'idiots savants' have excelled in one of them (Tredgold and Soddy, 1956). For instance there have been quite a number of persons of low intelligence who were arithmetical prodigies.

Tests of reasoning take two main forms – group tests and individual tests (Anastasi, 1958). The former involve a number of items of similar type which are usually presented so that the examinee has only to underline a word or figure. These test capacity to recognize synonyms, similarities, opposites or analogies, to find relationships between numbers, a sequence of shapes or words, to classify, and so on. Individual tests, on the other hand, are designed so that a psychologist can administer each item and observe the reactions of his patient or examinee. The best known of these is the Terman-Merrill revision of the Stanford-Binet tests which were devised early in this century (see Terman and Merrill, 1937). The six items which an individual must pass to be a superior Adult III, i.e. to be in the top thousandth of the population, require him to define at least thirty of a list of forty-five words ranging from orange, envelope, straw, puddle to . . . casuistry, homunculus sudorific, retroactive and parterre, to solve a problem involving orientation in space, to complete some opposite analogues, e.g. '(c) A debt is a liability; an income is . . .'; to watch the folding and cutting of a square of paper and to draw its appearance as it would be if opened again; to solve a numerical problem involving the finding of a law in order to extend a series of numbers and, finally, to repeat sequences of nine digits read slowly by the examiner.

Since these tests cannot sample innate ability but only what has been made of it by experience, different cultural groups tend to excel in different kinds of item and, whereas girls usually do better in verbal items, boys often do best in mathematical, spatial and mechanical ones. School children are quick and perform well in items requiring rote memorization, whereas the middle aged are relatively slower and poorer in memorizing by rote but, if they are highly educated, they continue to gain in ability to learn concepts and meaningful organizations of knowledge (Terman and Oden, 1947).

Differences in perception

Certain perceptual differences have also been identified, although these may represent preferences in ways of perceiving the world or those derived from experience, rather than differences in innate abilities. The majority of people use visual, auditory, kinaesthetic or tactile perceptions as required and may use verbal mediators to assist them in describing and memorizing what they perceive. But in recalling perceptions, a small proportion, some 10 to 15 per cent each, tend to favour exclusively either visual or verbal representations and conduct much of their thinking in their chosen modality. Some scientists, for example, claim to think primarily in visual terms whereas specialists in arts subjects are more likely to think verbally. This may be one reason for failure in communication, for one visualizes and may not give a complete description, whereas the other describes but possibly does not appreciate the value of visual illustrations.

M. D. Vernon (1962) distinguishes between 'synthetic' and 'analytic' problem solvers. The former sees the perceptual field as an integrated whole, without much regard for detail – it is they who, for example, may quickly survey a number of blocks and see at once what large figure they form; the latter concentrate on detail, building up a solution systematically step by step. But a 'plastic' type using both approaches is more successful than either extreme type in problem solving and probably also in making diagnoses.

Other well-authenticated perceptual differences are those found by Thurstone – of speed, or flexibility of closure – and by Witkin of field dependence. Thurstone and his students found that subjects who could rapidly interpret incomplete pictures differed in personality from those who were good at recognizing one geometric figure within another. The former tended to rate themselves as sociable, quick in reactions, artistic, self-confident, systematic, neat and precise, and disliking logical and theoretical problems. The latter had high self-ratings on such traits as: socially retiring, independent of the good opinion of others, analytical, interested in theoretical and scientific problems and disliking rigid systematization and routine (Pemberton, 1948). Outstanding administrators were found to excel mainly in the second kind of test (Thurstone, 1944).

Witkin tested subjects' capacities to indicate the vertical in abnormal perceptual situations. Those who did poorly he called 'field dependent'. He found some evidence that these were generally less confident individuals, as well as a sex difference showing men and boys to be usually less 'field dependent'.

Personality differences

The chief personality differences likely to affect study methods and choice of subjects in which to specialize are those between the extrovert and introvert, the dominant and submissive, the independent and dependent and between 'convergers' and 'divergers'. The well-known extrovert–introvert distinction was first made by Jung. Since extroverts tend to be sociable, they are likely to prefer methods of study which involve discussion and personal interaction whereas extreme introverts who tend to be shy, persistent, rigid, subjective and irritable may well prefer lectures and seminars to discussions and tutorials since these are less personal; also, there is evidence that the introvert's persistence in study results in better examination marks (Furneaux, 1962; Walton and Drewery, 1967).

Dominant and submissive students may like the same situations although they will naturally assume different roles; the dominant student normally chooses a position where he is in command – the submissive where his services are of value to others. The independent may prefer research since he is then entirely his own master. A distinction made more recently is that between the converger and the diverger: the former enjoys thinking about technical impersonal matters, likes argument to be clearly defined and logical and to know when he is right or wrong. He is not interested in probing into topics of a personal emotional nature nor in controversy. The diverger is the reverse. He likes discussion to be personal, he enjoys controversy and uncertainty, but is not interested in the technical nor in argument which is purely a matter of impersonal logic. Convergers tend to specialize in physical science, whereas divergers favour the arts, law or business where decisions are made on the basis of probabilities (Hudson, 1966). Despite the convenience of this distinction, it is perhaps unfortunate to have named these qualities as though they constitute a dichotomy. It is possible for individuals to do well (or badly) in tests of both 'convergence' and 'divergence', indicating that they are independent factors in personality and not the opposite ends of a bi-polar factor.

However, the majority of people do not tend to extremes but assume a position somewhere along each personality dimension.

So many sources of differences in skills and abilities leads to the conclusion that we have already drawn in discussing objectives – namely, that courses should be flexibly organized with a diversity of choices and teaching methods, or evaluative techniques should be varied so that students have some choice of methods, as well as of content, in their studies.

In the next five chapters different teaching methods will be considered in turn. It is assumed throughout that the choice of method will be determined by the objectives teachers have although, of course, it may be limited to some extent by the capacities of students and the teaching resources of a particular college or department.

Chapter 4
Advantages and Disadvantages of the Lecturing Method

Lecturing as a method of teaching is so frequently under attack today from educational psychologists and by students that some justification is needed to retain it. Critics believe that it results in passive methods of learning which, as we have seen, tend to be less effective than those which fully engage the learner. They also maintain that students have no opportunity to ask questions and must all receive the same content at the same pace, that they are exposed only to one teacher's interpretation of subject matter which will inevitably be biased and that, anyway, few lectures rise above dullness. Nevertheless, in a number of inquiries (Marris, 1965; Schonell *et al.*, 1961; University Grants Committee, 1964) this pessimistic assessment of lecturing as a teaching method proves not to be general among students although they do fairly often comment on poor lecturing technique. Students praise lectures which are clear, orderly synopses in which basic principles are emphasized but dislike too numerous digressions or lectures which consist in part of the contents of a textbook. Students of science subjects consider that a lecture is a good way to introduce a new subject, putting it in its context, or to present material not yet included in books. They also appreciate its value as a period of discussion of problems and possible solutions with their lecturer. They do not look for inspiration – this is more commonly mentioned by teachers – but arts students look for originality in lectures (Marris, 1964; University Grants Committee, 1964). Medical and dental students who have reported on teaching methods, or specifically on lecturing, suggest that there should be fewer lectures or that, at the least, more would be unpopular (Stavert and Wingate, 1966).

Predictably, the views of university teachers are somewhat

more favourable to lecturing as a method. Teachers of science consider that lecturing is the best method to open up difficult topics which students cannot undertake unaided and that, where subject matter is quickly outmoded, lecturing is the most economical method to make new topics available. Many teachers, in any case, believe that students are too immature to study independently (University Grants Committee, 1964). Despite students' criticisms, nearly all teachers claim to cover the syllabus in broad scope and principle, using only sufficient illustrations for the principles to be understood. They claim also that in lecturing they can respond to students in a way that teaching aids cannot do, that they are able to show their students how to build up a complex argument or diagram, sharing their enthusiasms for the subject while making reference to recent developments or indicating topics for further inquiry. Australian lecturers express similar views but, in one investigation (Schonell, Roe and Meddleton, 1962), 15 per cent of students were relying exclusively on lecture notes while the majority depended primarily on notes with little further study. Thus, there is an unintended danger that students will learn entirely, or largely, at second hand.

An aspect of lecturing rarely, if ever, mentioned by its critics is its efficiency. With the aid of microphones and closed-circuit television it is possible to reach large audiences within one building; and, as we know from national television, lectures of great interest, employing expensive visual aids and a high standard of preparation, can be made available to millions. Moreover, video-tapes may enable other audiences to see and discuss the same programmes subsequently at times convenient in their own courses. Had there been little else to say in their favour, these advantages of economy and availability would certainly ensure their continuation, but, even without the aid of television, lecturing is still an economical method; comparison of methods in one college led to the following conclusion:

For tutors the size of class is relevant to the economics of teaching, and the figures amount to 0.05 hour per session per student for lectures (assuming an audience of sixty); 0.3 hour per session per student for discussion groups of twelve students, and 0.33 hour per session per student for practical classes on the same scale . . . these estimates

. . . are probably reliable enough to emphasize the economy, both to students and staff of lecturing compared with practical classes and discussion groups . . . (Joyce and Weatherall, 1957).

Styles in lecturing

One might suppose from the students' comments on lecturing that clarity in presentation was not only the greatest but the only virtue they looked for. Perhaps this is because lack of clarity is so disastrous. However, observation of a large number of lecturers shows that a variety of styles stressing different skills in presentation and organization of subject matter is possible. Thus, in observing short lectures in courses for university teachers during the last year or two in London, many have fallen into the category of well organized and clearly expressed expositions; but, in addition, we have heard lecturers outstandingly good in handling evidence, in dramatizing a situation, in evoking a mood or in arousing interest in a problem. A teacher of medicine had his class (on this occasion of university lecturers) thinking with him as he produced evidence for and against successive theories. He spoke as though thinking aloud, whilst including his audience, and by this method demonstrated how to weigh evidence and ask questions. It would have been impossible to describe such a lecture as didactic or to criticize the lecturer for advancing a biased point of view. This lacked the finality of a 'clear exposition' which may enumerate points for and against a question without inciting students to think for themselves, but left the audience prepared to discuss the matter further and to seek new evidence. Some of our lecturers on courses have also shared this approach of raising a subject for consideration and further discussion and inquiry which seems wholly suited to the needs of university audiences. Indeed, it seems questionable as to whether a lecture which answers all the questions it raises can be advantageous at this level.

A different kind of experience is afforded by the lecturer who is a showman or whose style is dramatic. A lecturette on a legal topic delivered in declamatory style that captured the attention of the audience would certainly be memorable; but there is a possibility in such a case that the audience may be so impressed by the lecturer that they neglect to criticize or to think on their own account. However, in a subject such as law where the style may have its uses in practice, it serves as an example for students to copy.

A third style, aimed rather to widen experience, or to enable students to give expression to their own experiences, aims to evoke a mood or to transport the audience to a situation. This has the danger that it may not quite succeed. For example, in a lecturette on anthropology by a new lecturer who tried to convey his small audience in imagination to a society where surroundings and relationships were substantially different from those in Western Europe, we felt that he had not painted the scene quite graphically enough wholly to transport us there. Perhaps this was due to his attempt to achieve too much within the short space of time allowed. But it is worth the attempt where understanding is the objective. In some cases, a film or tape would help set the scene. Yet verbal skill can suffice. Trenaman (1967) mentions in his study of different media in broadcasting that audiences sometimes gained as much from a verbal account of travel as from television except, of course, specific visual memories.

A different approach again is achieved by the research worker or teacher engaged in current problems who gives an informal talk on his work. In such a case students see new applications of their knowledge and gain an insight into professional expertise. The engineer or architect who explains just why a bridge has failed or the difficulties encountered in a particular building, or the lecturer in political science who casts fresh light on current conflicts all help the students in these ways. It is true that they hear and see experts expound such topics in television programmes, but the opportunity to ask questions and to be involved greatly increases interest and motivation.

Perhaps the most effective style of lecturing is one based on comprehensive consideration both of the subject matter and of interests and differences within the audience. In a course for new lecturers in London University in 1966, for example, W. Gray Walter delivered a lecture designed to appeal both to eye and ear – for visual and auditory impressions reinforce each other in most of us, while some people have a marked bias to dependence on one or the other; thus both should be provided where possible. He asserted that essential ingredients of a successful lecture were humour, horror and sex. To provide for this alleged desire for sensation, in an erudite lecture on 'Brain mechanisms and learning', he used coloured backgrounds for tabulated data in which such outlines as bathing beauties were engraved in white. His admirably lucid and well expressed lecture in itself commanded interest but, if such additions will rivet attention to the less attractive numerical data, it may seem worthwhile to follow his example.

If the emphasis is put, as it should be, on learning, the possibility of modifying the form of the lecture more considerably deserves consideration. We have already mentioned the shortened lecture followed immediately by problems to work, or questions to answer, which are discussed among the students before remaining difficulties are put to the lecturer. This is a method of ensuring that students obtain immediate feedback on their learning. A different development is that favoured chiefly by students, namely the 'teach-in', which consists in a series of short talks followed by discussion: this, too, has the advantage of allowing immediate clarification which facilitates understanding before proceeding to the next topic.

A third method designed for a large audience is that of Betts and Walton (1970) who cooperated in preparing lectures in basic science for six hundred first-year students. Betts provided the straight exposition whilst Walton interposed questions, entertaining illustrations or demonstrations. Discourse of this kind, or indeed any method which offers more than one point of view – a succession of speakers perhaps – is too little used; it is likely to stimulate interest and may arouse the more passive students to undertake some genuine thinking. Nevertheless, with so large an audience, it seems improbable that questions from a second teacher could simultaneously meet the needs of the most advanced students and of those having a weak scientific background. It is hard to justify such large classes, so long as the staff-student ratio remains one to eight, unless all the students begin from an equal state of ignorance so that division on the basis of past performance is impossible. In his book *What's the use of lectures?*, Bligh (1971a) presents fairly extensive evidence which shows that lecturing as we know it is effective mainly for imparting information. He found little evidence that students learned to *think* as a result of listening to lectures. To do so they need to use information and to discover any inadequacies in their thinking in the course of some relevant activity. For this reason, and because it maintains or revives interest, Bligh suggests mixed methods of teaching during what is normally a lecture period. For example, buzz sessions may be used in which small groups of two to five students discuss a point for a few minutes, or larger groups of six to ten students might discuss a problem, presenting their solution to the entire class, prior to concluding remarks by the teacher. Either of these methods can work well in classes of up to about ninety.

Nevertheless, the traditional method of teaching by lectures and note taking may still reasonably have its advocates; but criticism of excessive note taking with consequent loss of time for thought or discussion is growing more vociferous. Quoting from Marris again (1964):

In effect you write your own textbook during the year, without understanding any of it at the time. The notes are good but what annoys me is that I'm expected to write them all down myself, and you spend about twelve hours a week doing it.
. . . Note taking is always a handicap to discussion. The advantage of typewritten notes is that you don't lose track if you engage in discussion.

The recent report of an inquiry by students among themselves amply confirms these criticisms (National Union of Students, 1969a). 'The opportunity to grasp basic ideas is hindered by the necessity to take notes' was rated as a major criticism of lecturing as a method by more than 63 per cent of students. Yet a very small proportion of lecturers was giving duplicated notes to its students. The argument normally advanced against this practice is almost invariably that it is 'spoon-feeding' or that if given notes students do not attend the lectures. But the loss of twelve hours per week copying notes without understanding seems to require more justification than this.

If, in addition, preparation and presentation of lectures is poor, students indeed have reason for complaint; and, since unfortunately this is not uncommon, what follows in the rest of this chapter is largely advice that is given (at our course for new lecturers) to young graduates who are beginning university teaching.

Preparation of the lecture
Defining its purpose

The first essential in preparing a lecture is to state clearly what its purpose is. Although this seems so elementary as to be hardly worth mentioning, criticisms by students of lectures which are ill prepared, badly presented or just repetitions from the standard textbook (Marris, 1964; University Grants Committee, 1964) suggest that this necessary step in preparation does not always receive the attention it requires. Since one purpose of a lecture, as in all teaching, is that students should learn something, the first step is to state what the students may be expected to know or be able to do as a result of it. Curiously, some university teachers seem to think of 'good teaching' as though it is unrelated to students' learning! That is to say, they do not consider teaching to be a form of communication which fails if it is not understood, but see it as a kind of performance in which well organized material, audibly presented, in itself constitutes 'good teaching' – whether it is understood or not! Possibly this arises from the tradition that it is up to the student to teach himself, for it is then a short step to say that meeting him at his own level is 'spoon-feeding'. Yet, if his needs are not to be considered, there seems little justification in taking his time for an hour when he might study more profitably alone in his own way.

Some of the most common failings are to prepare far more material than can be covered comfortably in the time, or to go at a pace too rapid for the class – or both may be combined. Haste and 'inability' to pause are often justified on the grounds that it is necessary to get through the syllabus; so the lecturer writes at a speed which makes a fair copy difficult and thought impossible, rubbing the board clean immediately he has reached the bottom, starting again, and so on.

A visitor might suppose that the purpose was that students should obtain a copy of an inaccessible or unwritten text. Yet in the absence of a text for the students to consult it is essential that they should understand at the time, whilst should a text exist, it is difficult to justify the use of their entire time in writing. Presumably, speed-writing is not a main objective in university teaching! And, if the truth is that the lecturer cannot accept an account of the subject matter other than his own this would seem to be a case for full duplicated notes in readiness for discussion or application to problems in class.

Content

What evidence there is suggests that too much detail, or a lecture too condensed in content, militates against sound learning. Erskine and O'Morchoe (1966) who compared a class that was taught essential principles with little detail with one to which considerable detail was presented found that the former did better; similarly, in experiments with programmed texts, students following a version containing only essentials tend to do as well, or better, than those who are given many more examples or illustrations (Wallis, Duncan and Knight, 1966). This is what we should expect from the study of learning theories, for too much material promotes interference which militates against memorizing it. However, if the material is already partly familiar, good organization may enable students to comprehend and remember subject matter from an entire field. It is in the early stages of learning that the pace should be slowest to give time to take in basic concepts and principles.

A second recommendation which has general application, regardless of subject matter, is that the content of the lecture should not be too abstract. In the investigation by Trenaman of broadcasting media and reading, for listeners of every level of education and intelligence, comprehension increased markedly for concrete subjects which were understood well even if they were initially felt to be uninteresting. Beginners especially require illustrations and applications which relate a new subject to their prior knowledge and experience. This does not imply that the lecturer should provide a session of amusing illustrations and stories, for someone who sets out simply to entertain his students not only fails in his purpose of teaching but is also likely to lose their respect.

A matter which is usually inadequately considered is presentation of material to a class of very mixed abilities and backgrounds. This is likely to be the problem of a teacher required to give a series of lectures to a class from outside his department on such topics as statistics, computational methods, economics for engineers, etc. For example, I talked with a class of adults after they had attended ten lectures in elementary statistics which were given with a view to helping them to comprehend statistical data when reading and, perhaps, to use simple statistics in research projects. They reported that they had found the lectures amusing; yet, when one member added: 'But I didn't understand a word of it after the second lecture', others immediately agreed that this had been their case also. Since the range of ability and knowledge within the class was very great one might question the wisdom of grouping all of them in a single class; but even so, had the lecturer considered his task from the point of view of what each student should learn, he might have arranged group work in each session or have sought programmed books to meet their different needs. By any standards, giving a series of lectures to them all was unrealistic. But many lecturers are required to give such series in statistics throughout the country and there is rarely an attempt to assess knowledge gained by the students. In the case quoted there was no reason to think that the humorous anecdotes and illustrations were irrelevant – on the contrary; it was simply that the subject matter was above the heads of most of the audience.

Unfortunately, even adult students are too long suffering. It is rare that they complain. If they do, it is usually because an entire class has reached desperation. Moreover, their complaint is likely to be made not to the well-meaning offender but to the head of department – who then has the problem of trying to understand the causes of difficulty as well as avoiding embarrassment to his colleague. For this reason it is advisable to plan for students to pass on any complaints to staff early in a course and at intervals subsequently. Even so, since students tend to suppose that a confident teacher knows best, they accept too difficult, hurried or overcrowded courses without complaint, blaming themselves for failure, and even join in the rush to 'cover the syllabus' in the erroneous belief that in this way they will learn more. The alternative seems to be a more flexible arrangement in which a minimum attainment is set which should ensure a good pass (if the content is learned) but with further work for more able students. In this way, there should be a general rise in standard due to increased understanding by average and less able students and greater scope for the able to go further than they are normally allowed to do.

Organization of material

When objectives and content are clear it remains to plan and organize the lecture itself. The beginning deserves careful thought and, perhaps, rehearsal. There is a number of opening gambits according to subject matter and objectives. Thus, if the purpose is to direct attention to a particular problem the introduction may take the form of a question, an arresting quotation or slides showing consequences of failure in development or construction. In this way, the attention of the audience is captured. If, however, the lecture is one of a series a brief reminder of previous material and how the next lecture fits into the course may be helpful; or a question relating to the last lecture or work arising from it may be discussed. If the subject is a unit in itself a very brief summary of what is to follow will help the audience to organize the content and give advance warning of topics which are of special interest.

Next, organization needs careful attention. It would be tempting to say that some subjects organize themselves had one not listened to a few lectures in mathematics which were far from lucid and which were represented by a chaotic collection of data on the board in place of the orderly exposition a class should expect. Perhaps the only answer for a lecturer who cannot organize data logically in front of the class is to prepare it in advance either for presentation on an overhead projector or in the form of duplicated notes. In most subjects where a selection of data and illustrations must be made, the lecturer needs at least a list of headings and main points; and in a small class of up to fifteen, say, where the lecture may in fact become in part a response to questions, or even develop into discussion, he may need little more. For a large group, however, the lecturer needs careful preparation of points under section headings, and it may be wise to keep each section together with relevant subheadings and illustrations on separate pages or cards. A variety of different forms of lecture organization is discussed by Bligh (1971a). A very full account of the lecture method as compared with other teaching methods has recently been written by Costin (1972).

Preparation of the lecturer's own notes is an individual matter and may well vary somewhat with subject. When lecturing in mathematics I kept continuous notes but rarely referred to them; in psychology I kept collections of notes in files under headings and drew on these, adding new material or further examples and illustrations as required. Sometimes I used separate sheets and, provided that they were numbered, they worked very well. The lecturer who reads his lecture must have the complete script available (whether one approves of the method or not) – in this case, a roll-backed notebook is useful. Although this method is usually regarded as reprehensible there are a few lecturers capable of reading very effectively. Other lecturers favour loose-leaf files which make addition or substitution of pages a simple matter and still others use cards. If the lecture extends to more than four or five pages or separate sheets of illustrations it is almost certainly wise to have them linked together in order within a file.

Visual and auditory aids need similar careful preparation and should be tried out in advance. Inexcusable faults are that slides, or the acetate sheets for the overhead projector, provide illustrations too small for the greater part of the audience to see clearly. Drawings should be bold and simple with few and brief labels and, above all, letters should be large enough to read. Far too often typewritten data suitable for showing to a class of thirty is used in a hall where it is illegible to the majority of the audience. It is true that it is better than no aid if the lecturer then reads the data, but a duplicated paper or a specially prepared slide or sheet with larger printed letters would be greatly superior. In any case, it is wise to have a blackboard available in the event of aids failing to work. Some automatic slide projectors, for example, jam if a change of slides is a trifle too rapid, or the class may find the noise from an overhead projector so distracting that they prefer imperfect hand-drawn illustrations in order to hear the lecturer clearly. Cassette tapes or film loops are, perhaps, easiest to handle; and, since audio-tapes can now be used with inexpensive players, their many uses may be more fully exploited.

Three-dimensional illustrations have become much easier now that closed-circuit television is fairly commonly used in universities. Where it is not available, either large models or sufficient models for several students to share are required. It is important in the latter case that the teacher should make certain that both he and the students are observing the same things, perhaps with the aid of diagrams. Lack of a model, or a verbal exposition whilst pointing to parts of a small model, may render a lecture incomprehensible to most of the audience. This tends to happen when the lecturer is, himself, very familiar with three-dimensional illustrations and fails to realize that his students are not yet capable of visualizing these for themselves. For example, I was present at a lecture on the development of the soft palate before birth in which one or two small diagrams were drawn, but otherwise only a verbal description was given for half an hour. At the end of this time the lecturer turned to the audience and inquired, 'Did you understand that?' When they laughed heartily in reply he offered to repeat what he had said – and did so, entirely verbally, in fifteen minutes. Finally he showed a few slides of deformities which could arise from incomplete, or imperfect, development. Both the structure and the presentation of this lecture could have been improved greatly. The slides which were shown at the end would have made a far more satisfactory introduction. 'These show what a doctor might see in his surgery; the question then is how it happens.' The subsequent lecture should have answered this question both visually and verbally, using a succession of large, carefully prepared illustrations on slides or overhead projector, sufficient to cover every critical stage in the development.

Presenting the lecture

When presenting his lecture the speaker should remember that it is his responsibility to keep the level of arousal of his audience at a high level. Evidence from studies of lecturing shows that if the lecturer presents his subject verbally, with little illustration, the initially high level of arousal falls steadily until just before the end, when it rises somewhat, only to fall finally with his concluding remarks (Lloyd, 1968). His lecture plan should therefore include various methods of stimulating attention. A good lecturer uses illustrative stories and examples or visual illustrations, or builds an outline on the board to enable members of the audience to keep track of the argument; he also varies his pace, pausing before important names or statements, raising his voice or speaking more deliberately to give emphasis. In these ways he keeps the arousal of his audience at a high level. Despite this, the audience will still experience micro-sleeps which result in temporary losses of attention (Bligh, 1971a). For this reason, a written record is needed, or repetition by presenting the subject matter in a number of different ways, to enable the audience to follow an argument without missing important points or, if they are making their own notes, to do so without serious omissions.

A brief account of the main faults perpetrated by lecturers at courses for university teachers will serve to illustrate the requirements for satisfactory presentation. The first, most disastrous, error is for the lecturer to put his notes on a low table and talk to them, never glancing at his large audience. A lecture given in this way is almost certainly inaudible to the majority and irritating to the remainder, for there is a lack of rapport with the speaker as well as difficulty in hearing him. Yet this is by no means an uncommon error. Indeed, on one occasion, when a demonstration lecturette was given in this way to a large audience at the Institute of Education, one participant described it as typical of lecturing in universities. Even should such a lecture be audible owing to the use of a microphone, it is evident that some members of the audience feel very strongly the speaker's apparent indifference to them, for they make such comments as, 'Tell the professor that he entirely lost contact with his audience.'

The second most serious error is poor organization. It is rarely so poor that the lecture is meaningless but it may be so ill planned that it is difficult to tell what the lecturer hopes the class will get from it. Or the lecturer pays so little regard to time that when he is stopped by the chairman he protests that he has not yet completed his introduction !

A third error, somewhat less serious, but responsible for much distraction, is that of wandering about the room, rocking back and forth, from foot to foot, or, as a new university teacher commented, 'One of your lecturers danced.' Since the offender inevitably moves his head in these cases, possibly even turning away from the audience, the difficulty in following what he says without omissions may be very great.

So far, then, we may deduce that the lecturer should sit or stand upright, remain reasonably stationary, at least most of the time, and speak directly to his audience.

Other serious errors may occur in speaking. A habit of addressing the board, with back to audience, is, perhaps, one of the most exasperating of these since it makes the speaker inaudible and simultaneously indicates that he has less regard for the class than the subject matter. Another common and irritating error is to become inaudible as the end of every sentence. In the latter case, expert advice may be required since it is possibly a matter of incorrect breathing; this may also apply when the delivery is utterly monotonous, a fault which can render a lecture tedious to the point where it becomes unendurable. One might suppose that this could happen only if the lecturer felt bored or uninterested but, surprisingly, he may *look* interested. Again, it is desirable that such faults should be detected before the lecturer begins 'unaccountably' to lose his audiences. However, a less dull speaker may keep the attention of his audiences by the use of illustrations, whether visual or on tape, or by pausing from time to time to invite or ask questions.

From this variety of errors we may deduce that it would be desirable for all lecturers to attend a course prior to taking up their posts and, if necessary, to attend subsequent classes in effective speaking. In the case of minor errors, a friendly arrangement with another new lecturer to sit in and criticize might well be sufficient. Failing all else, the use of a well-placed microphone will at least solve the problem of poor audibility.

Errors of a different kind occur when the lecturer obscures his own visual aids by poor positioning or by absent-mindedly interposing himself between them and the audience. For this reason it is advisable to use a pointer and to practise using visual aids with a friendly critic present. It is also wise to invite audiences to say if they are unable to see since all too often they suffer without complaint.

Aspects of communication which are rarely considered are the non-verbal ones. Recent studies by Argyle (1967) suggest that these have important consequences. They consist of facial expression, eye-contact, tone of voice, posture and gesture. Through these means it is possible to convey the impression of superiority, of friendly concern, rejection and so on. It is, therefore, of interest to recall an occasion when sound failed to operate in playing some short lectures on video tape, so that we observed non-verbal communication alone. The lecturer who had been most successful was looking arund his class, smiling from time to time, using his hand to make gestures, digressing to tell a story and so on, whereas those who were less successful were comparatively wooden. Indeed, in one case a lecturer who seemed to lack rapport due to timidity proved to have been looking either at the board, his notes or to one side of the front row of seats.

Since non-verbal communication is evidently important it is, perhaps, desirable that every lecturer should have the opportunity to see himself in action and to be provided with a list of points to check, enabling him to rate different aspects of his performance. And he should see himself as the class sees him, and not only in close-up, for close-ups tend to maximize the effect of even slight facial movement and so may misguide a dull lecturer into supposing that he is really quite interesting to watch whereas, in fact, his non-verbal communication is minimal.

Modified forms of the lecture

Considerations based on learning theory suggest that in certain kinds of learning the traditional lecture, in which subject matter is not discussed or used until later, is not very effective. If the purpose is to impart information and to ensure that concepts and principles are understood, it is likely to be considerably more effective to require members of the class to use the subject matter immediately. In this way they discover what they have misunderstood and can correct their errors before leaving the class.

Several very successful approaches have been devised in university schools and, although they were used initially in medical sciences, it is not difficult to think of suitable applications of the methods in other subjects, including the arts. One method is to give a somewhat shortened version of the usual lecture followed by questions, either on duplicated papers, or projected onto a screen for students to answer. Correct responses are immediately read out and errors are discussed. This is used in teaching anaesthetics (Davies, 1968) where the introduction of problem sheets has made progress so much more rapid that additional topics are now included in the syllabus. In a veterinary school, the use of a specially prepared room enables students to convey their choice of answers to multiple-choice questions to a panel on the lecturer's desk (Appleby and Poland, 1968). Thus he has prompt feedback on his teaching, from items the class got wrong, as well as on the learning of individuals in the group. A more carefully planned approach is to give a short, highly organized lecture outlining main principles and a few applications, followed by two or three questions for students to answer briefly. Their answers are immediately discussed by pairs or trios of students and any outstanding points are finally raised with the lecturer. This method proved so effective in a course of clinical medicine that almost all the students gained full marks in an end of term test (Mosél, 1964). Other methods are described by Bligh (1971a).

Evaluation of lecturing

Evaluation of learning by questioning and discussion will provide only part of the information a lecturer requires to make his teaching as effective as possible. There are some things that students will hesitate to tell him; for example, that his voice does not carry, or that he speaks too rapidly. Yet it is necessary to know these things, or excellently prepared and otherwise well-presented material may not be appreciated to the full. For this reason a group of lecturers in the sciences from nine of the colleges in London University co-operated in preparing a questionnaire which students could fill in anonymously early in a course. It covers the information which they wished to have but leaves space for comments to enable students to add points or to elaborate criticisms they make. The lecturer gives out copies of the questionnnaire, probably at the second or third lecture, explaining that he would appreciate the co-operation of the students in telling him how, in their opinion, the course could be improved. Lecturers who have done this, report that students are pleased to be consulted and take the matter very seriously. They say, for example, that the lecturer spoke too fast or that he ignored the audience, that they would welcome more illustrations and applicants or better notes. All of the lecturers report that one result of using the questionnaire has been improved relations with their students (even if they were already good) as well as increased interest. Students have also made some very helpful suggestions under the heading 'advice for the future'.

One lecturer who wrote a detailed report, commented on the value of the different items in the questionnaire. He found items which required merely a tick among five choices were easy to interpret (McVey, 1968). Possibly this was because different behaviours were described and were fairly easy to identify. On the other hand, some items seemed irrelevant to his classes and could possibly be omitted when using the questionnaire in that department in future; but as this is likely to vary for different individuals, it is as well to use it in its entirety at first to modify it in the light of experience. A point of considerable importance is that the items used should be as specific as possible. To ask students to rate the general ability of a teacher, for example, could mean such a variety of things to different students that it would be difficult to interpret; and knowledge of the student's response to this would be as unhelpful to the teacher as is a literal grade on an essay. What the teacher needs to know is in what ways he can help the students to learn more effectively.

In America a great variety of evaluating techniques has been tried. Some of these are summarized by Simpson (1965) and may be of interest to any teacher who wishes to devise methods most suited to the evaluation of his own courses.

When running courses for new lecturers in London, we issue in advance a list of points to bear in mind when criticizing a lecture. Since this is equally useful in preparation, whether of a lecture or a short course, it is reproduced here, followed by the questionnaire which the scientists devised.

Points to bear in mind when criticizing a lecture or
evaluating a short course of lectures
Timing. Did the lecture begin promptly? End promptly? How long did it last? Was any section of the lecture too drawn out, passed over too quickly?

Content. Could the subject matter have been followed more quickly, and profitably, in a book (or books)? Was it descriptive? If so, was it interesting? Was it explanatory? If so, did everyone follow? Was it inspirational? Was there too much/ too little content? Was part irrelevant? If so, was it valuable nevertheless?

Organization. Did the lecture have a perceptible form or structure (e.g. an introduction, examination of a case or problem, elaboration of principles, and a survey or conclusion)? Or was it rambling and rather incoherent? Did the lecturer state clearly what he intended to do – and did he do it? Was it easy to follow?

References and notes. Did the lecturer dictate notes? Did he go slowly enough for notes to be taken? Did he pause while note takers caught up? Did he distribute notes or a summary beforehand? If so, did he make use of them in class? Did he indicate precise references to printed material?

Visual aids
(a) *The blackboard*
Did he use the blackboard – to put up
names which were not well known?
formulae?
skeleton notes?
outline of a proof?
stages in the solution of a problem?
illustrative diagrams?
If so, were they clearly visible? Well arranged? Were they rubbed off too soon?

(b) *Charts, flannelgraphs, magnetic board, slides, film strips, film loops and films, TV pictures on monitor*
Were they clearly visible to all the class? Interesting? Informative? Relevant? Were they awkward to handle so distracting the audience? Were they *used* or merely displayed?

(c) *Specimens or models*
Was there one big enough for all to see? Or were they distributed to all the class? If so, could the teacher and students be certain that they were talking about the same thing?

Other illustrative material. Did the lecturer mention case history material; an industrial application; examples from his experience or experience of students; similar experiences met before, etc.? Did he use tapes of interviews, of a previous lecture? If so, was it relevant, interesting, useful? If irrelevant, was it nevertheless valuable?

Delivery. Did the lecturer appear to speak spontaneously, without notes? With few notes? Or did he read from a prepared manuscript? Was his manner stilted, nervous, rhetorical, conversational?
Did he speak clearly? Mumble? Drop his voice at the end of each sentence? Shout? Had he an accent difficult to understand? Were his pace and tone varied? Monotonous? Did he speak too fast or too slowly?

Rapport with audience. Did the lecturer appear aware of his audience? Did he react to it in any way? e.g. by jokes, humorous asides, examples from his experience, ask questions of the audience or invite questions? Was the audience afraid to ask questions? If questions were asked was the lecturer welcoming, sarcastic, indifferent, cold? Did the answers appear to satisfy the questioners? If not, did they give up? Did the lecturer make certain that he had answered the question which the student meant to ask?

Did you understand what the lecturer said? Did most of the audience? Did the lecturer have a pleasing appearance? An agreeable manner?

Evaluation. What means, if any, did the lecturer take to ensure that the purpose of his lecture had been achieved, e.g. asking questions of students, a class, setting homework, setting a test (e.g. multiple choice), etc.?

What would you advise this lecturer to do on future occasions (i.e. suggestions rather than pure criticisms)?

Table 6

Questionnaire to evaluate lectures

Surroundings and other factors Please comment on any of the following (e.g. excessive, good, slight, poor . . .)

Noise	Ventilation	Seating	Fatigue
Light	Space	Temperature	Hunger

The lecturer

Voice

Audibility: very clearly audible	easily heard	just audible	sometimes audible	almost entirely inaudible
Quality: lively varied tone and pace	fairly lively	satisfactory	rather dull	very monotonous
Speed: spoke much too fast	spoke rather quickly	about right	spoke rather slowly	tediously slow

Comments, if any

Appearance and grooming	very good – a pleasure to look at	good – a pleasing appearance on the whole	satisfactory	rather poor	poor disagreeable/distracting
Manner	very agreeable	pleasant	satisfactory	rather disagreeable	unpleasant
Rapport with class	excellent	good	satisfactory	fair	poor

Comments, if any

Table 6 – continued

Content and presentation

Amount of material:	Far too much	rather too much	satisfactory	rather little content thin	practically nothing worth saying
Clarity and organization:	very clear and easy to follow	clear	only fairly clear	rather difficult to follow – somewhat muddling	could not understand. Less clear than before
Use:	will help me greatly in the future	helpful	of some use	practically no use	absolutely no help
Stimulus and interest:	I shall certainly follow this up (by reading/practice . . .)	I shall probably follow this up	may follow this up	uninterested, would have been better occupied elsewhere	very bored, shall avoid subject whenever possible; less interested than before
Comments, if any					

Audio-materials

Blackboard:	materials very clearly and attractively presented	material well presented	satisfactory	untidy, rather crowded, partly illegible	far too crowded, illegible
Slides or other visual illustration:	very clear and attractive	well presented	satisfactory	lettering too small, slides rather crowded	almost illegible
Sound:	very clear and agreeable	clear	satisfactory	not entirely audible	almost inaudible
Comments, if any					

Chapter 5
Teaching Small Groups

The use of group discussion in higher education has become considerably more common in recent years. This seems to be partly on account of recommendations in the *Hale Report* (University Grants Committee, 1964) and of the findings of Marris (1964) that students would almost all welcome more tutorials or discussion groups, but it is also due to the increasing size of some departments and the consequent wish on the part of teaching staff to maintain contact with their students through small group teaching. Nevertheless, it is evident from comments by university teaching staff in an inquiry within London University (Beard, 1967) that by no means all teachers appreciate the value of discussion and, of course, very few have been trained to deal with it. In extreme cases, the teacher sees no use in such methods at all. One lecturer in chemistry, in the London inquiry, gave as his reply to a question asking his objectives in using discussion: 'To comply with "... will perform such duties as the College Committee, after consultation with the Head of Department, may from time to time require" ', and added bitterly: 'any further information may be obtained from the above'. Evidently, in his case no adequate reason can have been advanced to convince him that discussion with students could serve a useful purpose; and he cannot have received advice or training in how to perform a task for which he probably had little natural aptitude. In case the reader should think that this was a typical response from chemists, it is fair to add that the remainder of those who replied – and it was a large number – mentioned a greater variety of objectives in holding group discussions than teachers in any other subject field.

Before considering experimental evidence as to the effectiveness of group discussion for various purposes, let us look at the aims in using it of about five hundred university teachers (mainly from departments of science), who were circulated during the inquiry mentioned above. The objective which outweighs all others in importance (although this varies from subject to subject) is that students should be helped to discuss and to clarify difficulties arising from lectures or other teaching sessions. It appears in various guises: 'to provide opportunities for questions', 'to help understanding of lecture material', 'to ensure that students are not getting lost in lecture courses', 'to answer any problems arising from lectures and practical classes', 'to search for areas of ignorance and to direct attention to these', 'to promote understanding of concepts and principles', and so on. Another objective mentioned by a sizeable proportion of teachers in all subjects is to obtain more intimate and personal contact with students than is possible in lectures, which many consider to be one of the greatest advantages in holding group discussions. Then, with varying emphases in different subjects follow more specific objectives such as: to promote critical and logical thinking, to aid students in solving problems or making applications of theory, to give practice in oral presentation of reports, to discuss students' work such as essays, designs and plans, experimental results etc., to survey an entire field, to consolidate work already done, to take a closer look at one type of problem or to study one topic in depth, revision and preparation for examinations, to ensure that principles and concepts are understood, to extend studies to topics beyond those covered in lectures, to survey literature relating to one field or one topic, to widen interests, to change attitudes – an important aim in a field such as social studies – and to provide feedback to staff on students' progress and attitudes or as to the effectiveness of teaching. Although rarely mentioned as an objective, many university teachers consider that the feedback obtained on the success of learning and teaching is one of the main advantages of the method.

By using the term 'group discussion' throughout, the difficulty of defining 'tutorials' and 'seminars' is deliberately avoided. 'Tutorial' is commonly used for discussion of a student's work with his tutor or, possibly, with one or two other students as well as his tutor, whereas 'seminar' is normally used of a question-and-answer session directed by the tutor with from six to a dozen students. However, since some teachers use these terms interchangeably, or reverse the meanings, it seems more clear to employ 'group discussion' for either, or for any oral method involving discussion, and to specify the purpose and corresponding organization in each case.

The use of discussion to overcome difficulties

It is of interest that the objective most commonly mentioned, that is, to help the student with his difficulties, is also the least clearly defined. The uncertainty lies in the meaning of 'difficulty'. Should the tutor verify that the student knows the principles and theories or that he has as much information as possible? Should he ensure that his students learn to solve certain kinds of problems or assist them in developing an approach to solving problems in general? Or, as common sense at first dictates, should he perhaps ask the students what their difficulties are? Many teachers say that they do in fact do this, but experience shows that it can be in the nature of a difficulty that the students cannot identify it. For example, if they too readily accept assumptions without questioning them, or if they are illogical, this must be demonstrated to them to make them aware of it. Thus, to say that an objective in holding group discussions is to meet students' difficulties is inadequate without further elaboration, unless the teachers already know the kinds of difficulties students have or are knowledgeable about ways of discovering and overcoming them. However, this is unlikely to be the case if the tutor is young and inexperienced or if he has neither analysed the difficulties of weaker students nor experimented to see how they can be helped. In the great majority of cases to elicit difficulties involves setting problems in the form of written exercises or questions to which answers must be thought out and at least jotted down. Such methods will expose ignorance or misunderstanding, for a comparison of students' answers may be sufficient to demonstrate to each individual his own omissions, unjustified assumptions and errors. Discussion then arises naturally between the students and tutor provided that the latter resists any temptation to give an additional short lecture and has sufficient confidence not to wish to appear as an infallible authority. In the case of oral work such as making a report, or in chairing a meeting, tapes of the students' own efforts make a stimulating introduction to discussion of their performance: these may be supplemented by tapes of other groups at work. Videotape should be used if at all possible, since the non-verbal elements in effective communication, or in interactions within a group, then become apparent.

Thus if group discussion is to be used to elicit students' difficulties it should be based on some activity on their part. This may be simply listening to a lecture and thinking about it, or reading, but is more likely to be some common experience such as a visit, listening to discussion of a case-study, or viewing a film, or it may be based on solutions to problems which the students have already attempted or answers to questions set in the first ten minutes or so of the discussion period. In each case the kind of activity will be determined by the tutor's objectives.

A second point which seems not to be generally appreciated is that the way in which the group is conducted, and the role the tutor plays, also depend on the objectives. This may reflect differences in subject matter or in personality; for instance the accounts of social scientists seem to assume that discussion is necessarily of a free kind in which the tutor plays a minimal part, whereas physical scientists are more likely to see themselves as authorities to whom answers should be directed by the students.

Some examples will serve to show how the tutor's role may change in pursuing different objectives. We will begin by considering those in which the degree of direction on the part of the tutor is greatest and proceed to those in which the aim is maximum freedom of discussion between the students themselves. However, it is inadvisable to conclude that each tutor should proceed in the same way with every group, for personalities of tutors and the needs of groups of students differ so greatly that methods used to attain the same objectives may vary appreciably. What is required is not only the subjective judgements of those who participate but also objective means of assessing the learning which takes place during discussion. If objectives have been specified in advance and it can be demonstrated that they have been substantially achieved, some latitude is permissible in the intervening discussion methods.

Objective 1: development of mental skills
Promoting understanding

This objective is so broad that one might say it is an essential ingredient in most discussion. Nevertheless, it appears that when teachers mention this as a main objective, scientists' aims are to ascertain that students know new concepts and principles in the field, that they can interpret graphical, visual and statistical data or, perhaps, that they obtain a grasp of relationships within the subject; whereas, in the arts the purpose may be to ensure that students gain a knowledge of the social and political setting of a text, learn to appreciate the originality of a writer in relation to his time, to recognize differences between discursive and dramatic writing, and so on. In teaching biology, and subsequently economics and chemistry Epstein's method, which was described in Chapter 1, proved particularly effective in promoting understanding (Epstein, 1970). Discussion of the purposes of research in these subjects and clarification of terms, in response to students' questions, enabled them to gain an extensive vocabulary, sufficient for them to read journals and, in some cases, to attend post-graduate seminars with profit.

In all of these situations, the teacher's role tends to be that of an authority. Common practice is for him to give a brief introductory talk, and then ask questions; the resulting discussion, therefore, tends to be between individual students and the teacher. Alternatively, he may hand out duplicated graphs or tables, or require each student to have a copy of the text and ask questions immediately.

A variant of the method, recommended by the British Medical Students Association in their report of 1965, is the C O R L A B. In this method, which originated in Canada, a printed booklet is issued to each student in advance of the discussion; this contains a detailed clinical history and questions to indicate profitable areas of inquiry. During a series of discussions, students make additions to the booklet and teachers trained in a number of specialities are present to answer questions and to take part in discussion. At the end of the session, mimeographed abstracts of recent relevant papers are distributed. An advantage of the method to teaching staff is that they hear the views of different specialists in the field and see a number of approaches in discussion with students. The students gain in a number of ways: a wide field is covered in a short time, each student participates by prior reading and by making additions to the booklet so he has a permanent record of the discussion. But, above all, many aspects of the subject can be raised simultaneously, instead of considering different aspects at intervals during the course; in this way, they are provided with a coherent body of knowledge which is easier to remember and, in addition, spend less time on the topic. This seems to be a method suited to any subject in which cooperation between experts is important.

Where the teacher does most of the talking it is, of course, essential that students should follow up the discussion with further activities – in writing, interpreting graphs or whatever the task may be. In the case of statistical data it seems likely that teaching by programmed text would be at least as effective since each student would then be fully occupied and free to work at his own pace. But students enjoy question-and-answer sessions with a teacher capable of making them entertaining, and the opportunity to learn from other people's errors without embarrassment to themselves!

Developing intellectual skills through discussion of essays, designs, experimental findings, etc.

Discussion groups, or tutorials, to evaluate students' essays are most usual in the older universities but designs or plans are frequently criticized in the course of discussion in some schools of architecture or engineering, and discussions of reports on projects or experimental work are not uncommon in departments of science or engineering. Despite provision of time for these purposes, complaints by some students that time intended for discussion of their work is used as an opportunity for another monologue by the tutor suggest that even where the tutorial system is well established its purpose is not always fully appreciated. It is intended, of course, that the student should receive the maximum of criticism while defending his views, conclusions or prepared design.

In a group this works admirably when a student displays a design, briefly reminds his audience of the purpose it was intended to fulfil and explains how, in his view, it does so. A tutor and students of comparable standing are then in a position to ask many leading questions and to offer criticism. The whole group is likely to be fully engaged, their interest being greater if the students are comparing a number of their own different solutions to the same problem. There may be some difficulty in objectively evaluating a student's contribution but there is none in providing the criticism he needs from which to learn.

In the case of written work, however, students' complaints suggest that the situation is often very different. One student's essay, which is not accessible to the rest of the group, is discussed while they sit uninterested and unable to take part. A solution might be to duplicate one or more essays, giving the writer an opportunity to speak on it briefly before all the group joins in questioning or commenting on it. A list of points similar to that on page 202 could serve firstly as a guide to the writer, if he required it, and subsequently to assist students and tutor in framing criticisms of an indifferent piece of work. The essay chosen for discussion should not be of such outstanding merit as to discourage the group and might well be selected for an unusual point of view or for its illustration of errors many students were currently making.

Reporting on a project may be dealt with similarly, except that one or more students are likely to report at some length and there may be other groups of students and several tutors present to ask questions and to offer criticisms.

Teaching problem solving
Physical sciences and mathematics. The teaching of problem solving to less able students seems often to be ineffectual although, we must assume, they were reasonably successful

in solving problems at school. Comments such as 'they are not able to think' do nothing to explain their disability nor do they suggest remedies for it. Two main explanations are possible for the increasing weakness of some students in this respect. The first is that they have been drilled in solving specific kinds of problems without learning a problem solving strategy. In this case, they may get by in examinations which are of a highly predictable kind. The second possible explanation for failure is simply that less able, or less well-prepared students, are hurried too much by class teaching and need provision to work at their own pace.

In the former case, students may be led to developing a strategy by approaching the solution to problems through well-defined steps: clarification of the question by asking students to explain exactly what is required (they should not be told); discussion of principles which could be used in such a problem and why (this should lead to consideration of several possible approaches to the solution); and, as each of these is explored, a quick review of formulae, standard integrals, techniques, etc. which may be useful. Finally, when a solution is obtained, it should be discussed to see whether it can be improved in method, brevity or lucidity of expression. If the tutor feels that able students in the group will be bored by this treatment they may be invited to solve the problem independently, checking subsequently to see whether their solution was superior or not to the class solution, and a list of other problems should be available to keep them occupied. A student who obtains an unusual solution to the problem can be invited to present this to the group for discussion and comparison with their solution.

An alternative approach is simply to present students with an assortment of hard problems without a guide as to which principles may solve them. Hammersley (1968) reports that in teaching problem solving in pure mathematics at Oxford, about half the students attended problem-solving classes where very difficult problems were set whilst the remaining half continued to attend tutorials. In subsequent examinations the performance of students attending the classes was significantly superior, at all levels of ability, to that of students attending tutorials. But in applied mathematics, where easy examples were set, this was not the case. Presumably a combination of the stimulus of difficulty, discussion with other students, and the necessity to find a way into a hard problem results in development of problem solving strategies; but these may not be needed if a tutor is at hand, or if problems are known to be soluble from information in a particular section of a textbook.

Even these methods may work indifferently for less able students where most of the group is superior to them. For this reason, a number of departments 'stream' students by ability. However, since a really weak group tends to become seriously discouraged it seems advisable to stream only very roughly, if at all. If this also fails, problem-solving sessions in which students work independently, or occasionally in pairs, while staff circulate to discuss any difficulties with them, are said to be a satisfactory method and are fairly commonly in use. Surprisingly, the amount of discussion encouraged between students seems to be slight; yet this can be a valuable step in becoming independent of the teacher's aid, for each student then sometimes plays the role of adviser and will discuss his difficulties more openly than he would do in a group.

The inquiry into group discussion methods in London University (Beard, 1967) shows a wide range of success; there are groups which arrive unprepared, expecting their tutor to do the work for them, others who make no contributions except brief replies to questions, and yet others where able students are said to be bored and unprofitably occupied while the leader questions weaker members of the group. In contrast, there are groups which are described as profitable or enjoyable. In one, a volunteer begins to write his attempt at a solution on the board, prompted by suggestions from the rest of the group and, if he fails, someone else takes over.

Passivity and inactivity on the part of students are thus partly, or largely, due to the organization of the group within itself, but they may also be due to the attitude of the tutor. His role should essentially be to inspire confidence, to incite students to action by questioning or by praising them for making contributions. Students' suggestions, however poor, need to be treated with respect; if the tutor makes even a single caustic comment he will diminish the response of the group except, possibly, undesirable responses from aggressive members. If a student makes a poor suggestion, the tutor should not condemn it, though he may question it. Preferably he should ask the class: 'What do you think of that idea?' or 'Could anyone get further than that; what else should be taken into account?', etc. If other students attack the suggestion by condemning it, the tutor may come to the rescue saying, 'Well, it is better to try than to be silent; one learns that way' or 'Some creative workers are noted for throwing out improbable suggestions while they are looking for a solution', or anything which will encourage the first student to try again. In this way he promotes discussion and avoids lending his authority to condemning or praising a contribution; for, if he does this, there is no further need for the group to weigh it up and they tend to fall silent. Indeed, whenever the tutor contributes too much, the attitude of the students may become one of resignation leading them to say, 'If he wants to do all the work, let him!'

Social sciences. Procedures in solving problems in the social sciences are basically the same for they also require the capacity to discern the nature of the problem, knowledge of resources, and ability to organize available resources and techniques to a satisfactory solution. However, they are more likely to require good personal relations in cooperating with, or helping, other people, and the emphasis in such courses can be on changing students' attitudes. In this case, free discussion in which attitudes can be exposed and discussed is preferable to discussion in which the tutor plays a large part. There is also the difference that there may be no uniquely best solution, or even a good solution, and that, indeed, no two problems are quite alike. Thus there is little danger that students will be drilled in specific types of solutions, but rather that they will find problems too nebulous and ill-defined for confident action. This is one reason for the introduction of 'games' or simulated problems involving fewer complications, for in these ways the problems students meet can be limited to make them more readily comprehensible and thus easier to solve.

Making decisions and diagnoses

In some practical fields such as medicine and social sciences, engineering or management, skill must be developed in summing up a situation, perhaps before full information is available, and in making decisions on the basis of probabilities. Wherever possible this is best learned in practice but, if decisions by a beginner could be disastrous, or if it is too time consuming to wait for their consequences, or if suitable situations cannot be found at will, 'games', simulation systems and related methods of role playing are being introduced in an increasing number of fields as an intermediate stage in learning. A 'game' provides a model of the real situation or certain relationships within it. Exercises follow prescribed rules which, together with the model itself, give a structure to the participant's decision making. In this way, 'players' or participants are placed in roles which simulate those they would play in the corresponding real-life situations such as planning an advertising campaign, making decisions as to land uses, diagnosing an illness or injury and treating the patient, etc. (see Australian College of General Practitioners 1968b; Banks, Groom and Oppenheim, 1969; Hendricks *et al.*, 1966; Taylor and Carter, 1969). The cycle of studying a problem, making decisions, feedback as to their results and discussion of these decisions in the light of their consequences, may be repeated in successive situations, in as little as a day, where corresponding events in real life would occupy weeks or months. As in life, it is possible to introduce 'chance' occurrences which give opportunity for the players to exercise ingenuity or to learn to accumulate a reserve for any unexpected demands on their resources.

The role of the teacher in this kind of group work is to prepare, or to provide, a suitable activity. Discussion between participants consists largely in co-operative planning initially but subsequently in criticizing the way in which players have fulfilled their roles or in analysing causes for unsuccessful interactions. The tutor's presence is, therefore, not essential, although his greater experience and objectivity is likely to result in the group inviting his criticism.

A department of architecture has introduced study of a village and design of plans for its future development as a simulation project for the students (Hendry, 1971). This engenders enthusiasm since the problem is 'real' and leads to better understanding of how a local authority functions and its limitations. In addition it teaches survey and research techniques, whilst the presentation of an exhibition at the conclusion of the project is an exercise in communications.

In general, simulation systems are enjoyed by the participants. Less able members probably welcome the structuring of the situation and its limitation to a more manageable number of relationships, whereas able and experienced players take pleasure in varying their approaches in 'play' and in competing with others of similar calibre. A few people claim that they dislike models of situations, finding them too unrealistic to match living situations, but it may be that they have experienced simulation systems lacking sufficient complexity to interest them; alternatively, real situations may exist in which they would learn and they therefore feel, justifiably, that models are superfluous.

Developing critical thinking
One of the major objectives of teaching in higher education is usually said to be to train students to think in a disciplined rational fashion. However, evidence suggests that teaching students the basics of logic or expounding rational argument has little effect since their difficulties lie largely in preconceptions and misconceptions in their thinking of which they are unaware. It is, therefore, essential that they should state their views, whether in writing or in discussion, and discover through criticisms made by their teacher or fellows the faults in their argument. Abercrombie (see 1960), in a most interesting account of an experiment in group discussion in which students of biology were asked to define words such as 'normal' or 'average' or to read a controversial passage and to comment on it, to describe two X-rays, etc., showed that it was only through fairly prolonged discussion among themselves that

students eventually became aware of their own errors in thinking. Intervention by the teacher had little effect:

One or two might listen as though they understood what I said, but most were quiet only to save their breath and reverted back into their own confusions as soon as they could without being obviously rude. It seemed as though the associations that each person had to the word were extensive and tangled; the teacher could make it possible for the student to recognize that there was a muddle, but could not do much to help tidy up. That a long struggle is necessary to do this is indicated by the fact that students went on discussing the subject long afterwards.

She observes that the kind of change which has to be effected is the reassessing and rearranging of what is already in the mind, rather than the receiving of new 'facts' and this is a change which has to be made by the student for himself. She suggests that the central problem is one of changing from a state of dependence on authority to that of full acceptance of adult responsibility and that in this process the role of the teacher is a modest one – that of arranging conditions to facilitate the change.

In her experiment a subsequent test showed that students who had attended eight such periods of discussion, as compared with those attending the usual anatomy classes, made fewer false inferences and fewer inferences unaccompanied by descriptions. More of them considered two hypotheses instead of one only and a smaller number of them were inappropriately biased by one test item in dealing with the succeeding one. Since all these differences were highly significant (that is to say, such large differences would have been extremely unlikely to occur by chance) it is reasonable to infer that discussion of this kind is an effective method of promoting reflection by the student on his own modes of thinking and so facilitates criticism of argument and experimental evidence in what he reads. Continuing use of this method confirms experiments Abercrombie carried out in the 1950s (see Barnett, 1958; Beard, 1967).

Some of the virtues of this method are reflected in a use of group discussion in teaching French in a college of London University (Uren, 1968). It is employed to discourage too great eagerness on the part of students to give their own opinions on views of an author before ascertaining what they really are. The work is designed in three stages so that students are confronted with each others' assumptions. First, they get straight about the meaning of words (*éclaircissement*); second, they study what sentences mean or imply in the particular context (*interprétation*); and, third, they make personal judgements (*évaluation*). This leads naturally to précis writing or 'critical' essays.

Tutors using this method for the first time need to be warned, first of the possibility that some students will resent their apparent withdrawal from the role of teacher to that of observer unless they have been advised of its purpose and, secondly, that those who prefer to be given information to memorize will dislike the apparent aimlessness of discussion. For these reasons it is advisable to explain to the students something of the purpose of discussion of this kind – that it helps to uncover assumptions, mis-conceptions and errors in argument and so makes for improved performance. Tutors might also agree to warn students in advance that discussion may prove upsetting and frustrating, and to point out that if he, the tutor, takes notes, it will be only in order to draw attention at the end to good contributions which were neglected or to questionable statements which were received uncritically. The truth is that learning to think is not painless and that students, or teachers, who have come to feel that they should never be detected in an error and who find themselves obliged to give up this or other cherished belief, tend to suffer in the process.

Objective 2: group discussion to survey a field

Let us now turn our attention to a kind of discussion with yet a different objective. The purpose is to survey a whole field which may already be partly familiar or, in rare cases, may be wholly unfamiliar. Although understanding of concepts and principles is certainly one objective, the main one is the organization of subject matter in a coherent way so that it is readily accessible when required. Thus the emphasis is on the various interrelationships between topics and their structuring and on the common applications of methods and techniques. Since this is something teachers must know thoroughly in order to attain their position, they should be well able to act as guide to their students by demonstrating how to organize the subject matter; but, at a later stage, students must be encouraged to organize new topics for themselves and, at all stages, the teacher must ensure that they can use or apply their knowledge.

Three main approaches in discussion of this kind are in fairly common use. In the first, students make some preparation with their tutors prior to a 'grand tutorial' in which invited experts discuss different aspects of the topic while the students add to outlined notes already provided (British Medical Students Association, 1965). In the second, the tutor outlines the field in an initial session and assigns different topics to individual students for them to inquire into. In a third, less structured method, a subject area is decided in advance and during questioning from students topics are discussed and interrelationships, etc., are developed.

The first of these methods has certain advantages in that it brings together experts from several fields and gives students an opportunity to coordinate their different viewpoints. The printed outline provides a ready-made organization of subject matter and, when completed, forms a useful record for further study and use. Usually students are also advised as to further reading, or relevant visual material in the sciences, or may be set problems or questions to consider. The second method has the advantage that each student is fully involved in seeking information and that he gives an oral exposition of one aspect of the subject; but there is a danger that each student will tend to remember only those aspects which he has himself prepared. For this reason the method is best suited to inessential subjects in which some general knowledge and, perhaps, a special interest is desirable. The third method is most suited to revision and enables each student to organize new data, or points he previously failed to understand, into his pre-existing store of information. In the last case it is important not to sum up in too final a way but to provide flexible organizations which allow many different combinations and which will provoke further thought.

Objective 3: Developing oral skills through discussion

Until recently oral skills have been comparatively neglected in the British educational system. At the present time, however, new methods being used in primary schools, based on the findings of Piaget and other psychologists, stress the importance of discussion among children and of verbalizing much of what they learn, while in secondary schools oral work is increasing in both the arts and science fields. In the universities where departments are small discussion is said to be part of the normal commerce of the day and may continue throughout 'lectures'. The increasing demand for scientists capable of reporting on projects to colleagues from other specialities in industry, a new emphasis on spoken language since the advent of the language laboratory, and a demand for more skill in oral communications as a result of high standards of performance in televised programmes, have all led to a greater emphasis on students' skill in chairing meetings, conducting discussions and reporting on prepared projects. Moreover, since discussion has a valuable contribution to make to the student's mental development there is reason to think that it should be extended.

In some university schools, however, oral skills have already become an important objective in group work; for example, engineers prepare projects, present them to the group and defend their recommendations in subsequent discussion, while in management and political studies skills required in committee are practised and discussion of policies takes place in simulated situations. Students preparing to teach children in school have always received advice on how to speak to an audience and how to project their voices effectively without strain. Linguists, too, have always practised the speaking of languages but, since the introduction of the language laboratory and increasing demand for skilful performance in conversation and discussion in the foreign language, new techniques have been developed to give intensive practice in elementary language; increasing use is made of discussion to promote fluency in different kinds of vocabulary.

It is of interest that the effect of assessing students' contributions to seminars in the English department at York has been entirely good. Jones (1969) reports that the work is more thoroughly prepared than ever before, although as he says, the 'high quality of discussion led to our forgetting all about the examination'. He claims that this method recognizes that a student's activity is to a large extent a collaborative one, and that sustaining informed discussion is a central and essential function of a university.

Objective 4: using discussion to change attitudes

Since change in attitudes requires that students should become aware of and examine their existing attitudes one might infer from a previous consideration of the development of critical thinking in discussion that similar methods would be appropriate. Evidence tends to confirm this view. It seems that participation by students, exposure to views different from their own and to criticism from their fellows together with some withdrawal of the teachers' authority, are needed if attitudes are to be changed. Thus in a medical course devised to develop in students a concern for the social and psychological aspects of patients' illnesses it was direct contact with their own patients' homes which led to changes in attitude about social aspects of care, while comprehensive case conferences encouraged them to coordinate their knowledge of social, psychological and medical aspects of illness (Hammond *et al.*, 1959). This evidence suggests, therefore, that a new experience combined with free discussion is crucial in changing attitudes where a breaking down of prejudices and misconceptions or increase in awareness of factors which have been habitually ignored is desired.

A third factor which may well be important is that the individual should commit himself to a new mode of behaviour as well as being prepared to admit to earlier misconceptions, prejudices and so on. During the war years, Lewin (1947) found that housewives could be persuaded by discussion to say that they would try new kinds of food and, having committed themselves to do so, about one third in fact did whereas lectures had practically no effect.

Discussion of a fairly free kind, but with a tutor present, is also effective in changing attitudes towards others in the group. Several experimenters report that group members learned from their fellows' criticisms to be less aggressive or less voluble and that some participants remarked a change in themselves towards the end of a series of discussions.

There is a more traumatic practice used in some managerial colleges of throwing a new group of course members together, leaderless and without direction. The unexpected neglect gives rise to aggressive feelings in the group so that those who speak or attempt to lead the group tend to be the subjects of verbal attack. The justification for the method is that this proves a salutary experience since individuals become acquainted with some of their faults and, in subsequent discussion, if not before, gain insight into group dynamics and so into better techniques of management. Critics of the method report that, on the contrary, the method in some cases undermines confidence even to the point of inducing breakdown and cannot be recommended because of its effects on personal relationships. This suggests the value of having a staff member present even if he never participates since he acts as a check on hostility and so protects an unpopular individual or minority. On the other hand, where students know each other and get on tolerably well, free discussion without a tutor can be beneficial.

In all of these methods designed to influence attitudes the role of the teacher is to plan the right kind of experience for the group and to elicit contributions from them. If, for example, he shows a film of committee meetings, plays a tape of a patient's interview with a doctor, or of a class getting out of hand with a student teacher, he does not offer the interpretation; instead he invites this from group members and if they fail to observe a critical incident he will replay it and ask further questions until they see its significance for themselves.

The most recent and systematic development in the use of group discussion to change attitudes is that of 'T-groups' (Smith, 1969) in managerial training. These methods differ from most other group methods in that trainees spend a considerable proportion of their time talking about their relationships with each other on the training course. By discussing together the consequences of having behaved in particular ways, they transform prescribed learning into something which each person learns from experience for himself. Changes in an individual result from a complex interplay of his own goals with the reactions he obtains from other members of the group; thus a too retiring member may learn to show more aggressiveness when he finds that this is expected of him in a position of leadership. With groups of strangers, these types of training have three main goals: to increase sensitivity in accurately perceiving another person's reactions to one's own behaviour, to increase diagnostic ability in perceiving relationships between others, and to increase 'action skill' or flexibility in choosing the right behaviour from a range of possible behaviours. After an initial introduction by the staff trainer, indicating goals and meeting times, his contributions tend to be infrequent and a new structure, therefore, emerges taking account of goals of group members as well as those indicated by the trainer. As meetings proceed, members increasingly give feedback by expressing their reactions to one another sometimes, thereby, helping individuals to gain a more accurate self-concept. Attempts to evaluate the effects of these methods show a marked tendency by T-group members to gain in ability to respond relevantly and flexibly to group situations.

The use of T-groups within a single company or institution presents more problems. Friedlander (1967) suggests that it is only where trust is initially high that other benefits such as group effectiveness develop. But this leads us to a point where further research is needed to explore factors influencing group interaction and cooperation.

Personality factors in discussion

Whether group discussion goes well, particularly if it is of the free, less directed kind, inevitably depends to some extent on the personality characteristics of the students and the tutor. A number of tutors, especially in the physical sciences, complain of taciturn students; but an even larger number complain that group discussions tend to be monopolized by students seeking to impress the others or those who persistently argue. Findings in investigations by sociologists and psychologists into the effects of seating position and eye contact may sometimes be used to exercise a little control in such situations. It has been shown, for example, that individuals tend to talk most to people opposite to them and to those they can easily see rather than to their immediate neighbours (Hare and Bates, 1963). Thus it is worthwhile rearranging the group on some pretext so that persistent talkers are adjacent to each other or on either side of the tutor and opposite to the least talkative members. If this fails more positive measures should be tried, such as thanking the most persistent speaker for his interesting comments and inviting the views of other members, individually, on the same topic. As a last resort the persistent speaker may be asked to take notes of the discussion for the group's use or to write a brief account of his helpful observations.

Silent members of a group may be induced to contribute by pausing occasionally for a buzz session during which neighbours discuss points more fully. In this way a student too shy to address the whole group has an opportunity to contribute indirectly through a question or comment by his neighbour based on his inquiry or suggestion. However, if each student is at intervals asked to introduce a topic and to answer questions, all but the most persistently silent are likely to make worthwhile contributions. Perhaps it would also be beneficial to acquaint the students with research findings concerning the status of talkative and taciturn group members. It seems that the most frequent speakers (with a few exceptions) tend to be popular and are almost universally perceived as contributing more and as being more influential in getting a solution, or view, accepted than the least frequent speakers (Klein, 1965; Riecken, 1958). Even when given the best solution to a problem to offer to the group, infrequent speakers fail to get it accepted unless they gain the support of a talkative member. Ability to influence the group results from gaining their attention, so infrequent speakers tend to be ignored and any contribution they do make is undervalued. However, in one attempt to make the taciturn speak, talkative and untalkative students were separated (Knutson, 1960). Although untalkative groups proved even quieter than anticipated and tended to dislike their groups, whereas vocal groups were well satisfied, it was the quiet groups who presented better organized and inter-related reports of their proceedings. Thus taciturn members may make efficient group secretaries or prepare very good reports to present to the group and, in the latter event, they must inevitably give answers to questions.

Other psychologists have looked at the difference between group members with 'authoritarian' and 'egalitarian' person-alities. Among groups of students the former behaved more aggressively, were less effective in cooperative tasks, more con-cerned with status and liked a more authoritarian leader than groups of 'egalitarian' individuals (Haythorn, Couch, Haefner, Langham and Lannor, 1956). Emergent leaders in egalitarian groups were more sensitive to others, more effec-tive teachers, more prone to making suggestions for action, subject to group sanctions, and less likely to give direct orders to others. Where groups were organized as competitive by rating performance individually, or cooperative by rating the work of the group as a whole, cooperative groups per-formed better in a variety of respects, including greater under-standing of, and attentiveness to, fellow members, more co-ordination of effort and greater productivity (Deutsch, 1949).

Findings concerning leadership mostly relate to groups dis-cussing industrial disputes and probably have little relevance to teaching. In an interesting experiment with students, how-ever, in groups with either 'permissive' leaders or observers, group members more often changed their minds from be-lieving a wrong answer to accepting a correct one in groups with leaders and, when someone was given a correct solution it was easier to get it accepted in a group with a leader (Maier and Solem, 1952); also, in these groups, right answers were more readily worked out. However, minority views had greater influence in groups with leaders; when a strong minority held an incorrect view a leader tended to 'protect' them whereas in groups with observers, and no leaders, such minorities were obliged to change their views. Perhaps the moral is that when a difficult small group will not be convinced it may be better to find an excuse for withdrawing, such as an urgent telephone call, and leave them to their peers.

Encouraging students to talk

Since one of the most commonly reported problems in group discussion is that students do not participate, or that only some students do so, it is worthwhile to consider how to promote and to sustain discussion.

Findings discussed in the previous section suggest that the environment in which the group is held, arrangement within the group itself, placing of the tutor and the role he assumes may all have an influence on the group's performance. It is easier to talk in a small common room which is already associated with friendly conversation than in a corner of a lecture room. But if it is the tutor's room and he sits in his customary position behind his desk, he has already assumed a position of authority unsuited to the less directed kinds of groups. Arrangement of seating is important because students will not talk to those they cannot see, and physical distance may suggest intimacy if the group is crowded together, or an individual may choose to be both physically and psychologically remote (Abercrombie, 1971).

If the group are beginners in the use of discussion as a method of learning, they may need to learn in this way. Bligh (1971b) suggests that the rule is 'start with simple tasks, with small groups for short periods. Then gradually increase them.' He suggests further: 'Some students think that discussion periods are occasions for general relaxation and "chit-chat". If the tone of the course is set by making them work on a problem on the first day, teaching is easier later on.'

He stresses the need to promote confidence at this stage and to foster curiosity by use of problems which apply principles of the subject in a practical way or talks involving acquisition of facts and simple interpretation of them. Alternatively, they may be asked to solve a problem and to discuss their methods when the first one or two students have reached a solution. In this way everyone has something to contribute. Meanwhile if the teacher circulates amongst several subgroups, or withdraws and listens if the group is working as a whole, he may learn a great deal about his students' capacities and thinking.

As group size and task difficulty increase so does the problem of keeping the group active. It is essential that the teacher should withdraw so far as possible from a dominant position. He may use eye contact to bring in silent members who appear to have something to contribute so avoiding the danger of speaking again and being left to continue. Bligh (1971b) suggests these prohibitions: (i) 'Don't correct or reject the first contributions' even if they are wildly wrong. (ii) 'Don't state an opinion rigidly', it may inhibit students even if it is an outrageous statement intended to arouse disagreement. (iii) 'Don't answer questions that could be answered by another member of the class.'

If more mature groups will not participate the difficulty may lie in unsuitable topics, lack of preparation or in unconscious inhibition of discussion by the tutor. The last is easily diagnosed by introducing the topic and withdrawing for a time on some pretext such as a phone call. If the group is talking fluently on the tutor's return ten minutes later, then one solution is to divide the group into two and to alternate between them. This allows the leaderless group to become animated before the tutor joins in.

Lack of preparation is overcome if one of the mixed methods is used in which the tutor sets a task on completing a shortened lecture. Alternatively the group may be given more responsibility. Black reports (1971) that in one of their groups, degeneration into sporadic staff monologues led to student reaction and the formation of a student committee which asked to be allowed to run the discussions – a request which was readily granted. Subsequent discussion was more brisk because at least some students felt responsible and came prepared.

Unsuitable for discussion are topics which are simply a matter of acquiring fairly straightforward information. These are better learned through reading, a lecture followed by questions, or one of the modern self-teaching techniques. It is wiser to change the method or to choose a different subject which raises difficulties which can be profitably discussed.

Skill in leading group discussion needs to be developed. It involves considerable understanding of students as well as of subject matter and may well justify attendance at a course designed to develop expertise in group methods.

Chapter 6
Practical and Laboratory Teaching

A diversity of skills is taught in universities: engineers learn to assemble circuits and complex machinery or to design and build intricate constructions, architects and designers demonstrate solutions to the problems they solve by means of diagrams, drawings and models, students of dentistry and medicine acquire a wide variety of practical skills to diagnose and treat their patients' ills, whilst scientists learn skills in using apparatus, in observing phenomena or in obtaining experimental results with reasonable accuracy. Indeed, there is no reason to limit the list here. Linguists must acquire auditory and oral skills, while artists learn to express themselves in a variety of materials. In each subject perceptual abilities are called into play, whether visual, kinaesthetic and tactual, auditory or oral; but in all of them a basic theoretical background is required and in the majority, as knowledge advances, increasing skill in abstract reasoning is also involved. Training in most skills has been studied to some extent; but, since the emphasis has been on the simpler, more mechanical skills required in industry or for military purposes, findings concerning those with considerable theoretical content are comparatively scarce. In considering training in complex skills, therefore, we must depend on a modest number of experiments by teachers in universities, since the findings of psychologists studying training are not fully relevant although they may sometimes be illuminating. Acquisition of skills in aesthetic subjects presents special problems, for agreement as to what looks or sounds 'good' may be poor and there is, therefore, no possibility of training in the sense of producing a standard, measurable performance.

Before looking at the special problems of teaching in the

laboratory we will survey very briefly some more relevant findings from industry and the forces. Many of the former are outlined and discussed by Seymour (1966) in his excellent book *Industrial Skills*, whilst a book edited by Glaser (1962) in the United States describes training experiments in industry and, to a lesser extent, the forces, as well as discussing at some length the problems which psychologists must define and solve in studying training. In both books 'knowledge' and 'skills' content in learning practical tasks are distinguished; the former involves memory for symbolic material such as words, numbers or diagrams and is said to be learned when it is memorized and appropriately recalled; the latter involves non-symbolic information which must be acquired through motor and perceptual learning. If the 'knowledge' content can be readily memorized, the control of the motor activities can proceed unimpeded by reference to a guide. But difficulty arises when diagrams and written texts have to be consulted as the task proceeds or when the level of discrimination required (such as between two closely similar shapes, colours or sounds) is near the threshold for that particular sense.

Even in the simple matter of using names for components, experiments show that ability to memorize them readily, due to some prior knowledge, facilitates learning the skill but that, if the names are initially unfamiliar, then learning some of them assists learning of the tasks, but attempting to learn all the component names in this case results in poorer performance – presumably because either there is interference in recalling similar names or there is difficulty in discriminating between 'meanings' (Saltz and Newman, 1960). This suggests that in teaching the names of instruments to nurses, for example, they will perform better if they have already heard some of them named in the ordinary course of their work than if the names are introduced for the first time with all the instruments.

It is also of some importance to see that verbal cues can operate effectively, either by an explicit training procedure or by numbering the parts in the order in which they will be issued in an assembly, etc. Difficulty in following instructions is now commonly overcome by use of an audio-tape with pedal control, so that the student can stop it when he wishes. Alternatively, a tape dealing with the entire process, but with additional material to emphasize difficult points, seems to be highly effective. In a personal communication, Dr Goodhue of the Zoology Department at Trinity College, Dublin, reports that tapes, together with diagrams and other illustrations he has prepared, have proved so successful in teaching first-year students to dissect rats that their initial attempts which formerly took three hours, with many errors following a demonstration, are now completed almost perfectly in one hour.

A method emphasizing intellectual content in teaching anatomy has been proposed by Lawrence (1962), but has not been experimented with. Its advantages seem to be that – like the method employed by Uren (1968) in teaching French textual criticism – it would induce a preliminary 'set' conducive to more intelligent observation, and that an emphasis on function would give coherence to what may easily deteriorate into memorizing a list of names. Thus he suggests: firstly, naming and demonstrating the movements of joints, flexion, extension, etc., in a skeleton; next, demonstrating on a 'lean and muscular student' the tensing and use of muscles involved in a few joint movements; and then setting the class to study the muscles, their origins and insertions used in various movements, by inspecting and palpating themselves and fellow students, thus working out their own myology. After this he proposes that by the use of dissection or an illustrated textbook they would discover what nature had produced and learn the accepted nomenclature. This, he considers, would not only stimulate the imagination but would probably imprint the necessary facts more easily on memory than 'many hours of the present weary swotting'. On every system he suggests that the student should make his own discoveries and then compare them with the facts of nature.

Experiments suggest that it is wasteful to practise too intensively initially. Henshaw, Langdon and Halman (1933) did an experiment with three groups of thirty subjects employed on chain assembly for eighty minutes each morning. In the afternoon, group I did another eighty minutes chain assembly, group II practised a different operation and group

III did no assembly, yet the performance of the three groups remained almost identical; but it is a common experience that rest periods improve performance – in learning to drive a car, for instance, or in learning to swim. Seymour suggests that the optimum period of practice initially is half an hour, extending to two hours when the individual is already practised.

An observation in many of the more complex skills is that the learner reaches plateaux, where he appears to make little or no progress, but that these are followed by rapid improvements, possibly owing to the synthesis of a number of skills. Whether the skill transfers to another task seems to follow from the extent to which it depends on selecting similar groupings of activities of the muscles, and the skill the individual shows in 'selectivity', i.e. in more frequent selection of optimum responses.

Contradictory results have been obtained in studies of learning by part or whole methods. Woodworth (1922) favoured the 'whole' method with special attention to and repetition of difficult or important parts. This may account for Goodhue's success since his method consists in showing the whole dissection, but with coloured diagrams for critical stages. Experiments at Birmingham University Department of Engineering Production (Seymour, 1966, ch.8) suggest that a more useful distinction is between perceptual content of different parts of the task than between 'part' and 'whole'. Results of one experiment suggest that elements of a task with difficult perceptual content require longer training and that, therefore, methods which enable greater attention to be concentrated on these are advantageous.

As in other fields, knowledge of results leads to more rapid learning. What is needed is an exact and prompt indication of what went wrong and the direction from 'wrong' to 'right'.

In teaching the assembly of apparatus, or its effective use, programmed texts accompanied by practical activity are proving effective. But many simpler skills are taught in essentially this way. For example, a trainee may be asked a question in the teaching programme, required to press one of twenty buttons on the teaching machine indicating which procedure he chooses, and if he chooses correctly a green light comes on. By arranging questions in an appropriate order, he can be led to indicate what to do first, what next and so on. This is a method suitable for training an engineering 'trouble-shooter' who must learn to discover faults in complex machinery or circuits.

The content of trouble-shooting is, of course, largely theoretical and can be taught as a set of principles applied to specific situations or to simulated situations initially. G. L. Bryan (1962) outlines methods of training through obtaining solutions to problems of malfunction and checking these with solutions provided, or by solving problems of a more general nature (e.g. problems involving logical relationships), but of a similar kind, in the belief that the skill will transfer to the specific problems. Other psychologists advocate that the trainee should structure the problem for himself since no two technicians solve a problem in the same way; this method depends entirely on experience and the evidence is that although the trainees' performance does improve, those who are also given guidance improve still more.

One method used by G. L. Bryan (1962) and his colleagues to teach 'trouble-shooting' used a teaching machine. Answers were provided in advance by an expert. The trainee examined the symptom material given to him to decide what initial tests to make, ranging through about one thousand alternatives from simple knob twisting to complicated test-equipment reading. On making his selection he recorded it by pressing buttons. If his selection exactly duplicated that of the 'ghost expert' the green light on the face of the machine came on. If not, a prompting device was available to remind him of appropriate principles until he 'discovered' the solution. By working with this machine students learned within one week to think like the expert by following his footsteps and retained the skill on re-testing four weeks later.

Bryan points out that there is a similarity between 'trouble-shooting' in electronics and diagnosis in medicine. The specialist must conduct diagnosis without unnecessary recourse to expensive and time-consuming laboratory tests, deciding what information to obtain, interpreting the information obtained with a pattern consistent with the syndrome of a known malady. He suggests, therefore, that techniques used in training trouble-shooters should also prove useful in training physicians.

Current methods of teaching clinical medicine on ward rounds, of course, stress learning by 'sheer experience'; and, since there is much to learn in communicating with patients as well as in diagnosis of disease, there are certain advantages in this. But there is some evidence that the method is unnecessarily slow since students have insufficient practice and feedback. Moreover, teaching methods during ward rounds are not always conducive to effective learning despite the natural advantages of the situation. These arise because everyone wishes to know what is wrong with the patient and because, as information is elicited by testing, it is naturally organized in relation to the patient's body; there is therefore no need to devise an artificial system for organizing information. Nevertheless, students are sometimes taken to see so many patients that they cannot recall everything they have seen; some specialists tell them what to do or what to look for instead of eliciting this from the students by questioning, and there may be too few reminders via diagrams, X-rays or discussion of previously learned information to reinforce what the students know and to associate it with the cases they view. For these reasons a simulated technique such as Bryan suggests could be a useful supplement to teaching on ward rounds. One such method is discussed in Chapter 7.

Teaching in laboratories

In laboratory work theoretical content frequently takes precedence over practical skills. This is usually the case when a research worker uses experimental methods to test hypotheses he has set up in the course of solving a problem. However, the evidence from a number of publications on laboratory teaching is that many students are given practical work in which the need to think is minimal. In discussion between teachers in higher education one reason for this appears to be that some of them think of laboratory work simply as a means to developing faculties of observation and manual skills, or acquiring familiarity with equipment through performance of set experiments. They do not consider the need of specialist students to learn to apply scientific method, nor do they ask, in the case of students who will never employ laboratory skills in their professions, whether it is worthwhile for them to spend many hours verifying results in the laboratory or, indeed, any time at all.

Objectives in laboratory teaching

The main purposes of laboratory teaching are to some extent agreed, however. Teachers of physics at one international conference (Gavin, 1960) were unanimous in stressing the need to develop appreciation of the significance of measurements, for instance, understanding the difficulty of attaining a degree of accuracy of the order of 1 per cent when using apparatus readily influenced by vibration or draughts. They therefore condemned laboratories where getting the so-called 'correct' answer seemed to be judged more important than doing the experimental work itself. In any case they felt that although much was said about the importance of teaching children and students to assess errors, too little was done about it in practice.

Other objectives stressed by different physicists were familiarity with equipment, development of practical skills and accuracy in observation, inculcation of scientific method, evaluation of results and learning to record observations or to present findings. But one speaker mentioned his surprise when an industrial friend – of considerable scientific and technical status and an employer of graduates – suggested that much of the time spent by students on practical work in physics laboratories could be more profitably devoted to mathematics, in particular the numerical kind of mathematics (Gavin, 1960). Although the majority of conference members did not view with favour any considerable reduction in time given to practical work this led to discussion of its limitations: choice of experiments less on educational grounds than on those of expediency, limitations of space and equipment, shortage of staff, and the necessity for students to work in groups, or even large groups. They also repeated the charge that much experimental work is set with too precise instructions and is, therefore, dull and uninspiring.

Although this discussion relates only to physics, similar questions could be, and are being, raised in other fields – among chemists, biologists and engineers, for example, so that, as we shall see at the end of the chapter, new modes of teaching are being introduced in every field.

A further question raised by physicists and recently by medical biochemists (Wills, 1969) is whether non-specialists need to do any experimental work in order to appreciate the methods in relevant sciences. Macdonald Ross (1971), in discussing Epstein's work (which we have already outlined in Chapter 2), raises the question whether many important aims could still be attained even if practicals were abolished. He suggests that this depends partly on our view of science – as established human knowledge, a problem-solving activity, concerned with the relation between theory and specific instances or experiments, and so on. Arguments for practical work are that it gives students direct experience of basic material of the subject and of complex apparatus; it is important, too, since science rests on complex and varied links between theory and empirical tests. The physicists suggested that appreciation might be gained as effectively by devoting some of the practical time to other things, such as discussion or demonstrations or experiments done on a much bigger and more impressive scale by the teachers. Whilst in a course for medical biochemists (J. Jepson, 1969), students are already given a choice in the fourth term so that those who enjoy laboratory work do more of it and those who do not spend this time in tutorials. In support of diminishing the amount of practical teaching, Wills (1969) quotes results of a survey of students' opinions on the teaching of practical biochemistry in which about half the students showed little, if any, enthusiasm for laboratory work. He suggests a number of reasons why it might be reduced: firstly, many of the techniques used, such as pipetting and titrating, should have been mastered in an introductory chemistry course; secondly, it is difficult to teach modern techniques in biochemistry practical work because essential equipment is expensive and the problem is aggravated by large numbers of students who must be taught in relatively short periods of time; thirdly, only a very small percentage of clinicians ever again undertake active laboratory work after qualification; fourthly, theoretical understanding is gained relatively slowly through practical work – one student, for example, complains of the amount of time required to construct an enzyme activity/pH curve and compares this with the few minutes necessary to study a suitable textbook diagram; fifthly, tests required in chemical pathology are best done on actual clinical samples, where the patient involved is visited, for this has the advantage of relevance to the students' work; sixthly, students stress the poor reward in knowledge gained for the time spent, the lack of value of the techniques learned for their future medical career, the repetitiveness of much of the work and the apparent lack of medical relevance.

Similar points could be listed where any groups of applied science students study pure sciences in order to provide a basis of knowledge; there is a tendency for specialists to think in terms of presenting their subjects rather than of meeting the students' needs. This results in time ill-spent since many students dislike the irrelevance of the work to their objectives and tend to study ineffectually. Basic courses geared to students' needs, with optional more advanced courses for enthusiasts, would therefore be a more sound alternative. An additional cause of difficulty is that many such courses are essentially dull because specialists assume that students of applied sciences do not have sufficient background or ability to do anything more stimulating than to follow simple instructions, to study slides observing what they are told to see, etc. But, in fact, the course needs to be devised so that it is essentially interesting – leaving things for students to find out, not telling them all the answers, provoking thought by well-chosen questions and so on – for many of these students are not motivated to study the subject matter in the first place and therefore need every encouragement to their curiosity.

For this reason the view that theory and practice should be closely related is now less popular than formerly. J. Jepson (1969), for example, remarks:

We used to be proud of the inter-relation of our biochemistry lecture course and practical work – never was a student asked to perform an experiment that had not been covered by previous lectures. Then we realized how deadly dull this was for all concerned – no scope for initiative or prolonged laboratory sequences, no relation to reality and, above all, no feedback into the whole course. So we scrapped the lot. The obligatory biochemistry laboratory time was halved. . . .

Other teachers have developed different ways to foster interest and understanding. Tubbs (1968) works with groups of about eight students to help them to learn more about experimentation. A problem is outlined by the tutor, suggestions are invited from students and these are discussed in some detail. The students then choose apparatus and spend three or four hours in making measurements, each in different ways. Finally they discuss reasons for differences in their results and sources of experimental error. Tubbs considers that first-year students can profitably spend up to 20 per cent of laboratory time in this way, and the method proves economical of staff time, and usually of apparatus; but no evaluation has been undertaken. Martin and Lewis (1968) have attempted to clarify the purpose of experimental work for students by designing each experiment to achieve just one objective instead of the usual variety. They claim that this has resulted in considerable improvements in laboratory teaching. Read (1969) attempts to inculcate scientific method by insisting that his students should attempt to formulate and to test hypotheses to account for deviations they obtain from expected results. Griffiths (1971) described some novel methods used with scientists at Surrey University at a conference of the University Teaching Methods Unit in London on 'Varieties of group discussion in university teaching'.

Organizing laboratories and experimental work

The organization of a laboratory is not normally the concern of members of staff who do not already have considerable experience, and those who plan new laboratories are likely to view the most modern developments, such as multi-purpose laboratories or those designed for rapid dismantling prior to reorganization, before they decide on the construction and equipment of new laboratories. Thus the important matter of planning the laboratory itself can normally be left to senior staff and to a comprehensive guide such as Guy's *Laboratory Organization and Administration* (1963). The kinds of responsibilities most teachers undertake relate to maintenance of discipline, use of equipment, planning of experimental work and to organizing groups of students in their successive tasks.

Although most teachers consider that ideally students should work independently, and mention considerable improvement in their understanding when this is possible (Gavin, 1960; Jenkins, 1968), large numbers and limited space in laboratories usually make group work inevitable. However, some teachers turn this to advantage by using discussion within the group prior to and subsequent to the experimental work (Jenkins, 1968; J. Jepson, 1969), or before the writing of reports (Prosser, 1967), or commonly in the case of medical work by requiring students to conduct experiments on one another.

Very careful organization may be needed in planning group work with large classes. For example, J. Jepson (1969) describes the organization of a class of eighty-four on nine available afternoon periods, studying seven experimental topics, each requiring six sets of equipment as follows:

Students work in pairs (for reasons unknown, sets containing odd numbers always have someone with nothing to do!). Six pairs constitute a firm. During each three-hour period, the six pairs of a firm do the same experiment. Next period, each firm moves round to a different experiment, and so on for seven laboratory periods. . . . The whole process is under the care of a Laboratory Director with seven Supervisors, one for each topic, each Supervisor thus seeing all the firms in turn.

In an engineering department students work in groups of three, three such groups per lecturer being in the laboratory during any one three-hour period (Jenkins, 1968). At intervals of six weeks students are given sets of questions to solve using any tools available. The laboratory is open to each group in alternate weeks at set times, but students may use it at any other time provided that there is adequate supervision. Four lecturers as a group are responsible for the first-year instruction of a student in the subject but each normally deals only with his own group of fifteen to eighteen students. Thus in this case a looser type of organization has proved feasible.

Teachers running these courses stress the need for 'efficient' laboratories; that is to say, laboratories in which both students and staff are kept very busy, and planning is so good that no one is kept waiting for an appreciable time for access to apparatus or to consult the tutor. Technically this requires good supervision and maintenance of equipment, and normally it is essential that a senior member of staff is in charge.

Advising students on practical work and reports

The problem in providing instructions to students is to avoid, on the one hand, telling them so much that interest is lost and, on the other, telling them so little that they do not know what is expected of them. The advice required falls under three headings: organization of work within the laboratory, laboratory sheets or questions to guide specific experiments and points to note in writing reports. In addition, where projects are undertaken, the tutor's help is needed in choosing the topic, in suggestions for reading and in providing help, should this be required, in times of difficulty.

These kinds of advice are essentially the concern of the staff in the department. It is up to them to see that students have sufficient information, that laboratory sheets are kept up to date – leaving some room for thought on the part of students – and that they receive guidance as to the form reports should take. However, if a junior member of staff finds that such advice is lacking there are volumes to which he can direct his students or which he can use as a model in providing guidance for them, for example, the section on 'Practical classes' in *A Students' Guide to Efficient Study* (D. E. James, 1967) would be useful as it stands but is likely to provoke him into writing his own guide in preference to one which necessarily covers a variety of subjects.

Macdonald Ross (1971) gives examples of faulty communication in practical schedules and suggests new techniques to improve them. He mentions the use by David Rees of the Biology Teaching Project of a programmed text to guide students in the use of complex apparatus, and suggests that networks should be used to ensure that vital information about the timing of experiments receives due prominence. In pre-

ference to instructions written in prose, sometimes at far too
great length, he recommends algorithms to do the job better.
He suggests, too, that students should be advised to construct
their own algorithms to guide them in designing and carrying
through their own experiments. However, that traditional
methods of presenting instructions can be admirably clear, and
the experiments interesting, is evident, for instance, from the
books of instructions provided by the Nottingham Medical
School for the departments of Biochemistry and Physiology.

Since students often complain that writing reports takes too
long and some writers comment on excessive requirements, it
seems probable that some teachers need to reconsider the purposes for which they are required. In a manual for engineering
instructors, Morris (1950) mentions report writing which develops into a tedious mechanical operation and suggests that
printed forms are useful for computations, since they teach
order and procedure and that it would be helpful to include
suggestions on report writing and a list of approved reference
books on the subject in the set of laboratory sheets. However,
in some courses detailed reports may now be required as infrequently as once a term, a brief report, or discussion and
comparison of results, sufficing on other occasions (Elton,
1968a). Teachers wishing to prepare directives for their students
on the writing of reports, or research students writing theses,
will find *Writing Technical Reports* (Cooper, 1964) useful and
comprehensive. Younger students may be profitably directed
to advice on writing English in Gowers's *The Complete Plain
Words* (1962) or Maddox's *How to Study* (1963).

Some new laboratory courses

The result of reconsidering objectives in courses in all the main
sciences and applied sciences has led to some departments re-
directing laboratory courses to 'open-ended' experiments and
to research projects. Experiments vary considerably in their
extent: in some cases a single year is involved, in others an
entire three- or four-year course has been redesigned.

In an experiment in the physics department at Birmingham
group projects were introduced with third-year students during
seven weeks of the year, three prior to and four succeeding

the Easter vacation (Black, Dyson and O'Connor, 1968). Students were assigned to groups of twenty-five members who were often subdivided into mixed ability groups of five, each working with one member of staff. The purpose of the new course was to give the students first-hand knowledge of scientific research through study, discussion and individual or group attempts at problems and laboratory investigations within the topic they had chosen. The work aroused a lively interest, the main difficulty being to persuade students to leave the laboratory late in the evening, and a substantial amount of work was done during the vacation. Almost all of the students who replied to a questionnaire at the end of the experiment expressed approval or enthusiasm, students making comments such as: 'I hated the cramming for finals and felt I knew nothing. I very much enjoyed group studies and felt I was really sorting something out and learning things,' or, 'They are the only way in which any originality could creep into our undergraduate life – without them our course is like a machine taking in students, filling them with information which they pour out in examinations and forget soon after.'

Individual student projects, including research projects, have been introduced for clinical medical students in one London medical school (E. Wright, 1968). In this case students choose their own subjects with a tutor's guidance and have two years to complete the project. They are advised to start within the first six months and to finish well before their final pathology examinations to avoid a clash with revision. After three full cycles almost all students were achieving something worthwhile, 50 per cent were attempting a subject potentially capable of advancing knowledge while the remainder wrote case histories or carried out reviews. An increasing number of students were publishing work, usually with their tutors, in science journals.

In engineering, numerous projects are employed, but one with a strong practical bias is the 'design and make' project devised in a college of London University (Allen, 1968) which combines work in college with visits to industry. This was proposed by young graduates who wished to see activities relevant to manufacturing engineering introduced during undergraduate training. The object of the scheme is to simulate the actual industrial process of designing and manufacturing from customer's specification to finished article, but it is not obligatory to take part. Students work in 'teams' which interview customers, consider different design possibilities and their effect on cost, and make detailed working drawings of the final designs. Their work is written up in the form of a report to the customer. Results so far show that such projects arouse considerable interest and enthusiasm and give students opportunities to solve unfamiliar problems and to exercise a measure of creative thinking.

The chemists also are represented in the move to introduce more 'creative' work for students. G. Jones (1965) reports carefully chosen projects in organic chemistry undertaken by third-year students.

The complete reorganization of entire courses to demand more creative thinking, or more initiative at least, seems so far to be rare. Jenkins (1968) reports on a sandwich course on fundamentally new lines for engineering students at City University. The objectives for this course are outlined as follows:

It should promote a true spirit of inquiry and ordered thinking, provide maximum student involvement and hence motivation, demand the active participation of all students in both planning and performing experimental work, encourage students to criticize and to accept criticism, provide an environment where the maximum level and standard of work is limited only by the students' ability, enthusiasm and the time available, develop a sound basis for tackling real engineering situations, in particular, concepts of engineering compromise, provide a forum for general discussion and teach correct use of library facilities and other reference sources (University Teaching Methods Research Unit, 1968, p. 26).

To achieve this in the first year, lectures are limited to two a week on fundamental topics, there are large group tutorials to discuss problems and three-hour periods are allocated to students for experimental engineering. Carefully prepared questions and problems, some of which can be answered by reference to theory, whereas others can only be solved experimentally, are issued at intervals of six weeks. If a student decides to carry out an experiment he must first of all design it, then select the equipment, carry out the work and produce the results. The answers to all questions are recorded in a laboratory log-book. By the third year, teaching is centred in the laboratory, lectures being used only to explain fundamental concepts. A major project is undertaken during the fourth year.

Like other similar courses this provokes active interest among students (after initial disappointment owing to the simplicity of the apparatus) and student participation is said to be striking. To staff it involves harder work than supervision of set tasks would do but also the satisfaction of seeing students' interest and development as scientists.

The course devised by Jepson for medical biochemists is also of a fundamentally different character (J. Jepson, 1969). He lists four points concerning the laboratory work:

1. Every experiment produces a surprise, or generates a further question, or teaches a technique which will be used subsequently in another laboratory study.

2. All experiments are designed to have a tangible end-product for each member of the pair – an electrophoretic strip of his own plasma proteins, a photocopy of a chromatogram of an abnormal urine, a copy of his report on a patient's enzyme pattern. Nothing ensures a student's cooperation more than knowing that his teacher actually *cares*, that he has something at the end worth studying and showing around.

3. We think that medical students should experience venepuncture at an early stage of their course. Within six weeks of entering our Medical School, each student has taken and provided blood, under the tutelage of our chemical pathologists in the teaching laboratory, and has studied his own blood in various ways.

4. Only apparatus and technique actually operated in our research and routine laboratories are used. We have made several closed-loop eight-millimetre films to illustrate the procedures, and the students can view these films in the laboratory periods, or at any other time, and over and over again. Considerable improvement in experimental technique has resulted, and demonstrators' time has been saved.

He adds:

An important aspect of our laboratory work is to add a *social* dimension to the student's biochemistry studies – to develop team work, the interaction of students with staff and with each other, and a certain degree of lightheartedness. To this end, each pair has to prepare a report on the experiment they performed in the *third* laboratory period, and present this report verbally to a group of fellow students and staff.

He comments that on the social side the new laboratory studies have been outstandingly successful since students enjoy them more than they do traditional courses, but he has not tested whether students learn more biochemistry this way. However, there seems to be a very real probability that if a subject is enjoyed it will be studied with more alacrity in the future.

Comprehensive changes have also been made in the Civil Engineering Department at Heriot Watt University where new methods are in use to direct students away from dependence on teachers to a student-centred process of genuine education. Learning sessions replace technological lectures and supporting tutorials. Objectives include development of skill in writing and reading, in answering questions and solving problems, making observations and inquiries and in writing reports of observations and deductions. Students make experiments of their own choosing and open tutorials are used to deal with unanswered queries (Cowan, McConnell and Bolton, 1969/70).

The growing complexity of practical work in the laboratory has recently resulted in a development in the United States of 'preparation laboratories' (Johnston and Fiel, 1967). Their purpose is that complex equipment and intricacies of procedures should be mastered before students undertake a difficult experiment, thus avoiding loss of time and attention in the process of familiarizing themselves with new equipment, becoming proficient with surgical procedures, and so on. Experiments suggest that for the majority of students 'preparation laboratories' are well worthwhile since they lead to a saving of time and improvement in performance.

To complete this survey of practical and laboratory work it remains to mention preparation for inspection and field trips but, since no research findings are available, the following remarks are directed to lecturers undertaking these tasks for the first time.

Preparation for inspection and field trips

Inspection and field trips are usually closely related with work in the laboratory. They depend for their success on careful preparation and on full information to the students, and need to be timed so that students will understand and appreciate what they see; alternatively, if the time cannot be carefully chosen, students must be prepared to enable them to ask intelligent questions and to benefit from the answers. Instruction should be prepared so that they know what they are to observe and how to use the time available. If a schedule of instructions exists from previous years it should be carefully examined and brought up to date if necessary.

Where the time of the trip is open to choice it may be wise to consult the plant manager or field-centre warden as to the most suitable time for the visit. For example, Morris (1950) recommends that student engineers should visit a plant at a time when it is disassembled for inspection and maintenance, since a better knowledge of internal parts is then possible. He finds that plant managers are usually glad to notify instructors in engineering schools when such a disassembly is to be carried out.

Prior to the visit, the teacher needs to consider what exactly the students should see, or do, to clarify and give meaning to the theory they are studying in their department. The details of observations or investigations should therefore be considered, preferably on the spot, and students should be consulted for any relevant questions they would like answered. From this information a schedule should be prepared and issued to each student a few days before the visit. In this way students can become largely independent of the teacher except to return to him for essential information and final discussion.

Chapter 7
Instruction without Teachers: Some New Techniques in Teaching

A new development, introduced in the mid-1950s, is that of systematic instruction in the absence of a teacher or the supplying of information to poorly informed people enabling them to follow complex instructions and so make difficult decisions without reference to an expert. The best known of these methods is programmed learning, originally devised by Skinner in 1955 (see Skinner, 1958) and now employed in programmed texts, teaching machines or computerized learning. During the 1960s systematic exercises, based on a careful analysis of subject matter, were devised for teaching foreign languages by tapes or, again, in learning by computer. A less well-known development is the extension of 'games', originally played to teach military or managerial tactics, to structural 'simulation' systems for teaching in the social sciences; but these latter methods do not entirely dispense with the need for the teacher's presence for he is still required as a critic. During the 1960s algorithms also came into being originally to guide decision making in telephone kiosks or in making applications for government allowances, but latterly the method has been developed to aid decision making in industry, medicine and law.

These methods are similar in that they can be used at the students' own pace in the absence of a teacher and their carefully structured forms make them ideally suited to research into different ways of presenting subject matter, for example, amount of material, order in presentation, the number of responses required for effective learning, number of examples needed, the complexity of rules given in 'games', and so on. It is, no doubt, for this reason that many of the best-planned researches into teaching methods in higher education have been made with programmed texts. Nevertheless, there is too often a tendency merely to compare teaching by one of these new techniques with traditional methods instead of experimenting to develop the best forms of presentation when employing new techniques.

Programmed learning

Programmed learning in higher education has, so far, been developed only to a modest extent and then mainly in medicine, chemistry, elementary statistics for psychologists or mathematical topics for engineers, the elements of foreign languages, and, to a lesser extent, topics in physics (Biran and Wakeford, 1967; Cavanagh and Jones, 1966). It seems well suited to imparting factual information on subjects which have clearly recognized procedures and 'correct' answers; but it is difficult to write programmes in poorly structured subjects or in those where the subject matter has not been, and perhaps cannot be, clearly defined. Thorndike already observed in the 1920s how hard it was to teach imagination, force and beauty in literary expression because it was difficult to be specific about the evaluation of these characteristics. This is still true despite the development of programmed learning; for no one has yet analysed these qualities and it is possible that teachers would not agree as to their nature.

An argument against extensive development of programmes even in the sciences is that with knowledge growing so rapidly, their content may soon be out of date. Since it is estimated that at a minimum it takes about eighty hours to prepare three hours of a programmed text, it must be assured of a reasonable life span to justify the use of so much of an expert's time. A way partly to overcome the problem of excessive time spent in preparation is to share the work. In London, groups of chemists have combined to write new programmes which are tested in their own and other departments (Beard, 1971).

The reader who is not familiar with programmed learning may like to know that there are two kinds of programme: the linear programme devised by Skinner (1958) and the branching programme originally advocated by Crowder.

Skinner based his early teaching programme on findings relating to the learning of animals. He found, for example, that pigeons could rapidly be taught to walk in a figure of eight if movements in the required direction were rewarded with grain whereas 'wrong' responses were ignored. Believing that learning would take place in fundamentally the same way in human beings, he argued that the 'reward' of knowing a response was correct would suffice to reinforce it in the case of children and adults. A good example of a linear programme shows how this method works. What follows are the first six frames from 'An introduction to physician's liability for battery, negligence and acts of others', prepared for physicians in America by Pfizer Laboratories.

A few introductory paragraphs on the nature of battery precede these frames.

The legal importance of consent

1. Any treatment to which a patient has not consented is a battery. Therefore, the only matter at issue when considering whether a given treatment constitutes a battery is whether or not the patient has been given his—.

   Complete the sentence above. Then look at the correct response. (consent)

2. If a patient is given treatment to which he has not consented, the physician may be liable for— .(battery)

3. A patient consents to X-ray treatment for eczema on his ankles. The X-rays are carelessly administered and the patient is burned.

   ☐ An action for battery will probably be successful.

   ☐ An action for battery will probably be unsuccessful.

   Place checks in the appropriate boxes. Then look at the correct response. (An action for battery will probably be unsuccessful)

4. In the consideration of liability for battery, the question of whether or not a course of treatment benefited a patient:

   ☐ is relevant.

   ☐ is not relevant.

   (is not relevant)

5. If a physician is to avoid liability for battery, he must obtain his patient's—. (consent)

6. A physician gives a patient treatment to which the patient did not consent. The patient sues the physician for battery. The physician points out that:

   (a) he was trying to help the patient;

   (b) the patient was not harmed by the treatment;

(c) the patient was cured by the treatment.
Which defence(s) will protect the physician from liability?

☐ (a) ☐ (b) ☐ (c) ☐ none of these
(none of these)

It is interesting and, provided that the programme is so prepared as to emphasize what is important, the reader learns very effectively.

However, if the subject matter is already partly familiar, or so difficult that elementary concepts need to be revised first, a branching programme would almost certainly be preferable. The beginning of a programme in electrocardiography (Owen, 1966) illustrates this method.

Basic concepts
You will probably remember that, under normal conditions, all living cells have a positive electrical charge on their surface, the inside of the cell being negative relative to the outside. Because the two sides of the cell membrane thus have polarity, like the two terminals of a battery, the cell is said to be polarized.

The reason for this electrical difference across the membrane – or 'membrane potential' as it is usually termed – is that the extracellular concentration of positively charged ions (cations) is somewhat higher than that inside the cell. You will also remember that the chief extracellular cation is sodium ($Na+$) and the chief intracellular cation is potassium ($K+$).

Normally, the cells in adjacent areas of tissue carry surface charges of identical magnitude. But maintenance of the unequal ionic concentrations on which the membrane potential depends is an active metabolic process, requiring the expenditure of energy and the utilization of oxygen (the so-called 'sodium pump'). Should cell metabolism become compromised, e.g. by traumatic or inflammatory injury, by oxygen lack or by enzyme poisons, the membrane will no longer be able to function actively and will have only the properties of any non-vital semi-permeable membrane. Potassium will diffuse out of the cell, sodium will diffuse in; and the membrane potential will disappear.

Now decide whether the following statement is correct or incorrect: There is no potential difference between two adjacent areas of healthy tissue in the resting state.

Correct: page 39a. Incorrect: page 25b.

We will follow both answers to see how the programme proceeds: Page 39a reads:

because cells in adjacent areas of healthy tissue normally carry identical positive charges. Now consider the two statements below. Which of these do you think is true?

'Anoxic tissue is electrically positive with respect to an adjacent area of healthy tissue.' page 9a.

'Healthy tissue is electrically positive with respect to an adjacent area of anoxic tissue.' page 36b.

Whereas on page 25b we find:

Your answer was that the statement was incorrect or, in other words, that there is a potential difference between two adjacent areas of healthy tissue. But we have already noted that healthy cells of the same tissue carry positive surface charges of identical magnitude. If the surface charges are identical, there is no potential difference between two such cells, or between two groups of cells. Only if one of the cells, or one of the groups, is damaged to the extent that it can no longer maintain the positive surface charge, will a potential difference appear. Return to page 1a and select the right answer.

In this case the author has allowed for a number of different sequences in learning and enables a student who chooses a wrong answer to see *why* his answer was incorrect. More complex branching programmes may allow for four or more alternative answers but, in these cases, the programme is easier to handle in a machine. The student then presses a button corresponding with his choice of answer which automatically selects the next frame, so saving him the business of constantly turning pages. It also prevents him from cheating, but the evidence accumulating at the National Centre for Programmed Learning suggests that cheating has little influence on the ultimate effectiveness of learning.

The reader will begin to appreciate how much care goes into the preparation of a good programme. The shortest length of time so far recorded to complete a well-validated programme at university level was eighty hours' preparatory work for a programme which students, on the average, completed in three hours. In the first place the programmer specifies his objectives very exactly in terms of what the student should learn to do by the time he has completed the programme. He then lists the separate items of vocabulary, information, concepts, principles, and so on, which must be learned to achieve these objectives. Next, he studies their interrelationships in order to find the most logical order. (This is usually easy in a logical subject such as mathematics but may be perplexing and time-consuming in a subject such as medicine.) Fourthly, he plans a test, or two parallel tests, which the students will take before and after completing the programme to discover what they have gained from it. After that he writes the frames, making sure that the responses correspond with the most important facts, etc., to be learned, and avoiding the many pitfalls described in such books as Markle's *Good Frames and Bad* (1964). But in addition to careful preparation, a comprehensive programme of testing is undertaken. The completed programme is first tested on a group comparable with those for whom it is intended; frames or items are judged satisfactory if the majority of students respond with the correct answer immediately. Difficult or confusing items are replaced. Next, the corrected programme is used and the students' improvement recorded between the pre- and post-tests; if it is insufficient the programme is revised again. Finally a test of retention may be made by repeating the post-test some weeks or months later.

No doubt some programmes receive less careful preparation than that described above, but the majority of programmers are conscientious and the evidence that all these processes have been undertaken can normally be found in an introduction to the programme. And if it is interesting and easy to learn from, it is reasonably certain that it was carefully prepared.

Experimental studies of programmed learning

From experimental studies made so far the evidence is that programmes are at least as effective as teaching of the same content by an expert teacher and that it takes as little as two-thirds of the time for average students to cover the same ground (Stavert and Wingate, 1966; Teather, 1968). A number of experiments suggests that a programme need not consist in a succession of short 'frames' each requiring a response, as advocated by Skinner, but that variations using longer frames, complete paragraphs, or a continuous carefully planned text, may prove as effective, depending on the kind of subject matter and its level of difficulty to the students. For example, a psychologist found that it was more effective to present a programme in psychology to university students in the form of paragraphs followed by questions than in the usual short 'frames' (P. Wright, 1967). Indeed, if the latter were employed, students did significantly better if the answers were already filled in. This seems to be a function of difficulty, for in an experiment where a programme in electronics was used with three groups of students having markedly different levels of prior knowledge (Leith and Buckle, 1966), those with least knowledge did best when they not only gave frequent responses but made them vocally. Perhaps this reflects the kind of learning which was taking place, for it is a well-known finding that rote-learning is some 15 per cent more effective when it takes place vocally instead of mentally, and students tend to resort to rote-learning when the subject matter is too difficult, or too unfamiliar, to be readily understood. Presumably, the content of the programme was partly familiar to those who already had some qualification in the subject so that, in their case, the laws of meaningful learning would be more likely to apply. Thus when the subject matter is straightforward, questions in the text may not be helpful. In an American study (Cheris and Cheris, 1964) linear-type programmes were written for medical students in basic physics and in principles of diagnostic radiology, and a continuous text closely similar to the programme was also prepared for use with the same book of illustrations. In the subsequent experiment programme users learned more but retained what they learned rather less well than those who used texts. These findings suggest that, in this case at least, careful organization in preparing the text was more important than the mode of presentation.

The effect of programmed texts in facilitating understanding has been demonstrated frequently. For example, in an engineering department, programmes were prepared to cover courses in strength of materials and theory of structures which students had found the two most difficult subjects in their course; but with programmes, they considered them easy, covering the ground in considerably less time (Croxton and Martin, 1965) and subsequently gave additional attention to the next most difficult topics taught by conventional methods. A reduction in details and illustrations included in programmes also resulted in substantial time saving and it was found that students who used programmes containing only essentials learned as much as those who studied fuller versions (Wallis, Duncan and Knight, 1966).

The danger that learning in this way will reduce the flexibility of students' learning, or that they will cease to think for themselves, does not appear to be a real one. No one has suggested a curriculum consisting exclusively of programmes, except experimentally to see how the students would react and, predictably, they became bored from a surfeit of one method; at the end of a week rate of working had dropped and teachers were in demand again (Wallis, Duncan and Knight, 1966). In addition, evidence from a number of studies suggests that a programme should not usually last for longer than twenty-five minutes (Barrington, 1965; Mills, 1966; Wood and Hedley, 1968). But if used for the purposes for which they are well suited, good programmes result in sounder and more rapid acquisition of basic knowledge, providing ground-work and leaving a greater part of the course for more advanced forms of study.

Like programmed learning, most other new techniques for independent study are employed mainly to impart information effectively. Sequences using tape and slides are prepared in a number of centres to provide medical information for doctors and medical students (Graves and Graves, 1965; 1967; Harden, Wayne and Donald, 1960, Engel, 1971). Veterinary scientists have devised 'programmed' tapes to use with slides for postgraduate refresher courses (Appleby and Poland, 1968), clinical students may find that the hospital museum has questions to answer about the exhibits they view, film loops are used to present processes in biology or in first aid, and objective tests may be used to determine the student's grasp of the essentials of a topic he has studied. The modern tendency is to collect references to all of these techniques in a filing cabinet, or in the library, and to supply booths in which students can study with the aid of tape recorders, head phones and slide viewers.

Some systematic methods using these techniques are planned

and carried through with the same thoroughness that is applied to the planning and writing of a good programmed text. Engel (1971), for instance, has prepared a number of carefully designed sequences in medical teaching which include a test to enable the student to find out whether he has learned the material. At the Open University many courses use multiple-choice items to test students' acquisition of information provided in television sequences or course books (Lewis 1971a). In the Nuffield inter-university biology teaching project self-instructional methods are being developed (Dowdswell, 1970). These include 'bridge courses' for poorly prepared students, 'techniques courses', for example, at Bath, aseptic techniques, and 'main courses', for example, enzymes, which are short courses that can be inserted anywhere.

An American innovation of the early 1960s in which students worked in individual booths, receiving instructions, or being directed to draw conclusions, by audio tape suggests that these methods may be extended to teach techniques in problem solving and experimental design (Postlethwait, Novak and Murray, 1964).

Systematic methods are already being developed for use with computers to teach decision-making in medicine (de Dombal, Hartley and Sleeman 1969). Grubb (1968) used a computer to route mature students through sections of a statistics course which they chose after seeing a map of the entire course on a cathode-ray tube.

Uses of computers

So far extension of programmed instruction to computers has been developed mainly in the United States, but Flood-Page (1971) mentions that there are at least fifteen centres of Higher Education in Britain which are experimenting, or considering experiments, with computers in teaching. Both machines and computers are well suited to the use of branching programmes which provide for students to deviate from the main programme in order to understand the reason for an error or to make good essential information which they have missed or failed to learn previously. Advantages of either are that they may also provide a record of the student's errors as he learns, so indicating either weak parts of the programme itself or poor strategies on the part of the student. Following this analysis of the student's difficulties, the teacher is then able either to help the student personally or to recommend further programmes.

Games and simulation systems

During the last ten years or so social scientists have begun to employ simulation systems similar to, but more complex than, 'games' which were formerly used only in military and business studies. The value of 'games' as a serious part of military training had first been recognized by the German Army in the First World War and was extended to a study of crises in a military-political exercise by inclusion of Foreign Office officials in 1929. Games are now used in teaching pure and applied economics, planning land uses, stock market operations, political sciences, the making of medical diagnoses and the study of international relations and so on. A good simulation system replaces a real-life situation by substituting elements as closely similar as possible, for example, as in a simulated battle, or it replaces the real situation by a simpler, more easily manipulated system in order to facilitate study. The term 'game' is generally less favoured; partly because some simulations are so serious in intention that it is misleading, but also, as one author suspects, because of its strong connotation with levity and entertainment – connexions hardly likely to elicit respect and support from the uninitiated (Taylor and Carter). In business, 'games' seem to be acceptable, and 'Monopoly' is an elementary instance; but no one would be likely to approve the replacement of the 'simulated patient management problem' by the 'medical diagnosis game'.

Since these methods are still largely unfamiliar a few examples may be helpful. In one, the object of the 'game' is to expose students to selected situations which involve conflicts of interest which may occur in planning land uses (Taylor and Carter, 1969). Two groups, the planners and owners, represent opposing interests. The former, representing the professional advisers of a small community, attempt to ensure good planning while incidentally keeping their office in existence; the latter aim to make fruitful speculative dealings and to prevent the adoption of land-use regulations contrary to their interests. Both sides are supplied with a list of strategies which they may use in designated areas and specified situations, and an arbitrator, representing the Planning Commission, makes known to the planners the consequences of their selected strategies. Since monetary values are assigned to specific outcomes it is possible to measure success for planners or property owners in financial terms.

A more ambitious game may bring into play 'social', 'political' and 'economic' influences. This is the case in the 'North East Corridor transportation game' (Abt, 1967) set up to investigate these factors in regional transportation between Boston and Washington D.C. It involves no less than seventy players and four administrative staff in a two-day computer assisted role-playing simulation, using information from the actual area; but this represents only a small part of a government-sponsored research.

Other games of these kinds are described by Taylor and Carter (1969), Armstrong and Taylor (1970, 1971), Banks, Groom and Oppenheim (1969), in architecture, Rae (1971), in business games, Lovelock (n.d.), and in teacher training, Tansey (1970). In all of them participants gain relevant experience in roles resembling those of real decision makers and, through discussion as well as feedback from an 'administrator' or 'tutor', come to understand the effects of their own actions within the group or the group's actions *vis-à-vis* the interests of other groups. It is also an opportunity to play out hunches, even if they appear risky or unlikely to pay off and to gain some appreciation of the various consequences of alternative policies in terms of human relations or economics. As Banks, Groom and Oppenheim (1969) claim for the 'crisis game': 'Perception communication, consensus formation, timing, interpretation of documents, environment escalation, tension spirals are but a few of the topics that can be covered and *experienced* in a game-simulation.' Nevertheless, however much the participant may be involved in the model situation, it cannot make real the consequences of his decisions, and this, together with a degree of over-simplification, inevitably alters their character to him. Yet, on balance, this is a very useful teaching method which provides experiences which would otherwise be lacking, and has considerable potential as a means of evaluating students' aptitudes and performance. It almost invariably heightens interest, increasing motivation, and may promote reading and study of related subjects. Finally, in research into teaching methods, a 'game' can be used with many different groups under similar circumstances or under controlled variations so that the effectiveness of the method can be assessed, or the most effective method can be selected.

A simulated situation of a different kind, for individual decision making, is the Simulated Patient Management Test devised originally by the National Board of Medical Examiners in the United States in an attempt to provide an objective examination in patient management for clinical students. These problems, however, are well suited to teaching, and provide a unique opportunity to follow the student's (or doctor's) strategies in making decisions. A test prepared by the Australian College of General Practitioners and now published (1968b) contains the following:

Problem 2 Patient H.I.
A thirty-two-year-old man, recently discharged from the army, who has been in a motor-car accident an hour ago, is brought by ambulance to your small country hospital fifty miles from the Metropolitan area. The hospital has a well-equipped operating theatre. Your nearest colleague is six miles away.

On admission, the man is unconscious, his head and upper chest are covered with fresh blood and his extremities, lips and tongue exhibit some cyanosis.

Section A Question sheet

What would you do first?
(Then follow eight possible actions, e.g.:
201. Take brief history from ambulance driver and other occupant of car.

204. Perform a rapid preliminary assessment of the patient.

207. Refer immediately to the nearest hospital with full neurosurgical facilities.

208. Give oxygen intranasally.)

Opposite each question is an answer but concealed by a layer of black plastic. The candidate erases the plastic corresponding to a question to which he would like the answer and so reads the consequence of his actions. He may take as many choices as he wishes but is warned not to uncover any inappropriate or unhelpful item. Having completed this section he proceeds to more decisions in section B to K, in an order determined by his previous selections.

Although this approach would not be recommended if the student always had access to patients whenever he wished together with the presence of a tutor to criticize his decisions, it is a valuable supplement to the limited practice he, in fact, receives and enables him, or his tutor, to assess his mistakes.

'Programmed' teaching of languages

The development of carefully planned oral courses in languages based on tapes or the full facilities of a language laboratory, began with intensive language teaching in wartime in the United States. Since then it has continued in order to meet the needs of businessmen, scientists and tourists as well as to supplement language teaching to specialists.

Many elementary courses are devised for those who may have little background in learning languages and who desire only to use the language during short visits to the foreign country. For this reason there is no attempt to teach appreciation of the foreign literature, the method being based on a simple conditioning with repetition of learned phrases. Elementary courses are based on analysis of frequencies in use of phrases and of common structures in the languages; students are then trained to build up associations between pictures and phrases, or situations and phrases, repeating them until they are 'overlearned'. Reinforcement is used in various ways; thus meaning is maximized by presenting basic structures and linguistic items of the language in structural contexts in dialogue, for example. In this way a number of special patterns appropriate to the situations in which the student may find himself are provided as naturally as possible so that they are likely to be recalled when similar situations are encountered.

In one such course structures are expanded in exercises

based on visual materials, then manipulated until overlearned in structure drills, and finally recombined and applied by the student in guided conversation (Coggle, 1968). To give the student the intensive listening practice required for comprehension, every unit, after the third in this course, has a listening passage associated in theme, structure patterns and vocabulary with the other material in the unit. The context of the listening passages is freer since their purpose is not active use but simply that the student should comprehend some 70 per cent of it. The content may also be used to prepare students for material in the following unit. The authors include a grammar summary which, they say, is mainly for reference, but is a concession to those who like to classify and analyse in the belief that this will improve their performance. Written exercises are introduced as a useful check on assimilation of the grammar section and to provide an opportunity for testing structural comprehension not easily demonstrable on tape. Like writers of programmed texts, the authors state their objectives both in the course as a whole and in teaching, and work out their practical implications for the course.

Programmes for scientists are now being devised using the vocabulary of their own highly specific fields. Thus, at Essex, one linguist is concentrating on teaching groups of low-temperature physicists (Du Feu, 1968). He invited specialists to provide him with a suitable range of tests and used a computer to count frequencies of words and constructions prior to devising ways of teaching the required material. This method avoids waste of time on unnecessary vocabulary in physics and the consequent loss of motivation.

An intensive course in Japanese is being developed at Sheffield by Jelinek. Specialists achieve a reading knowledge of texts on their specialism in eight weeks under supervision. The course is programmed, comprising lecture-type instruction followed by drilling with feedback and supervised application of acquired material. An automatic analyser developing into a set of manual auxiliaries is used in place of traditional grammar teaching. Instruction is limited to reading knowledge of the technical and scientific style of Japanese; no speaking skills are developed. Knowles (1969) has made a detailed, contrastive analysis of Polish and Russian to enable students with prior knowledge of Russian to acquire speedily a good knowledge of Polish.

At Cambridge, a language laboratory is equipped with closed-circuit television to facilitate association of visual and aural programmes – individual monitors have been provided for the students to avoid interference from intervening visual stimuli between them and the screen (Bennett, 1968). This enables students to see close-up representation of material, for example, Chinese characters, so ensuring that they can copy detail accurately. Experiments have also been made in presenting fairly difficult texts at high speed whilst feeding a recording of the passage through earphones. In this way it is hoped that students will learn to read rapidly without 'verbalizing' the text themselves.

Other experiments in relatively elementary work for university students include programmed texts to teach Oriental scripts or aspects of linguistics and 'respect language' in modern Japanese, a dictionary for masterpieces of French literature and a reading series in French (Bennett, 1968; Healey, 1967).

At more advanced levels the elementary visual/oral or aural/oral drills described above are inappropriate both because they are needlessly time consuming and because they do not make use of the conceptual framework the students have already acquired. But at this level there is practically no completed research to assist in devising graded exercises for students and so there are few suitable courses of these highly structured kinds. Indeed, graded exercises would often be unsuitable. Blanc and Biggs (1971) have recorded spontaneous conversations, discussion, interviews, meetings (ranging from unprepared to prepared), in Orléans, in such a way as to provide a body of material suitable for research and study of the living spoken language, and for applications to the teaching of French at post-intermediate levels.

In addition, Blanc is conducting research. This includes as an aim realistic and explicit formulation of the aims of a first-year university French language course in the light of the overall purpose of a degree course, assessment of the students' initial linguistic behaviour, and definition of what terminal linguistic behaviour it is practical to aim at.

At Birmingham, Sieffert and van der Will are investigating the use of language laboratories in post-A-level teaching of German. They have developed two complete stages of language laboratory exercises: the first programmes oral practice leading from direct imitation to free oral discourse, the second provides varied types of aural comprehension and oral discourse with exercises in oral translation. These and numerous other studies in progress are outlined in the register kept at the Centre for Information on Language Teaching and Research in High Holborn, London, and in a review article by Perren and Hunt (1971).

Algorithms

Algorithms are an approach to decision making which arose from psychologists' preparation of 'flow-charts' of instructions enabling the reader to arrive at decisions by simply making a succession of single alternative choices. Gane, Horrabin and Lewis (1966) began work in clarifying decision making in industry and in government directives to the public, but they have also suggested applications in the engineering laboratory and in medicine, and, most recently, in decision making in law.

An interesting attempt to use this method in training students to solve legal problems has been made in Holland (Crombag, van Wijkerslooth, van Tuyll, van Serooskerken, 1970, 1972). Initially, with a view to developing a method, they asked legal teachers how they solved problems, but this elicited replies that it was 'an art', vague advice, or suggestions ill suited to inexperienced students. Next, they invited skilled problem-solvers to 'think aloud' but this tended to leave a chaotic and unsystematic impression as the experts often worked on several lines simultaneously, oscillating between them, or they might have a provisional solution at an early stage. Since beginners lacked experience to think of reasonable hypothetical solutions these methods were unsuitable for them. The authors were therefore driven to devising a step-by-step working programme. In order to do so they placed themselves in the position of a beginning student and considered what would be the most 'logical and economical' way to solve a particular legal problem, listing the operations which had to be carried out.

Seven such operations were defined and tested on other problems for general application.

1. Mapping the problem, i.e. rearranging the facts, chronologically or diagrammatically.

2. Translation of the problem into legal terms, allowing for all alternatives.

3. Selection of relevant principles from the total body of legal doctrine.

4. Analysis and interpretation of a statutory material.

5. Application of principles to the case in hand.

6. Evaluation of alternative constructions, derived from alternatives in 2, against each other.

7. Formulation of a decision and a presentation of the decision, or possible decisions, supported by arguments.

A later version recognizes the need to return to earlier stages as successive steps are considered. A third version which is dealt with in the form of an algorithm (Figure 4) is designed for application to somewhat more difficult problems. Students begin with the second version, progressing to the third, and a fourth amplified version; they are guided by corresponding manuals prepared in the law school. In this way they learn to ask the right question and develop a habit of consulting source books – as they will need to do in future professional practice – in order to clarify a problem or progress towards a decision.

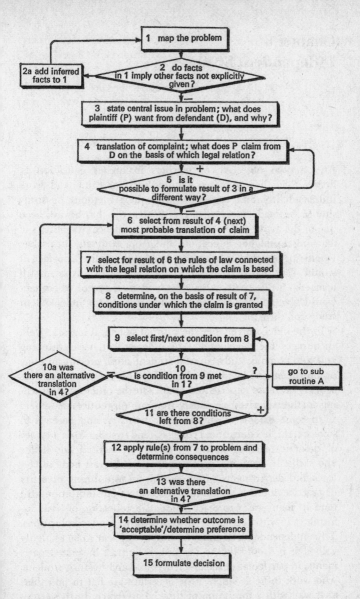

Figure 4

Chapter 8
Independent Study

An essential objective of teachers in higher education is, firstly, that their students should learn to think and work independently and, secondly, that their methods of study should be made more effective. Whilst this has always been one of the avowed aims in universities, evidence from critics of teaching in higher education and from students themselves would suggest that it has never been fully realized. In fact, it would seem that it is not the central aim of by any means all teachers; for were it so, courses and methods of assessment would give additional credit to the capacity for independent study and thinking.

In the older universities the tutorial system, if it works well, encourages the development of independent, clear thinking and autonomous study, since a student must present an essay or a problem and be prepared to defend his views or arguments against his more experienced tutor. On the other hand, teaching methods derived primarily from an apprenticeship system as in some schools of engineering, dentistry, and perhaps to some extent, in educational colleges, tend to suffer from a legacy of didactic teaching aimed to inculcate essential knowledge and skills. In between these extremes lie the vast body of colleges and departments which exhibit an astonishing diversity of practice but, if examination papers are a fair indication, still tend in many cases to teach students a collection of basic information with accepted interpretations and applications. Thus independence of thought does not appear to be as highly valued as it should be. As a complete contrast in some departments, in particular of social sciences and architecture, students who work in fields where little is certain are left to find their own way with a minimum of tutorial guidance. In these cases they can hardly survive unless they already have the capacity to direct themselves and to organize their own studies.

Whatever the attitude of teaching staff to students' development of independence, the skills they require in study – reading, note taking and organizing material in revising for examinations – tend to be taken for granted, while frequently those required in the writing of essays and reports receive little or no attention. Yet if the ultimate aim is that the students should continue their education without guidance, the methods by which this is to be achieved need to be developed until they are as effective as possible. But skill in reading receives no attention after the age of eight or so, with the exception of abnormally poor readers, effective methods of taking notes have never been investigated (it seems to be agreed by authors of books on study that full notes are most effective whereas some teachers advocate taking none), little attempt is made to help students to organize information systematically, and in some university departments no essays are written until the students sit for their final examination.

That students themselves feel the need for guidance in these matters is evident from the number of editions and reprints of books written to help them in their studies. R. W. Jepson's book on *Clear Thinking* has run to nineteen impressions since 1936, Maddox's *How to Study* (1963) is reprinted annually, a teacher's manual on *Teaching Faster Reading* has been reprinted since 1963, and the corresponding book for students was reprinted three times by 1967 (Fry, 1963a and b). The paperback version of *The Complete Plain Words* (Gower, 1962) is also reprinted almost annually and books on writing reports and essays show a similar, but somewhat less heavy, demand (Cooper, 1964; Harris and McDougal, 1956). However, whilst reading about these skills can be of some assistance in attaining them, what is most essential, as in learning all skills, is practice and feedback on the students' performance, that is to say, intelligent, detailed and prompt criticism.

That giving good advice alone may be quite ineffective was shown in an unpublished paper by Bassey which was reported at a Society for Research into Higher Education conference. During his experiment half a group of students attended a course on study methods for one term. The course included lectures and discussion on such topics as how to read, how to take notes, etc., and students were issued with a duplicated book of advice. In order to compare the 'trained' group with the 'untrained', students were matched initially on the basis of their results in A-level chemistry, physics and mathematics and, subsequently, in their end-of-year examination results. No noticeable differences resulted. As the author observed in a note accompanying his talk :

One of the characteristics of a skill is that practice is needed in order to acquire proficiency. My research results suggest that reading a book on study methods or attending a lecture on the subject are not satisfactory methods of improving performance. In order to help students we need to distinguish between 'telling' and 'teaching'; we must be prepared to teach students how to study effectively and not just tell them how to set about it.

In addition, of course, we need to find out how students *do* study and this will involve some patient investigation by psychologists. Research so far indicates that learning directions may have little influence on acquisition of a skill while those who acquire it may be quite unable to explain their methods (Belbin 1956). As we have seen in Chapter 2, activity on the part of the learner is essential in acquisition of skills of all kinds. Librarians who recognized the importance of practice in use of library facilities set exercises for students who were learning to use the library (Crossley, 1968). This resulted in a higher level of library inquiry and increased use of inter-library services.

In one interesting investigation still in progress, Jahoda and Thomas (1966) studied how a group of individuals read, what they considered should be noted down and when they took notes. In a pilot survey, twenty individuals were asked to study each of three passages – an introduction to cybernetics presenting a rigorously logical argument, a history text requiring memory for fairly unfamiliar names and a text on clinical psychology in common-sense terms – until they felt they had learned it. They were then asked to compose questions which would adequately test whether the passage had been adequately learnt and were themselves asked questions designed to test what they had learned and at what level of abstraction. During the course of study their progress from page to page was recorded. It proved that techniques differed widely: rapid scanning followed by study of selected passages, perhaps repeatedly, a careful first reading checking back only on a few important passages, constant reference to earlier paragraphs, and so on. Some used identical strategies for each passage whereas others generated strategies appropriate to the material. Questions set by members of the experimental sample in some cases dealt wholly with details while others concentrated on principles. As a result of this pilot study alone, the authors consider that staff time spent early in a course in individual tutoring, encouraging students to examine their learning processes, could save time later and increase the students' range. However, Bassey's experiment suggests that this may be inadequate, and that teachers must be constantly providing full information to students on their performance and showing alternative models for them to imitate. Thus as they gain in skill they should acquire knowledge and standards which enable them increasingly to criticize their achievement. We shall therefore consider various skills – reading, taking notes, organizing material or time, writing essays or reports and planning projects and openended experiments – in each case discussing what teachers can do to help students to improve their performance.

One method to achieve this might be to ask students to read a passage in class and to write questions which in their view adequately tested knowledge of the important points in the passage. Discussion among small groups of students, three neighbours perhaps, of the questions they had set would involve them all. In a small class questions set by each small group could be considered by all its members and the tutor. In a larger class several small groups might combine their questions to reduce the amount of reporting back; but, in either case, the teacher would learn a great deal about their initial capabilities in listening to their discussion in groups or in the class discussion and, at the same time, have opportunity to improve them.

Reading

Observation of students shows that inability to read quickly, or to 'skim', and lack of awareness as to the value of the index of a book are more common than would be supposed. In a Department of Education the writer found annually that graduates in sciences and mathematics did not think of looking up topics in the index of psychology books which were handed to them but began systematically to search from the first page. A suggestion to consult the index invariably caused initial surprise and some of these post-graduate students needed to be told where to find it! Since this is a 'skill' already familiar to many junior-school children it is astonishing that able graduates have either failed to acquire it, or have forgotten it. This surely reflects on the slight use of books demanded of students by their teachers, for were they required to look up topics as, for example, in preparing a long essay or in undertaking a project the use of an index would be familiar to them; and if their teachers' objectives had included that students should learn to educate themselves this would surely have been one essential 'skill'.

The desirability of using exercises to promote faster reading is still in doubt. Students and lecturers who have attended a 'faster reading' course are usually of the opinion that it was well worthwhile and cite considerable increases in their reading speeds as well as greater skill in 'skimming'. Experiments show many considerable increases immediately on completion of a course (Poulton, 1961) but, where further tests have been made it seems that only some students retained their improvements, individuals differing widely. The fact is that students read at many different speeds depending on difficulty of subject matter and the purposes for which they are reading; one does not usually understand mathematics or appreciate literature best by rapid reading; but there are occasions in seeking a quotation, for example, or in getting the gist of a passage, where skimming is advantageous. Fry (1963a) considers three speeds: a slow speed or 'study speed' for high understanding or good retention, an average speed for easier textbooks, novels, newspapers, etc., and a fast speed for skimming, when high comprehension is not required or time is at a premium.

No doubt, most of us use all these without conscious thought and probably acquire preferred techniques. The writer, for example, has the habit of skimming all difficult material before studying it, perhaps because this helps to put topics into context, calls to mind related subject matter which is already familiar, and indicates which sections of the book need most attention. However, in surveying studies of students' and adults' reading the poorest readers prove unable to skim at the beginning of courses and if they want to obtain 70 per cent comprehension can read only 150 to 180 words per minute of fairly easy material or 90 to 125 words per minute when subject matter is difficult or an 80 to 90 per cent comprehension is required. A good reader, on the other hand, achieves 50 per cent comprehension while 'skimming' at more than 800 words per minute, reads at 250 to 500 words per minute for 70 per cent comprehension and reduces to about 200 to 300 words per minute to achieve 80 to 90 per cent comprehension. It is evident, therefore, that poor readers will certainly benefit if they can be taught to 'skim' and that some good readers may benefit at least in terms of the time spent in study.

There are two methods available to promote faster reading. One involves the use of specially prepared passages which are read and timed, followed by perhaps ten questions to test comprehension (Fry, 1963b). The other is to show material on film at increasing speeds so that the reader must keep pace with it; again, comprehension is tested by questions (R. L. James, 1967). Either method is effective at the time, but evidence that increased speeds are maintained is conflicting or largely subjective. In skimming, however, some quite specific advice can be given which may lead to permanent gains. Fry advocates that the student should do the whole of a skimming exercise 'against the clock', perhaps reading opening paragraphs at average speed, in full, since they may supply an outline, then picking up main ideas from later paragraphs, probably in their first sentences, and skipping the rest except for figures and key words. If the student meets a paragraph which needs to be read in full to obtain the meaning, he makes up for loss of time by skimming faster subsequently until the last paragraph which he may read in full. Since this requires practice it is best done in a class or by pairs of students checking each other.

Wright (1968) suggests that efficient reading involves three stages: a preview which is often achieved by skimming, fast reading of the passage, and a review. She considers that the most important characteristic of written information is its structure; the reader must restructure difficult material to provide his own 'cognitive map'. But in the case of some students this is another skill they must learn or improve. Alderman (1926) found that exercises designed to increase the reader's ability to organize what he read resulted in greater improvement in a comprehension test than exercises intended either to develop vocabulary or to increase retention.

Taking notes

Relatively distinct problems arise in taking notes from books or during lectures. In the former case, subject matter can be read at the student's own speed and re-read if he wishes and, commonly, despite the exhortations of librarians, he marks passages which he considers important. Thus note taking can be carefully considered and completed at leisure, although a poor worker can lose the thread if his studies are too inter-mittent. One reason for poor comprehension from reading may be that students fail to make notes or to ask themselves questions about the text. Evidence obtained by Carmichael and Dearborn (1948) showed that whereas a reader normally seemed fatigued after one and a half hours, if the reading material was broken down every twenty-five pages by short tests, reminding him what he had read, he could go on without fatigue or loss of efficiency for periods of up to six hours.

In the case of lectures, however, complaints from students that they must write so fast that they have no time to think, or from staff either that students write far too much, or that their notes are scrappy and poorly kept, indicate, firstly, some con-fusion as to purpose and, secondly, failure in communication. Since memory for detail is generally rather poor, fairly com-prehensive notes are needed where the purpose of the lecture is to provide information, particularly if no textbook exists for students' reference; but if the lecturer discusses the interpretation of a poem, for example, the poem itself may suffice to recall what was said; or, again, if the lecturer's purpose is to discuss data which he provides duplicated, this with a few explanatory remarks may be all that is needed. If the material is already in books there seems little to be said for copying it out in a lecture except that for some people kinaesthetic, muscular and visual sensations are an aid to memory.

Controversy as to whether duplicated notes should or should not be supplied still depends on subjective judgements since adequate experimental evidence as to their value is lacking. In an experiment by Freyberg (1965) four methods were compared: taking no notes, writing full notes, making an outline or accepting a duplicated summary. His findings suggested that different methods suited different purposes. If material was required very soon and was not needed for examinations, taking no notes was most effective, but if the material was to be examined, learning from duplicated notes gave the best results. This, however, dealt with only one kind of subject matter and did not show the manner in which students' study habits would be affected over a period of time, so the results cannot be generalized. A possible advantage of supplying duplicated notes is that students weak in organizing material may follow the example of their teacher when they themselves make notes from books, but this has not been explored. The addition of questions with the notes seems to be advantageous. Elton and colleagues (1970) reported on the value to students of receiving lecture notes and self-testing devices. Students read and revised more and could follow lectures better. Provision of full notes in a basic science course for first-year undergraduates also brought benefits to the teaching staff, for they saw for the first time what their colleagues were teaching and were able to integrate courses. Although notes were provided in advance, lectures were well attended and students expected their lecturers to talk around the subject.

Some experimenters have investigated the quantity of subject matter students recorded from lectures and how much of this was subsequently remembered. In two experiments McLeish (1968) found that little more than 40 per cent of information was noted from lectures in psychology; but as they were not part of an essential course this could possibly be explained by lack of motivation. In a more detailed study, Hartley and Cameron (1967) recorded the number and kind of items in a lecture and checked how many and which of these occurred in students' notes. Rather less than one-third of what was said appeared in note-books but this included about half of what the lecturer considered important. References, definitions, names and words written on the blackboard were recorded, whereas experiments leading to theory were omitted. They suggested that the students regarded the lecture as a framework of ideas and theory in which to fit subsequent work, but, since inquiry showed that very few students studied the subject matter, they concluded that one weakness of lecturing as a teaching method was the discrepancy between the students' intentions and their achievements. Thus it could be argued that duplicated notes would have been more effective if followed by written questions requiring students to use the information, or any other method which involved more activity on the part of the students than is promoted by lectures.

Students' use of time

A problem which many students meet for the first time at college is how to plan their own work. Teaching staff can help considerably in this by setting up short-term and intermediate goals and by giving assignments which act as a challenge to their students. Where set work is too easy, or requirements unclear, there is a tendency for the majority of students to reduce their efforts. Thus in a comparison of two courses of engineering, in the one which included a great deal of revision during the first year, abler students were giving less time to work and more time to social activities – with the result that at the end of the year the least intelligent students did best in the examinations whereas the ablest did poorly (Beard, Levy and Maddox, 1964). In courses of clinical medicine, as we have already observed, it has been frequently said that students do not work hard; but if the course is demanding and the role of the student is clearly defined, this need not be so. In an inquiry in one school in Britain (Anderson, Burkitt, Geal and Cocker,

1968) students were fairly fully occupied averaging about forty to fifty hours per week, but their teachers felt that this did not represent hard work and that the course could therefore be more challenging. However an earlier study among students at the University of Birmingham (Thoday, 1957) showed that mean time used in work per day was six and a quarter hours, three and a half hours in timetabled work, and two and three-quarter hours in informal work. Contrary to belief, female and science students worked no harder than male or arts students, but the latter did more informal and less set work. Significantly, second-year students worked less hard except those studying medicine or modern languages who had important examinations then. Yet in most subjects, students did more work in their first year than in their final year.

Writing essays and reports

Whatever the subject in which the student specializes, if he is to write well he requires practice, opportunity to read and to discuss good examples, advice about faults to avoid, whether in argument or in use of language, and full, prompt criticism of his own performances. In the arts it is hardly possible that he will lack outstanding examples but he may not be required to practise sufficiently for maximum benefit and, as is common in sciences, feedback on his own performance may be too uninformative to help him. Often all that students receive by way of marks are literal grades. These are satisfactory if they are high but, if not, the students require guidance as to which points, for example, organization, argument or style, need improving. Indeed, there is a danger that unless the member of staff gives detailed criticism he may form overall judgements or 'halo' effects so that 'A' who has written a number of good essays always gets good marks whereas 'B' who wrote a few poor ones initially never receives high ones; and, since neither receives criticism likely to result in any substantial change in style, this state of affairs tends to perpetuate itself.

One student who received the mark of 'gamma plus plus' for an essay but no comment, resolved when he himself was a university teacher that his students should be better informed. He reported at a conference organized by the Society for

Research into Higher Education, in 1970, that he had formed the habit of writing two lists of comments at the end of students' essays under headings 'good' and 'could be improved'. Comparison of students treated in this way with those who received the usual uninformative grades showed that the former improved steadily whereas the latter maintained almost unvarying standards of performance.

For this reason it seems desirable that teachers should discuss points they consider important in the writing of essays and reports, perhaps even circulating a list of reminders. One such list considerably improved performance among a class of students of English, indicating that exposure to good models is insufficient alone to ensure excellence in practice. Possibly different teachers would stress different points, but this might have the advantage that students would be provoked into making their own list and giving some hard thought to the avoidance of possible faults and the achieving of greater clarity of style and expression. Thus the list prepared by a teacher of English which is cited below is simply an example of an aid which helps students and is not offered as a panacea for all subjects and all kinds of writing.

The virtuous essay writer:

1. Reads the question carefully.

2. Lists points that are to be made if the question is to be adequately answered. (He may not be able to deal with them all in time, but can indicate the range in an introductory paragraph or – perhaps better – point out untackled possibilities in a final paragraph.)

3. Arranges the points, if possible, in a logical order.

4. Has a business-like, to-the-point opening.

5. *Keeps* to the point throughout.

6. At each stage of the argument says explicitly what he is about.

7. Is concise.

8. Cultivates clarity of style (which is the result of clear thinking).

9. Is careful in his use of words, avoiding or defining those whose meaning is not precisely clear.

10. Gives exact references and quotations correctly: otherwise says that the passage is quoted approximately or paraphrased, and indicates its context.

11. When giving a quotation or paraphrase, makes sure that its meaning is not distorted by being taken out of context.

12. Does *not* generalize unless he can *and does* support the generalization with adequate evidence.

13. Understands what is and what is not evidence.

14. Remembers that his first duty is to produce literary criticism and not history, philosophy or – temptation of temptations – psychoanalysis, though these may all be included in so far as they are relevant.

15. Does not perpetuate anachronisms.

16. Thinks for himself, *not* swallowing down the opinions of others out of mistaken deference or sheer gullibility, and displaying a wholesome scepticism towards published criticism, very little of which is really excellent.

17. Knows that there is no substitute for having read his texts slowly, carefully and thoroughly, paying proper attention to every word.

A list of this kind may be turned to advantage in marking since it can serve as an aid to writing detailed criticisms or enables the teacher to say more tersely: 'potentially good work spoiled, note points 5, 7, 9, 12', perhaps indicating failures in these respects by appropriate figures in the essay as well as writing 'good' whenever justified.

In this way feedback on performance is at least moderately full even if it is not so prompt or frequent as Skinner suggests is necessary to 'shape behaviour'.

Probably the best kind of feedback occurs when the student is required to discuss his essay with fellow students and a tutor since this forces him to clarify his thinking and language; but by no means all students are offered this opportunity and, of those who are, some report that much of the time is occupied by a monologue from the tutor which of course defeats its purpose.

A parallel to tutorial discussion for helping students to write better scientific reports has been suggested by Prosser (1967). Since he was of the opinion that reviewing written reports of experiments after two or three weeks' delay was a poor method of instructing students, he developed the practice of discussing their work with pairs of students on completion of open-ended experiments. Each pair is given a problem to investigate and a list of points to consider in preparing for discussion and written reports. A tutor then questions the students, eliciting their criticisms, for example:

TUTOR: What did you choose for the solution composition?
FIRST STUDENT: Ferrous only.
TUTOR: Did you have any reason for your choice?
FIRST STUDENT: It was the easiest to prepare.
TUTOR: Did any of your later experiments indicate that this was, perhaps, an unfortunate choice?

Both students look blank.

TUTOR: Where did the e.m.f. change most rapidly with the addition of ferrous or ferric? Look at your graph of the influence of solution composition.

Eventually they established that, because of possible changes in the solution, the error in the results is a maximum when ferrous, or ferric, ions alone are used.

From this kind of informal discussion they are helped to interpret their experiments, to improve their ability in oral reporting and to acquire a basis for a written report of high technical standard.

Planning projects, experimental dissertations and research

A recent development in undergraduate studies is the extension, or introduction, of projects and research topics. Dissertations, or projects, are also a feature in some colleges of education both in the student's special field and in studying some aspect of education in depth. The purposes of these projects and researches are to give a student an opportunity for more intensive study of a topic, to challenge him to read more widely, and, perhaps, to give him the opportunity to solve a problem or to set up experimental work which he devises for himself. To the scientist this may be an opportunity of using an intuitive approach in asking the right questions initially and in setting up hypotheses, but he must then use scientific methods to verify them and is forced to become critical if his different hypotheses lead to conflicting experimental data.

The ways in which projects and researches are introduced differ widely in different schools and departments. Some teachers expect each student to seek his own topic, others give their students a list of suitable subjects but will consider any likely alternative, while others, again, choose the topics for their students allowing those who are dissatisfied with the topic they are assigned to choose a different one. Which of these is followed depends primarily on whether tutors feel that it is an essential part of the training that students should read widely initially and explore new lines of development, but it may be partly determined by availability of equipment and resources (Allen, 1968; Wooding, 1968). In a medical school where students must choose their own topic for a two-year study, their tutor comments, 'I really believe that this is the only time in their whole six years of training that medical students are asked to think of anything original for themselves and it seems to come very hard to many of them.' However, almost all of them achieve something, about 50 per cent attempting a project which is potentially capable of advancing knowledge and an increasing number of their researches are published. As a result of this work the students have learned to use the library in an efficient way, read original articles critically, may take a responsible and essential part in a research team in the hospital or work in institutions elsewhere, and develop a greater interest in non-examination subjects. A further advantage is that they, like students in other subjects who do similar projects, become more sympathetic towards cooperation with research workers and able to understand their language even if they do not themselves have any wish to pursue a research career (E. Wright, 1968).

In social science, Wakeford (1968a; 1968b) has reformulated the fieldwork method to develop an integrated, systematic and comprehensive approach to the teaching of method which links closely with other courses in sociology and elementary statistics. To achieve this he has introduced thirty-six short projects each of which is designed to focus the attention of the student on a single familiar topic in sociology and an appropriate methodological and statistical approach. The range of content is considerable. Some of the projects are classroom exercises such as the scaling of moral and legal evaluations of eighteen categories of activity, or drawing conclusions from the first half of a journal article. Some are class experiments, e.g. a scaled-down version of Preston and Heinz's experiment on the effects of participatory versus supervisory leadership on group judgement. Others involve work at home or in the library – for instance, documentary analysis on utopias in literature. A few involve a small amount of actual field work. In these ways the student encounters at first hand a wide range of the syllabus of the methods course.

From the point of view of effectiveness in teaching and learning this is obviously preferable to lecture courses on methods. Instead of merely hearing about the skills a sociologist needs, the student in fact employs them and finds out in discussing results how successful he has been. Wakeford notes that the variety of interpretations by students (and by tutors), many of them valid, is important itself, as the students argue their merits and attempt to determine which are acceptable. Thus the method motivates the students by involving them, it is adaptable since a large class can operate in small groups, it provides prompt feedback on performance, allows for different levels of prior knowledge, is fairly easy to operate and is versatile. Moreover, it is a method likely to inspire students to make further independent efforts in reading or investigation in addition to giving them an appreciation of how sociologists work.

A questionnaire on the first year's experiment in a school of engineering showed that most students were in favour of projects (Beard, Healey and Holloway, 1968). A popular kind of topic was one requiring a specific answer such as 'Recommend a suitable transport system for use between Central London and London Airport'. Many of the students were enthusiastic about working in groups of four to six but 85 per cent of them felt that it would be desirable for groups to meet from time to time without a member of staff being present and 74 per cent were in favour of students acting as chairmen with members of staff as observers available for consultation. Among the techniques and general matters learned by students from working on group projects were:

What makes for effective oral reporting to a group (39 per cent).
The best way to collect and classify information (35 per cent).

Sources of information, library services, etc. (57 per cent).

The internal organization of industrial or governmental bodies (20 per cent).

The problems of co-ordination between bodies working on different aspects of the same problem (52 per cent).

Chapter 9
Evaluation of Learning and Teaching

Lamentations by teachers in universities and technical colleges that students work only for examinations, or do not work until just before examinations, are surely a condemnation of their systems of assessment. A good system of assessment, after all, should encourage students to work at precisely what is important in a course and to make the best use of the time; conversely, if working to obtain satisfactory marks under the existing system is lamentable, then the system of assessment must surely be failing to test that which is of most consequence in learning. That this is so is emphasized by existing assessment systems to work to pass exams, instead of for broader educational objectives. The tenor of their complaints, in the NUS report (1969b), is that examinations are often irrelevant to what is important educationally, that traditional examinations are unreliable and thus unfair, that failure rates are artificially high and that standards vary from subject to subject and from one university school to another. The truth is, of course, that most examinations continue to consist of the kind of papers set years ago; few have yet been reconsidered to bring them in line with modern requirements or to take advantage of new techniques in examining or psychologists' findings as to the effects of assessment on learning. What is needed in the first place is a careful consideration of objectives in courses and relation of evaluation to these. The examples in Chapter 3 show how varied such objectives may be; but they serve also to show that even in these cases systems of assessment have not always been selected to match the objectives which teachers hope to realize. Yet if we have learned a new subject or skill in adult life we know from experience that to be told something is important in the course but to find that it is taken very little into account, and that it is not assessed – or not in any way we can recognize – is a frustrating experience which leads us to question the value of the course and, perhaps, the skill of the teacher.

Two main purposes are normally recognized in systems of assessment: to provide 'feedback' on the students' learning (both to them and to their teachers) and to measure attainments prior to entry to further courses or to conferring a qualification. It is the latter kind of assessment which is so much criticized and which has been more extensively studied. Since the former is normally used to aid students it tends to be welcomed; nevertheless, the marking of essays, solutions to problem or reports of experiments are often too inadequate and too late to improve learning effectively. Indeed, there are still many cases of lecturers who set problems which are never corrected or essays which receive no more informative mark than a literal grade. The influence of educational technologists, who hope to shape learning by constant criticism and by reinforcement of correct or desirable responses, is only now beginning to make itself felt. In time, continuous assessment in the form of full and prompt information to the learner about his performance may supersede tests and examinations as we know them; but this will depend on development of new techniques in teaching such as 'games' and simulation systems, new types of 'tests' such as the simulation patient management problems, computers to guide individuals in programmes tailored to their need and to follow their strategies in learning, and so on. If this proves feasible in directing all kinds of learning (and it seems unlikely if the objective is invention or direction by the student of his own studies) there will be a situation comparable with that in industry in which checking during production ensures a high standard while inspection at the end is a relatively unimportant function.

The content of examinations

Evidence as to the limited content of traditional examination papers, or even of early new-type tests, has been collected by a number of psychologists and teachers during the 1960s. In America, McGuire used taxonomies of educational objectives to analyse content of objective tests used in medical examinations. She found that 78 per cent of test items fell into her lowest category of 'isolated recall', 5 per cent required recognition of learning of a fact or concept, 11 per cent involved ability to generalize, leaving only 7 per cent in the five higher categories; of these, 'unfamiliar application' and 'ability to synthesize' remained unrepresented (McGuire, 1963). She felt that this reflected a relatively unconscious choice of factual material by examiners. In Britain similar results have been obtained from study of examination questions in traditional physics examinations. Spurgin (1967) found that O- and A-level papers put considerable emphasis on rote memory work, standard book-work, description of experiments and simple problems; but few questions were set which required intelligence and appreciation of principles. In his view the A-level paper was a 'kind of high-grade and rather specialized general knowledge paper', suitable as a predictor for the university. In 1968, Black reported results of his analysis of questions in physics finals. Among twenty-two courses he found that, on the average, more than 40 per cent of questions could be answered entirely from memory, while a further 40 per cent required memory for information together with ability to make fairly familiar applications. 'In general', he says, 'departments replied that they had not formulated rules about the style of questions, did not analyse systematically the abilities tested by the questions, did not ask for model answers and did not ask for a marking scheme.' He concluded that most papers were of a common pattern which enabled candidates to gain high marks through a well-organized memory and that questions were neither systematic nor searching. The absence of similar findings in other subjects is an indication simply that they have not been sought.

An argument still quite often put forward in favour of limited examinations of this kind is that those who do well in them are the best students who would do well in any other test. It has been claimed that some evidence points in this direction. For example, Illingworth (1963) who used an objective test as well as traditional examinations concluded, 'students who gain high marks in a test of factual knowledge in a particular subject [in this case surgery] are the same students who have the ability to succeed in any other type of examination.' He drew the conclusion – pleasing to those who dislike examinations – that the objective test could be used as a screening device for borderline failures or distinctions who should then be scrutinized more closely by means of oral and clinical examinations. Perhaps unfortunately, other investigators do not entirely agree with his conclusion. In a geography department at Newcastle (see Whiteland, 1966) it is true that outstanding examination candidates generally managed to achieve competent thesis marks but, on the other hand, less than half the undergraduates with a mark of A in research projects obtained examination marks as high as B+. This bears out the claim made by students as well as psychologists that creative individuals are not necessarily good examinees. Hudson (1966) found evidence that some distinguished men obtained poor degrees at Oxford and Cambridge, with a third of Fellows of the Royal Society having gained a second or worse at some time during their university careers. No doubt these findings are one reason for the introduction in recent years of open-ended experiments and research projects for undergraduate students; prowess in these is a better indication of ability in research than is ability to pass traditional examinations. In addition, such projects give an opportunity to exercise skills in posing questions and in devising experiments which have more relevance to work as a scientist than has the recall of information and ability to work familiar kinds of examples which are usual in traditional examinations.

Unreliability in marking

Criticism of the unreliability of traditional examinations cannot be taken lightly for, even if they were superseded by continuous assessment or more varied kinds of evaluation, the same sources of error and variability would still remain in marking. Moreover, these do not apply only in examinations which are known to be difficult to assess, such as oral work and projects, but also in marking of essay papers and the written notes followed by problems common in science exams. Many of the numerous studies which have been made are surveyed by Cox (1967); here it must suffice to mention a few recent or well-known investigations which serve to illustrate the extent of disagreement between examiners.

The first extensive study by Hartog and Rhodes (1967) of essay examinations showed considerable variability in any one examiner on different occasions and very significant difference in standards of marking between examiners. These findings have been confirmed many times since. It is generally known that examiners differ in being 'hard' or 'easy' markers; but this is simply adjusted by equating their mean average marks and the spread of the marks they give – provided that each has marked a fairly large sample. Nevertheless this cannot explain such considerable divergences in marks as ranges from 16 to 96 or 26 to 92 given by different examiners to single essay papers in an investigation of essays on mathematical topics (William, 1967). Conceivably such ranges may have been partly due to the examiners' reactions to the candidates' handwriting (Kandel, 1936), to the number of scripts already marked – for there is evidence that marks grow more extreme as times passes (Farrell and Gilbert, 1960), or to the effects of fatigue, or carelessness in adding the candidates' scores. Such considerable divergences between examiners are common as the National Union of Students (1969a) shows:

Fifty candidates sat one three-hour single-essay paper. The scripts were then marked out of 100 marks by five different examiners. When the five marks were averaged out all the candidates' marks were very close, so close in fact as to make it impossible to grade the results into 'classes'. But the difference in the marks given to individual candidates by separate examiners varied by as much as 36 marks out of 100. The average difference on an individual script between the five examiners was 19.

Thus marks could be expected to vary, on the average, by nearly 20 per cent dependent on who marked the script.

Correlations between marks of examiners, marking the same script, confirm that agreement is often poor. In a study in an English medical school, despite the factual content of the examination, Bull (1956) found negligible agreement between examiners, from which he concluded that a random allocation

of marks would have been nearly as useful. In surveying findings in a number of subjects in English universities, Cox (1967)
quotes consistently poor correlation between examiners. This
suggests that examiners were looking for different qualities
in the papers, valuing either style or content, or that they required different interpretations of events which resulted in
conflicting judgements. Nevertheless, if more attention was
given to obtaining consistent marking standards, as is the case
in marking O- and A-level papers, such extreme disagreements
would hardly be possible. Yet even with this precaution, two
pairs of independent examiners of dental students raised the
correlation between their marks only to 0·79 and 0·53, and
out of twenty-two students the first pair agreed to pass seven
and fail ten, disagreeing on seven (Heffer, Holloway, Rose and
Swallow, 1965). So large an element of disagreement as this
inevitably throws the decision for failure onto subjective judgements which may have little bearing on the candidate's factual
knowledge or his skill in using information but is as likely to
depend on the inflexibility of one examiner.

Investigations of oral and practical tests show similar sources
of unreliability in marking but to these must be added effects
of personality (Holloway, Hardwick, Morris and Start, 1967)
and, in particular, volubility (Evans, Ingersol and Smith, 1966).
In an American study of oral examinations, grading became
less stringent during the course of each day's examinations
and also on each succeeding examination day (Cotton and
Peterson, 1967). Reliability varied greatly between different
teams of examiners and within teams, but less reliable examiners could be identified. In a recent study of the marking of
clinical examinations (Wilson, Lever, Harden, Robertson and
MacRitchie, 1969) using fourteen examiners, candidates
needed to be in the top third to be reasonably certain to be
passed by all of them; fifteen of the candidates were failed by
at least one examiner but none were failed by all examiners.
However, reasons for their differences were not investigated.
In an earlier study, Bull (1956) found good agreement between
examiners of clinical work when they saw examinations of
the same patient, but only reasonably good when they saw
candidates with different patients. A study which offers an

explanation of variability between examiners is that of Natkin and Guild (1967) who asked six teachers to grade practical work of sixty-five dental students. They discovered that the teachers did not observe the same errors. Although there was greater agreement when a carefully planned marking system was issued, main causes of differences continued to be in what the examiners observed.

As teachers and psychologists have become aware of the extent of disagreement between examiners two main approaches have been made to overcome it. On the whole teachers have tried to obtain better agreement, whereas the psychologists have developed new types of tests which can be marked more consistently.

The teachers have attempted to use more examiners, averaging their marks (Bull, 1956), to devise more satisfactory marking schemes (Abrahamson, 1964), and to reduce the length of answers or the number of grades obtainable (Mowbray and Davies, 1967). The first of these solutions gives a high reliability if the marks of four independent examiners are averaged but it assumes the simultaneous availability of four suitable examiners and, in view of their difference, tends to reduce the final scores of the candidates to a dull mediocrity. The second, as we have already seen, leads to greater agreement; but, despite great care in arriving at a marking scheme which increased correlation between grades from 0.57 to 0.82, Abrahamson (1964) found that exact agreement as to grade occurred in less than 50 per cent of the cases. The third solution seems to be most satisfactory: Mowbray and Davies (1967) found that pairs of examiners agreed significantly better in marking short answers than in marking an essay but, if the number of grades for the essay was reduced to three, namely Honours, Pass and Fail, then agreement between the examiners was almost as good as for short answers.

Objective tests

Development of new types of examination began with the construction of objective, or multiple-choice tests. Since these required candidates simply to select the correct answer from a number of alternatives in a succession of items they are quick to administer and easily marked. Indeed, if there is only one right answer to each question, and marking is facilitated by scoring sheets, the reliability in marking should be perfect. Because reading and answering questions takes so little time a large number of items can be set to cover most of the syllabus; this gives rise to a wide range of marks which differentiate effectively between candidates. Results compare well with other criteria of success and have the advantage that they are available after the examination is completed. Recent programmes for computer scoring (Buckley Sharp and Harris, 1968) produce the results in half an hour or so, including detailed analysis of results in individual items for the information of teachers or their results in the whole test for individual students.

Critics of objective tests have claimed, and some still claim, that they are suited only to testing factual information, that guessing distorts results and that intelligent students may obtain answers by a process of deduction relating to the test constructor's strategy, without reference to the subject matter. But the last of these criticisms applies only to tests which are poorly constructed, so that they give unintentional clues, and there is a variety of ways of allowing for guessing (Cooper and Foy, 1967b; Cox, 1967). Moreover, objective tests can be devised which require students to apply principles, to match related items, to interpret data or to make a judgement (Bloom, 1956).

The further criticism that they are difficult and time-consuming to construct seems to be amply justified. But once a 'pool' of 5000 or so suitable questions has been collected and classified, it may be drawn on by different bodies to set their own examinations. In America, and more recently, in Britain (Buckley, Sharp and Harris, 1968), it is possible to programme a computer to select items for a 'pool' with proportions of questions relating to different subject matter (at stated levels of difficulty) as well as in different kinds of cognitive skills.

A point which should be noted is that foreign students seem to do worse in these kinds of tests than in many examinations (Anderson, Lennox and Low, 1964); but, since they were nearly all over twenty-one in the study quoted and older

British students show a similar, though smaller effect, it could have been due to age. The authors suggest, depressingly, that this may reflect loss of speed in learning new techniques after the age of twenty. In any case, it suggests that objective tests should be used with caution among populations of mixed ages and nationalities.

More complex types of objective tests now offer new possibilities in testing. The National Board of Medical Examiners in the United States and, within the last two years, the Australian College of General Practitioners, have developed simulation patient management tests. As the method is relevant wherever students must learn to make a series of related decisions before they can be trusted with full responsibility, it might be applicable in engineering or in any of the social sciences which now use simulation systems in training. If such tests are machine marked, or if they are used in teaching, the erroneous strategies of students can be studied. Thus McGuire (1965) reported that in medicine the decisions of many examiners coincided closely with the thorough and discriminating approach of a group of consultants. Others made a constricted approach, dealing with an obvious complaint but ignoring subtle and serious signs and symptoms, while a few (both students and doctors) made a 'shotgun' approach to the case of the patient, selecting clearly indicated measures but also many not-indicated or even contra-indicated procedures. Conceivably within the fairly near future an extension to teaching by computer will enable students and teachers to obtain such information immediately, and students' strategies in problem solving may be similarly studied.

In so far as tests of these kinds are applicable in higher education it may prove feasible to set up an absolute standard allowing comparisons between students of successive years or of different colleges. Since the tests used in examining are not normally made available to students it is possible to include some of the same questions in successive years thus providing a limited basis for comparison. This would go part of the way to meet complaints of variable standards and failure rates.

Failure rates and classes

If for no other reason than that marking is unreliable, failure rates and the proportions of different classes will be questioned; but high failure rates in some subjects – in the absence of an absolute standard – and very different proportions of first-class degrees from subject to subject deserve further inquiry. In addition, the habit in some departments of subjecting students to a series of examinations in successive years, which must be passed in order to continue, is itself highly questionable.

The Robbins Report (Committee on Higher Education, 1963) draws attention to different percentages of first-class degrees, ranging from 4 per cent in history to 14 per cent in mathematics. This is, no doubt, partly due to the ease with which high, or low, scores can be obtained in subject matter which is either right or wrong as compared with that in which a range of judgements is legitimate. Yet it would be a simple matter to adjust these proportions – as is done already for O- and A-level examiners whose standards differ in severity – if there was not evidence that university examiners tend to have preconceived ideas as to the proportions of failures and first-classes in their subjects. Hohne (1965), for example, showed that improved student quality was not reflected in better examination results. One reason given for high failure rates is that the 'standard' should be kept up. In the absence of absolute standards this is somewhat questionable except in so far as a subject may be recognized as an easy alternative which weaker students tend to choose; but observation suggests that this may be due less to a low standard in students' abilities than to few requirements for written work, or, indeed, demand for any written work during the course. As an instance, an adult student of theology who visited me recently described a three-year course in which the failure rate is currently 50 per cent; two years ago it was 70 per cent. During this course there are no examinations prior to the third year and there is little work set, what little there is being neither discussed nor marked in an informative way. In this department, therefore, it seems that a poor standard of performance by students is directly related to a poor standard in teaching or, rather, abdication from teaching together with neglect to make clear to the students what is expected of them.

That one reason for very different standards of performance in different departments is the teaching is indicated by Elton's (1968a) finding that in university departments of physics with identical entrance standards among their students, 42, 38 and 72 per cent of the students gained honours degrees.

There is evidence of the value of setting an examination at the end of the first term as an early warning to those who are likely to fail later on. In an investigation by Nisbet and Welsh (1966) students most likely to fail in finals were in the bottom third of the class in two or more subjects at the end of the first term. Rates of failure could be reduced by warning these students, for feedback as to the probability of failure resulted in a redoubling of their efforts.

The effect of intermediate examinations which must be passed before students may proceed to the next year's course is often not fully appreciated. An extreme example was mentioned in a meeting in a technical college where, in a four-year course, only half the students could hope to pass each year. An elementary calculation shows that only one sixteenth of the students who began the course could hope to complete it satisfactorily. The effect of this was that the most intelligent students, seeing how poor their chances were, withdrew, so leaving a small proportion of mediocre but persistent students to succeed. Thus this system lowered standards instead of raising them.

A more general criticism of exclusion of students from the next year's course as a result of a test at the end of the preceding one arises from a study by Furneaux (1962). He calculated correlations between examination results for students at the ends of their first and second years of a course; on the whole correlations were poor. Attainments in first-year applied electricity, for example, correlated more highly with second-year mathematics (0.69) than did first-year mathematics (0.47). Thus the practice of insisting that a student should pass in first-year work before proceeding to the second seemed unjustified. Unreliability of the tests would also account for a fairly high proportion of errors (i.e. in a parallel test, even the next

day, some borderline candidates would change places and even
a few candidates from extremes of the distribution might do
very differently). Thus sending a student down, or holding
him back a year on grounds of failure in such tests is unwar-
rantable except in rare cases. Where such an action is considered necessary it should be based on failure in a second
test after an interval for revision, together with assessments
of course work. Students themselves are in favour of an early
warning system in each subject (National Union of Students,
1969b).

Continuous assessment

An alternative which is sometimes suggested to the system of
intermittent examinations or tests is that of continuous assessment. In America this often takes the form of weekly or fort-
nightly tests in which grades are assigned to contribute towards
the students' overall assessment at the end of the year. Those
who favour this system claim that it encourages hard work. In
a recent inquiry, however, R. J. Burke (1968) found that
students assessed in this way reported adverse effects both on
their own work and on teaching, and in a study comparing
students frequently graded with those who were not, results
suggested that the former tended to cram for exams, cutting
courses not directly relevant to them (Johnson and Abrahamson, 1968).

When the NUS speak of continuous assessment they mean
'a system of assessment by which all aspects of a student's
work during his time at college are taken into account –
tutorial essays, practicals, seminar contributions, dissertations,
etc., as well as written examinations'. In this way, they claim,
teachers and students alike get continued feedback on performance. In discussing such methods they find different responses. 'On the one hand staff and students speak of the continued strain involved in this system, but others speak of a
reduction in nervous tension and a feeling that the individual
has a fair chance to demonstrate his capabilities. ... If judgement is based on a candidate's performance over three years it
is more difficult for society to brush aside.' They appreciate
the possibility that students may be more concerned about any

bias they suspect in tutors' judgements when marking current work, and the problem of the external examiner called on to compare essays or projects which are essentially different in kind, but they feel that such a varied form of continuous assessment is fairer and more meaningful to employers. But possibly the greater advantage is that it can be designed to direct the students' efforts to the activities which contribute most to their learning.

An alternative procedure, designed to avoid the continued strain on staff of marking, and on students of constant preparation, is to introduce intermittent assessment of course work. With a procedure of this kind, the five best essays for a term may be assessed, or three experiments are chosen for discussion in a viva, and so on. Staff agree that under such a system students may not always work hard, but they prefer this to continuous assessment if the latter leaves no time for thought or for intensive pursuit of a special interest.

Current techniques of assessment

In addition to the traditional techniques of examination: timed essay papers, timed 'essays' followed by problems, orals and practical examinations and the more recently developed objective multiple-choice test, a number of variations have been tried in examining. These include the open-book examination which matches more closely the situation in the professions for the student can look up facts and figures he forgets or find the relevant quotation, provided that his prior knowledge is sufficient to enable him to do so quickly. On the whole students welcome the opportunity to look up data which they would, in fact, have only for the duration of an examination, and anxiety as to forgetfulness is reduced. However, an investigation by Kalish (1958) of the open-book method showed no difference either in anxiety or success between students using this method and the traditional one. Those who argue against this system and in favour of the traditional one, claim that the stress of a timed examination is a better test of performance in a situation requiring quick effective action leading to prompt decisions and to production of rapidly prepared reports. But this implies that there must be a choice between the methods, whereas a consideration of objectives in relation to professional requirements may decide between these methods or show that both are desirable.

Other modifications of traditional examinations include the prepared time test which allows the students several weeks to look up the subject prior to a timed examination. When this was first tried it was claimed that results showed little difference in expected rank order of candidates but that performance was generally improved. However, some students claim that the method puts too much of a premium on memory or that, having plenty of time for thorough preparation, they try to scribble down everything they know once they get into the examination room (Flood-Page, 1967). The latter criticism suggests that this kind of test is most effective in showing whether students are able to select information, employing it to the best advantage; but their emphasis on 'getting it all down' indicates that they believe that their teachers give more credit for quantity of information than for its intelligent use.

Other forms of assessment which are becoming more common than formerly are long essays and projects. In some departments of education, for example, a large part of assessment is of essays in topics partly, or entirely, of the students' choice within each relevant field, in history of education, the teaching of a special subject, and so on. In sciences and engineering, projects are becoming increasingly important and a comprehensive assessment may include credit for a good survey of the field and originality in solving a problem, as well as oral presentation of the report and defence of ideas in discussion with staff and fellow students.

Assessment of practical work has also been extended to include originality in solving open-ended experiments, and thus takes into account wider objectives in the training of scientists such as ability to ask appropriate questions or to develop hypotheses and to set up well-constructed experiments to test them.

New approaches to examining practical work, such as proficiency in spoken language or the medical examination of patients, include the use of tapes and video-tapes to provide a permanent record which enables more examiners to see the performance and to assess it at leisure. But, although it is certainly possible to see or hear very well there is so far little evidence that the assessments of examiners are appreciably more reliable, probably because as we have seen, examiners tend to observe different aspects of performance. Nevertheless, a collection of permanent records will provide material which should make it practical to train some examiners to a higher level of consistency.

New systems of assessment

Although nowadays university teachers begin to say that objectives should be defined in behavioural terms before planning courses, setting examinations or deciding on teaching methods and techniques to evaluate course work, no professional body in England has yet systematically analysed the skills, information and attitudes it requires; thus no examinations have been systematically re-designed. The Open University is beginning to do so, however, as successive courses and their evaluation are planned (Lewis, 1971a, 1971b; 1972). An interesting attempt to match an examination with objectives has recently been made by the Australian College of General Practitioners who analysed what they meant by clinical competence before planning an examination in two parts to test it (Australian College of General Practitioners, 1969; Beard, 1969). This also involved them in searching for and designing new types of tests.

In the first part of this examination, which is written, there is a three-hour essay paper on medical practice, a two-and-a-half-hour paper on a speciality of the doctor's choice (e.g. obstetrics, industrial medicine), a two-hour multiple-choice test of essential information and a three-hour programmed simulation test of patient management. The second part of the examination tests the doctor in action. In a simulated diagnostic interview a member of the college plays the part of a normally difficult patient; secondly, there is a simulated patient management conference in which the contributions of each examinee are assessed both for effectiveness in working with other participants and with respect to medical knowledge; finally, there is a practical test in which X-rays, colour transparencies, etc., are viewed and the examinee is required to comment briefly on diagnosis, treatment and prognosis for a patient.

Modifications in testing occur in the kind of 'essay' question set which describes a specific situation and requires the doctor to say what he would do, for example:

Describe in detail your interview with a patient who presents with a trivial complaint which you feel sure is not the real reason for her consulting you. The case presentation is as follows:

Your secretary has allowed twenty minutes for Miss X's appointment with you. She has not seen you before and has not sought medical attention for twenty years. She is forty years of age, well-controlled poise, but a trace of nervousness is evident. She says she is concerned about a small mole on her neck, though she admits it has not undergone any change in years.

In the patient management group conference, careful attention is given to a marking scheme; identifiable behaviours and knowledge are outlined, for example:

1.2. Is passive, non-facilitative: Shows passive acceptance or rejection; concurs, complies, merely reports or ratifies suggestions of others, makes personal, private, idiosyncratic comments or expresses ideas ineffectively and unclearly.

5. Attitude toward emotional, family and social disorders: Demonstrates an interest in these disorders. Shows sensitivity to people and their problems. Exhibits a strong motivation towards an over-all diagnosis and total patient care.

This examination is designed simply to identify general practitioners whose knowledge and skills are inadequate but, as no less than 20 per cent fail, this possibly reflects the need for refresher courses; it may also indicate a need to look again at the examinations which clinical students take in order to qualify. Refresher courses will be needed increasingly as medical knowledge expands but meanwhile a valuable consequence of this examination is that practitioners buy copies of the papers to work through and revise skills required in practice; thus, like all good examinations, it serves to ensure that an essential range of skills, abilities and information is practised or acquired.

A departure from traditional anatomy examining methods has been made by Figge (1971). In an open-book examination the student is assigned an anatomically oriented article to read and is asked to answer a set of questions based on factual or conceptual knowledge of the anatomy involved. The consultation of textbooks and other references is recommended. The answers submitted by the student are evaluated according to the following criteria: are the anatomical facts and concepts expressed in the answer correct? Is the answer relevant, and presented in a well organized, logical manner? Have adequate sources been consulted to make the answer complete and in depth? A single answer may necessitate correlating knowledge from all the pre-clinical fields. It is reported that the examination convinces students that knowledge of anatomy will be useful and important in the practice of medicine and that it satisfies their demand for relevance.

In Britain there are several far-reaching innovations in assessment in progress and in a large number of departments assessment is made on a wider basis than formerly. Consideration of objectives in teaching English has led in one department of York (Brockbank, 1968; Jones, 1969) to five types of examining. Three-hour examinations with textbooks and dictionaries allowed test ability to work against the clock and provide evidence that the holder of a good honours degree is not 'paralytically incompetent to produce respectable work in a hurry'. Jones considers these unfair and unrewarding to mark. A paper of stated length prepared during fourteen days allows unrestricted use of books and is a more realistic test of abilities. Some students are said not to sleep for the last three or four days but this seems justifiable since it makes realistic demands on the students such as any author may experience and, in addition, it leads to more mature perspectives on returning to the course. Long essays are used to allow students to write about their optional topic: this, it is felt, gives students opportunity to make significant and fresh discoveries whilst working in a chosen field. His five best tutorial essays are also selected by each student and three of them are assessed by four wholly independent examiners; the remaining two are studied in the event of doubt or disagreement. Finally a form of viva is employed which consists in a continuous assessment of oral contributions to seminars and tutorials throughout the term. To achieve this, each seminar is conducted by two tutors which allows one to take the initiative in guiding discussion whilst the other operates mainly as an observer. The effect of this on seminars has proved entirely good since students realized that nothing would gain marks except responsive contribution to relevant discussion. The method is justified, of course, by the students' future need for oral and collaborative skills. It is of interest that assessors found it necessary and possible to give credit for 'the ability to hold one's peace' and found it possible to distinguish between different qualities of silence. Before silence is encouraged overmuch it may be wise to draw attention to the evidence for a positive relationship between frequency of contribution and status which is summarized by Sprott (1958)!

A new pattern of examining in physics is reported by Elton (1968b). In this department the final assessment is based on:

1. Examinations at the end of the sixth and the beginning of the ninth terms, which each carry about one-third of the marks.

2. Course-work assessments under five headings: (a) an essay written in the first summer vacation; (b) an open-book oral examination at the end of the fifth term; (c) full reports on three experiments selected by the examiners from those in the laboratory during the second year; (d) an oral examination in two other experiments, thirty minutes' notice being given as to which one; and (e) a project which is undertaken during the whole of the final term.

Account is also taken of the level of the courses chosen during the first two years (students may choose nine to twelve 'units' for study at either of the levels α or β). Elton comments that altogether the reliability of marks for course work is low; nevertheless, the examination has high validity since it represents the broad range of skills and knowledge required by physicists. As we have seen in Chapter 2 Professor Jepson's new examination in biochemistry is similarly based on skills and abilities required by biochemists (Beard and Pole, 1971).

The NUS (1969b) reports other modifications of traditional examinations in the English departments at Kent and Surrey, the sociology department at Essex, the mathematics department at Kent which is using 'pre-set questions' in part 1 examinations – but probably they no longer represent the full range of variations.

In the NUS report on examinations (1969b), students come out strongly in favour of a diversity of examining methods since they believe that only in this way can students be assured of a fair deal. The evidence suggests, however, that much more research will be required to make examination marking more reliable and thus fairer; the advantages of varied kinds of assessment seem rather to be in fully representing the range of skills and abilities which students should acquire and in directing their energies into everything which is important for them to learn in the field.

Assessment of teaching

The furore raised by the proposal in the PIB report, that students should help to assess their teachers, followed by its rapid cancellation, have combined to distract attention from the serious criticism such a proposal deserves simply on grounds of feasibility. It was that more careful questionnaires could be devised than the few mentioned in the report and that these could be used to mark teachers in order of ability. Could this in fact ever be done? Or could those who proposed it have ever seriously believed that it was feasible? The answer to the first question seems to be 'no' – if anything more than a very rough order of merit was intended – and to the second, 'no' – if they had seriously studied the evidence or understood the implications of statistical findings relating to testing.

Attempts to assess teaching performances in Australia (Schonell, Roe and Meddleton, 1962) showed, as might be expected, that teachers performed differently in teaching different topics or with classes of different abilities or in employing different methods of teaching; they might even perform very well in one university department but indifferently in another. Students and colleges also differed in the way they assessed teaching; some praised highly a conscientious teacher who covered the syllabus thoroughly in well-planned lectures whereas others looked for originality and provision of information which was not readily accessible, preferring that basic information should be obtained in private study. Thus of one series of lectures Falk (1966) reports that students said:

1. Made a fascinating period of history very flat.

2. Congratulations on an exceedingly workmanlike job of teaching as opposed to purely lecturing.

3. Gives students impression that they are back in the school-room. By this I mean over-simplification, over-classification.

4. These lectures were the best I've had this year.

Even when more detailed behaviours are specified, these variations in performance and basic differences in judgement still pertain. Like examiners, students observe different things and, like examinations, rating scales are unreliable. They may serve to identify 'failing' teachers and those of 'distinction' calibre (but these are probably well known already); the intervening order is hardly dependable. It is true that a varied form of assessment of all the different classes taken, and the different teaching techniques employed, may be said to add to the 'fairness' of such an assessment as a variety of assessments does for students; but the chief value of this kind of assessment is to inform the teacher of his prowess and to help him to improve his teaching. Indeed, the purpose of the majority of questionnaires concerning students' opinions of courses in America as well as in Australia and Britain is to provide this information to the teacher himself or to a head of department. In American colleges where teachers are rated by students, their reported attitudes of 'approval or indifference' suggest that this is of minor consequence in determining salary. In any case, students are considered competent only to judge effectiveness of presentation; content and organization are assessed by senior staff. However, it has been suggested that post-graduate student opinion might be sampled to confirm their judgements. But, whatever the outcome, the reliability of rating scales is normally fairly low.

The statistical naïveté of the Prices and Incomes Board suggestion that discretionary payments should be made to teachers ranking in the upper half of such a scale can only be a cause of astonishment. No one who has ever marked examination papers would attempt to distinguish in giving awards between candidates at the middle of the scale; for at this point many of them obtain the same score, or differences are negligible, so that a maximum degree of unfairness would result. Even to distinguish the highest quarter with any confidence, besides requiring a degree of accuracy in marking and rating which is unattainable, again implies many hard cases. Thus, although the suggestion of an award for good teaching is welcome to some teachers, this recommendation was impracticable to say the least. A scheme of graded increments such as those employed in the United States and Canada might, perhaps, be more acceptable. These normally depend on assessment by a committee of colleagues of each teacher's research and administrative contribution to the department and may include an assessment of teaching to which students' opinions have contributed. At present, however, the Association of University Teachers is opposed to such a scheme in Britain. There are obvious dangers. In many American schools this kind of scheme seems to be related with a rigorous system of student 'grading' in frequent tests which, as we have seen, tends to have detrimental effects educationally. Secondly, British teachers have already seen the ill consequences of 'payment by results' on teaching in schools at the end of the last century and would require considerable persuasion that this would not be repeated. Thirdly, a scheme of this kind might possibly result in a rush to publish as it is said to have done in the States or, perhaps, a similar determination to try out every new method in teaching and to 'prove' it successful. At present, therefore, it would be likely to distract attention from the important matters of providing some training for new lecturers and attempting to improve teaching throughout the university schools – even among those who would never be likely to gain a teaching award. Perhaps the most rational and scientific procedure would be to institute a few experiments in teaching assessment in an assortment of schools and departments in higher education and to consider their effects after the lapse of three years or so.

References

ABERCROMBIE, M. L. J. (1960), *The Anatomy of Judgment*, Hutchinson.

ABERCROMBIE, M. L. J. (1966), 'Perception and communication', in *Teaching Methods in University Departments of Science and Medicine*, report of a conference held at the University of London Institute of Education, January.

ABERCROMBIE, M. L. J. (1968), 'The work of a university education research unit', *Universities Quarterly*, March, pp. 182–96.

ABERCROMBIE, M. L. J. (1971), *Aims and Techniques of Group Teaching*, 2nd edn, Society for Research into Higher Education.

ABRAHAMSON, S. (1964), 'A study of the objectivity of the essay examination', *Journal of Medical Education*, vol. 34, no. 1.

ABT, C. C. (1967), *North East Corridor Transportation Game: Administrator Handbook*, Abt Assn Inc., Cambridge, Mass. (mimeographed).

ALDERMAN, G. H. (1926), 'Improving comprehension ability in silent reading', *Journal of Educational Research*, vol. 13, p. 21.

ALLEN, P. H. G. (1968), 'Engineering projects for engineering undergraduates', in *Innovations and Experiments in University Teaching Methods*, University Teaching Methods Research Unit, Dept Higher Education, University of London Institute of Education, pp. 81–7.

ANASTASI, A. (1958), *Differential Psychology*, 3rd edn, Macmillan Co.

ANDERSON, J. BURKITT, D, GEAL, M.A., and COCKER, P. (1968), 'How clinical students spend their time', *British Journal of Medical Education*, vol. 2, pp. 4–10.

ANDERSON, J., LENNOX, B., and LOW, A. (1964), 'Medical students' performance: analysis of selection procedures and examination marks in Glasgow', *Lancet*, vol. 1, pp. 96-100.

APPLEBY, E. C., and POLAND, J. (1968), 'Some observations on the use of tape-recorded programmes in teaching veterinary pathology', in *Innovations and Experiment in University Teaching Methods*, University Methods Research Unit, Dept Higher Education, University of London Institute of Education, pp. 30–32.

ARGYLE, M. (1967), *The Psychology of Interpersonal Behaviour*, Penguin.

ARMSTRONG, R. H. R., and TAYLOR, J. L. (eds.) (1970), *Instructional Systems in Higher Education*, Cambridge Monograph on Teaching Methods no. 2, Cambridge Institute of Education.

ARMSTRONG, R. H. R., and TAYLOR, J. L. (1971), *Feedback on Instructional Simulation Systems*, Cambridge Monographs on Teaching Methods no. 5, Cambridge Institute of Education.

ASCH, S. E. (1940), 'Studies in the principles of judgments and attitudes: II. Determination of judgments by group and ego standards', *Journal of Social Psychology*, SPSSI bulletin 12, pp. 433–65.

ASCH, S. E. (1948), 'The doctrine of suggestion, prestige and imitation in social psychology', *Psychological Review*, vol. 55, pp. 250–76.

ASCH, S. E. (1956), 'Studies of independence and conformity. I: A minority of 1 against a common majority', *Psychological Monographs*, vol. 70, no. 9, whole no. 416.

AUSTRALIAN COLLEGE OF GENERAL PRACTITIONERS (1968a), *Examination Handbook*, ACGP, Melbourne.

AUSTRALIAN COLLEGE OF GENERAL PRACTITIONERS (1968b), *Patient Management Problems* No. 2, ACGP, Sydney, New South Wales.

AUSTRALIAN VICE-CHANCELLORS COMMITTEE (1963), *Teaching Methods in Australian Universities*, J. A. Passmore, chairman, New South Wales University Press.

AUSUBEL, D. P. (1967), *Learning Theory and Classroom Practice*, bulletin 1, Ontario Institution for Studies in Education.

BANKS, M. H., GROOM, A. J. R., and OPPENHEIM, A. N. (1969), *Gaming, Simulation and the Study of International Relations in British Universities*, paper presented during a symposium at Birmingham University, 8 January.

BARBER, T. X., and CALVERLEY, D. S. (1963), 'Hypnoticlike suggestibility in children and adults', *Journal of Abnormal and Social Psychology*, vol. 66, pp. 589–97.

BARNETT, S. A. (1958), 'An experiment with free discussion groups', *Universities Quarterly*, vol. 12, pp. 175–90.

BARRINGTON, H. (1965), 'A survey of instructional television researches', *Educational Research*, vol. 8, pp. 8–25.

BEARD, R. M. (1967), *Small Group Discussion in University Teaching*, Dept Higher Education, University of London.

BEARD, R. M. (1969), 'Methods of examining professional competence', *Medical and Biological Illustrations*, vol. 19, pp. 127–8.

BEARD, R. M. (1968a), 'On evaluating the success of teaching', *British Journal of Medical Education*, vol. 1, pp. 296–302.

BEARD, R. M. (1968b), *Research into Teaching Methods in Higher Education*, 2nd edn, Society for Research into Higher Education.

BEARD, R. M. (1969), *An Outline of Piaget's Developmental Psychology*, Routledge & Kegan Paul.

BEARD, R. M. (1971), 'Programmed learning – cooperative ventures', *Chemistry in Britain*, vol. 7, pp. 324–6.

BEARD, R. M. and BLIGH, D. A. (1971), *Research into Teaching Methods in Higher Education*, 3rd edn, Society for Research into Higher Education.

BEARD, R. M., HEALEY, F. G., and HOLLOWAY, P. J. (1968), *Objectives in Higher Education*, Society for Research into Higher Education.

BEARD, R. M., LEVY, P. M. and MADDOX, H. (1964), 'Academic performance at university', *Educational Review*, vol. 16, pp. 163–74.

BEARD, R. M. and POLE, K. E. (1971), 'Content and purposes of biochemistry examinations', *British Journal of Medical Education*, vol. 5, pp. 13–21.

BECKER, R. A. (1971), 'The effectiveness of higher education', *Innovations in Higher Education*, proceedings of the anual conference of the Society for Research into Higher Education, 1971.

BELBIN, E. (1956), 'The effects of propaganda on recall, recognition and behaviour. I: The relationship between the different measures of propaganda effectiveness', *British Journal of Psychology*, vol. 47, pp. 163–74; 'II: The conditions which determine the response to propaganda', vol. 47, pp. 259–70.

BENNETT, W. A. (1968), 'The use of closed circuit television for second language teaching', in *Innovations and Experiments in University Teaching Methods*, University Teaching Methods Research Unit, Dept Higher Education, University of London Institute of Education, pp. 101–4.

BETTS, D. S. and WALTON, A. J. (1970), "A lecture match or 'Anything you can do I can do better' ", *Physics Education*, vol. 5, pp. 321–5.

BIRAN, L. A., and WAKEFORD, R. E. (eds.) (1967), *Programmes in the Health Sciences*, National Centre for Programmed Learning, University of Birmingham.

BLACK, P. J. (1968), 'University examinations', *Physics Education*, vol. 3, no. 2.

BLACK, P. J. (1971), 'Group discussion in the planning and reporting of group projects', *Varieties of Group Discussion in University Teaching*, report of the sixth conference organized by the University Teaching Methods Unit, University of London Institute of Education.

BLACK, P. J., DYSON, N. A., and O'CONNOR, D. A. (1968), 'Group studies', *Physics Education*, vol. 3, no. 6.

BLANC, M. and BIGGS, P. (1971), 'L'enquête sociolinguistique sur le français parlé à l'Orleans', *Le Français dans le Monde*, vol. 85.

BLIGH, D. A. (1971a), *What's the Use of Lectures?*' University Teaching Methods Research Unit; Penguin, 1972.

BLIGH, D. A. (1971b), 'Techniques in small group discussion', *Varieties of Group Discussion in University Teaching*, report of the sixth conference organized by the University Teaching Methods Unit, University of London Institute of Education.

BLOOM, B. S. (ed.) (1956), *Taxonomy of Educational Objectives I: Cognitive Domain*, David McKay, New York.

BLOOM, B. S., KRATHWOHL, D. R., and MASIA, B. B. (1956), *Taxonomy of Educational Objectives II: Affective Domain*, David McKay, New York.

BORGER, R. and LEABORNE, A. E. M. (1966), *The Psychology of Learning*, Penguin.

BRADLEY, R. L. (1965), 'Lecture demonstration *v.* individual laboratory work in a general science course', *Journal of Experimental Educational*, vol. 34, pp. 333–42.

BRITISH MEDICAL STUDENTS ASSOCIATION (1965), *Report on Medical Education – Suggestions for the Future*, British Medical Assn, London.

BROCKBANK, P. (1968), 'Examining exams', *The Times Literary Supplement*, no. 3465, pp. 781–2.

BROWN, S. C. and CLARKE, N. (eds.) (1960), *International Education in Physics*, Proceedings of the International Conference on Physics Education, UNESCO House, Paris, MIT Press and Wiley.

BRUNER, J. S., GOODNOW, J. J., and AUSTIN, G. A. (1956), *A Study of Thinking*, Wiley.

BRYAN, G. L. (1962), 'The training of electronics maintenance technicians', in R. Glaser (ed.), *Training Research and Education*, University of Pittsburg, ch. 10.

BRYAN, R. C. (1968), 'Student rating of teachers', *Improving College and University Teaching*, vol. 16, pp. 200–202.

BUCKLEY SHARP, M., and HARRIS, F. T. C. (1968), 'Automation in medical education,' in *Innovations and Experiments in University Teaching Methods*, University Teaching Methods Research Unit, Dept Higher Education, University of London Institute of Education, pp. 101–4.

BULL, G. M. (1956), 'An examination of the final examination in medicine', *Lancet*, vol. 2, pp. 368–72.

BURGE, R. E. (1968), 'Wider London, B.Sc.', *The Times Educational Supplement*, 1 March.

BURKE, R. J. (1968), 'Student reaction to course grades', *Journal of Experimental Education*, vol. 36, pp. 11–13.

BURKE, W. H. (1967), 'The new course and its development', *Design Education*, vol. 2, pp. 19–24, Hornsey College of Art, London.

BUTLER, R. A. (1953), 'Discrimination learning by rhesus monkeys to visual exploration motivation', *Journal of Comparative Physiological Psychology*, vol. 46, pp. 95–8.

CARMICHAEL, L. and DEARBORN, W. F. (1948), *Reading and Visual Fatigue*, Harrap.

CAVANAGH, P., and JONES, C. (eds.) (1966), *Programmes in Print*, Association for Programmed Learning, London.

CHERIS, D. N., and CHERIS, B. H. (1964), 'Programmed instruction versus a textual presentation of radiology', *Journal of Medical Education*, vol. 39, pp. 311–18.

CLARKE, G. K., and CLARKE, E. B. (1959), *The Art of Lecturing*, Heffer.

COGGLE, P. A. (1968), 'A programmed course in German for adult beginners', in *Innovations and Experiments in University Teaching Methods*, University Teaching Methods Research Unit, Dept Higher Education, University of London Institute of Education, pp. 101–4.

COMMITTEE ON HIGHER EDUCATION (1963), *Higher Education*, (*Robbins Report*), Appendix Four – Administrative, Financial and Economic Aspects, Cmnd 2154 HMSO.

COOPER, B. (1964), *Writing Technical Reports*, Penguin.

COOPER, B., and FOY, J. M. (1967a), 'Examinations in higher education – a review', *Journal of Biological Education*, vol. 1, pp. 139–51.

COOPER, B., and FOY, J. M. (1967b), 'Guessing in multiple choice tests', *British Journal of Medical Education*, vol. 1, p. 212.

COSTIN, FRANK (1972), 'Lecturing versus other methods of teaching: a review of research', *British Journal of Educational Technology*, vol. 13, p. 4.

COTSONAS, N. T., KAISER, R. J., and DOWLING, H. F. (1958), 'Adapting the group discussion technique for use with large classes', *Journal of Medical Education*, vol. 33. pp. 152–62.

COTTON, T., and PETERSON, O. L. (1967), 'An assay of medical students' abilities by oral examination', *Journal of Medical Education*, vol. 42, pp. 1005–14.

COWAN, J., McCONNELL, S. G., and BOLTON, A. (1969–70), *Learner Directed Group Work for Large Classes*, Department of Civil Engineering, Heriot-Watt University.

COX, R. (1967), 'Examinations and higher education', *Universities Quarterly*, June, pp. 292–340.

CROXTON, P. C. L., and MARTIN, L. H. (1965), 'Away with notes (programming in higher education)', *New Education*, vol. 1, pp. 25–7.

CROMBAG, H. F. M. and VAN TUYLL VAN SEROOSKERKEN, E. H. (1970), *Het CI-Kurriculum in de Fakulteit de Rechtsgeleerdheid: een tussentijds verslag* (The first-year curriculum in law school: a preliminary report), Leiden, Bureau Onderszoek van Onderwijs R. U. Leiden rapport nr. 2.

CROMBAG, H. F. M., DE WIJKERSLOOTH J. L., VAN TUYLL VAN SEROOSKERKEN, E. H. (1972), *On Solving Legal Problems*, full version in: Over het oplosson van casusposities (H. D. Tjeenk Willink, Gronignen).

CROSSLEY, C. A. (1968), 'Tuition in the use of the library and of subject literature in the University of Bradford', *Journal of Documentation*, vol. 24, pp. 91–7.

DAICHES, D. (1964), *The Idea of a New University*, Deutsch.

DALLAS, D., and PIPER, D. W. (1972), *Case Studies in Course Design I. Post Graduate Course for Biology Teachers* (in press).

DARKE, M. (1968), 'Teaching design methods', *Royal Institute of British Architects Journal*, January, pp. 29–30.

DAVIES, D. M. (1968), 'Teaching sheets as an aid to learning', in *Innovations and Experiments in University Teaching Methods*, University Teaching Methods Research Unit, Dept Higher Education, University of London Institute of Education, pp. 88–9.

DE DOMBAL, F. T., HARTLEY, J. R., and SLEEMAN, D. H. (1969), 'A computer-assisted system for learning clinical diagnosis', *Lancet*, pp. 145–8.

DEUTSCH, M. (1949), 'Experimental study of effects of cooperation and competition upon group process', *Human Relations*, vol. 3, pp. 199–231.

DOWDESWELL, W. H. (1970), 'Inter university biology teaching project', *Journal of Biological Research*, vol. 4, pp. 197–203.

DRESSEL, P. L. (1968), *College and University Curriculum*, McCutchan Publishing Co.

DU FEU, V. M. (1968), 'The language laboratory and minimal skills courses', in *Innovations and Experiments in University Teaching Methods*, University Teaching Methods Research Unit, Dept Higher Education, University of London Institute of Education, pp. 105–8.

ELTON, L. R. B. (1968a), 'Success and failure in university physics courses', *Physics Education*, vol. 3, pp. 323–9.

ELTON, L. R. B. (1968b), 'The assessment of students – a new approach', *Universities Quarterly*, vol. 22, pp. 291–301.

ELTON, L. R. B., HILLS, P. J. and O'CONNELL, S. (1970), 'Self-teaching situations in a university physics course', *International Congress on the Education of Teachers of Physics in Secondary Schools*, Sept. Eger, Hungary, pp. 11–17.

ENGEL, C. E. (1971), 'Preparation of audio-tapes for self-instruction,' *Medical and Biological Illustration*, vol. 21, pp. 14–18.

EPSTEIN, H. T. (1970), *A Strategy of Education*, Oxford University Press.

EPSTEIN, H. T. (1972), 'An experiment in education', *Nature*, vol. 235, pp. 203–5.

ERSKINE, C. A., and O'MORCHOE, C. C. C. (1961), 'Research on teaching methods: its significance for the curriculum', *Lancet*, vol. 1, pp. 709–11.

EVANS, L. R., INGERSOL, R. W., and SMITH, E. J. (1966), 'The reliability validity and taxonomic structure of the oral examination', *Journal of Medical Education*, vol. 41, pp. 651–7.

FALK, B. (1966), 'The preparation and in-service training of university staff', *Australian Journal of Higher Education*, vol. 2, pp. 200–206.

FARRELL, M. J., and GILBERT, N. (1960), 'A type of bias in marking examination scripts', *British Journal of Educational Psychology*, vol. 30, pp. 47–52.

FESTINGER, L., and CARLSMITH, J. M. (1959), 'Cognitive consequences of "forced compliance" ', *Journal of Abnormal and Social Psychology*, vol. 58, pp. 203–10.

FESTINGER, L., and MACCOBY, N. (1964), 'On resistance to persuasive communications', *Journal of Abnormal and Social Psychology*, vol. 68, pp. 359–66.

FIGGE, H. J. (1971), 'Relevant anatomy', *New England Journal of Medicine*, vol. 282, p. 633.

FLOOD-PAGE, C. (1967), 'Worrying about examinations', *Cambridge Institute of Education Bulletin*, vol. 3, no. 6, pp. 2–7.

FLOOD-PAGE, C. (1971), *Technical Aids to Teaching in Higher Education*, Society for Research into Higher Education, London.

FOY, J. M. (1969), 'A note on lecturer evaluation of teachers by students', *Universities Quarterly*, vol. 23, pp. 345–8.

FRENKEL–BRUNSWIK, E. (1949), 'Intolerance of ambiguity as an emotional and perceptional personality variable', in J. S. Bruner and D. Krech (eds.), *Perception and Personality: A Symposium*, Duke University Press, pp. 108–44.

FREYBERG, P. S. (1965), 'The effectiveness of note-taking', *Education for Teaching*, February, pp. 17–24.

FRIEDLANDER, F. (1967), 'The impact of organizational training laboratories on the effectiveness and interaction of ongoing work groups', *Personnel Psychology*, vol. 20, pp. 289–307.

FRY, E. (1963a), *Teaching Faster Reading – A Manual*, Cambridge University Press.

FRY, E. (1963b), *Reading Faster*, Cambridge University Press.

FURNEAUX, W. D. (1962), 'The psychologist and the university', *Universities Quarterly*, vol. 17, pp. 33–47.

GAGNE, R. M. (1965), *The Conditions of Learning*, Holt, Rinehart & Winston.

GANE, C. P., HORRABIN, I. S., and LEWIS, B. N. (1966), 'The simplification and avoidance of instruction', *Industrial Training International*, July.

GARBUTT, D. (1963), 'An investigation into students' understanding of some accountancy terms', *Vocational Aspect of Secondary and Further Education*, vol. 31, no. 15, pp. 69–169.

GAVIN, M. R. (1960), 'The place of laboratory work in physics teaching', in C. Darborn, S. Brown and N. Clarke (eds.), *International Education in Physics*, Wiley.

GERARD, H. B. (1964), 'Conformity and commitment in the group', *Journal of Abnormal and Social Psychology*, vol. 68, pp. 209–11.

GIBSON, J. N. (1970), Paper in a symposium on atitudes measurement in exploratory studies, *Bulletin of British Psychology Society*, vol. 23, pp. 323–4.

GILBERT, T. F. (1962), 'Mathematics: the technology of education', *Journal of Mathematics*, pp. 7–75.

GLASER, R. (ed.) (1962), *Training Research and Education*, University of Pittsburgh Press.

GORDON, W. J. J. (1961), *Synectics: The Development of Creative Capacity*, Harper & Row.

GOWERS, E. (1962), *The Complete Plain Words*, Penguin.

GRAVES, J., and GRAVES, V. (1965), *Medical Sound Recording*, Focal Press.

GRAVES, J., and GRAVES, V. (eds.) (1967), *Report on Second Conference on the Use of Audiotape in Medical Teaching*, Medical Recording Service and Sound Library, Royal College of General Practitioners.

GRIFFITHS, V. (1971), 'Group work in problem solving', *Varieties of Group Discussion in University Teaching*, report of the sixth conference organized by the University Teaching Methods Unit, University of London Institute of Education.

GROVES, P. D. (1968), 'Marking and evaluating class tests and examinations by computer', *Computer Journal*, vol. 10, pp. 365–7.

GRUBB, R. E. (1968), 'Learner controlled statistics', *Programmed Learning and Educational Technology*, vol. 5, pp. 38–42.

GUY, K. (1963), *Laboratory Organisation and Administration*, Macmillan Co.

HALLWORTH, H. J. (1957), 'Group discussion in its relevance to teacher training', *Educational Review*, vol. 10. pp. 41–53.

HAMMERSLEY, J. H. (1968), 'On the enfeeblement of mathematical skills by 'modern mathematics' and by similar soft tack in schools and universities', *Bulletin of the Institute of Mathematics and its Application*, vol. 4, pp. 1–22.

HAMMOND, K. R., *et al.* (1959), *Teaching Comprehensive Medical Care: A Psychological Study of a Change in Medical Education*, Harvard University Press.

HARDEN, R. MC., WAYNE, E., and DONALD, G. (1968), 'An audio-visual technique for medical teaching', *Journal of Medical and Biological Illustration*, vol. 18, pp. 29–32.

HARE, A. P., and BATES, R. F. (1963), 'Seating position and small group interaction', *Sociometry*, vol. 26, pp. 480–84.

HARRIS, R. S., and MCDOUGAL, R. L. (1956), *The Undergraduate Essay*, University of Toronto Press.

HARTLEY, J., and CAMERON, A. (1967), 'Some observations on the efficiency of lecturing', *Educational Review*, vol. 20, pp. 30–37.

HARTOG, P., and RHODES, E. C. (1967), 'An examination of examinations', *Universities Quarterly*, June.

HAWKINS, J. D. (1969), 'A survey of student opinion on practical biochemestry in the London medical schools', in E. D. Wills (ed.), *Practical Biochemistry in the Medical Coure*, Federation of European Biochemistry Societies.

HAYTHORN, W., COUCH, A., HAEFNER, D., LANGHAM, P., and LANNOR, F. C. (1956), 'The behaviour of authoritarian and egalitarian personalities in groups', *Human Relations*, vol. 9, pp. 57–74.

HEALEY, F. G. (1967), *Foreign Language Teaching in Universities*, Manchester University Press.

HEBB, D. O. (1949), *The Organization of Behavior*, Wiley.

HEBB, D. O. (1966), *A Textbook of Psychology*, Saunders.

HEFFER, P., HOLLOWAY, P. J., ROSE, J. S., and SWALLOW, J. N. (1965), 'An investigation into dental undergraduate examining techniques', *British Dental Journal*, vol. 118, pp. 334-58.

HENDRICKS, F., *et al.* (1966), *GSPIA Management Planning Decision Exercise*, Dept Urban Affairs, Graduate School of Public and International Affairs, University of Pittsburgh.

HENDRY, J. (1971), *The Village Study as a Live Project*, Oxford Working Papers in Planning Education and Research, Oxford Polytechnic, Department of Town Planning.

HENSHAW, E. M., LANGDON, J., and HALMAN, P. (1933), *Manual Dexterity: Effects of Training*, Industrial Health Research Board, no. 67, HMSO.

HERZBERG, F. (1966), *Work and the Nature of Man*, World Publishing Co.

HILL, B. J. (1969), 'The analysis of objectives for lecture courses in the physical sciences and engineering', in *Conference in Objectives in Higher Education*, University Teaching Methods Research Unit, Dept Higher Education, University of London Institute of Education.

HOHNE, H. H. (1965), 'Success and failure', *Scientific Faculties of the University of Melbourne*, Australian Council for Educational Research, Melbourne.

HOLLOWAY, P. J., HARDWICK, J. L. MORRIS, J., and START, K. B. (1967), 'The validity of essay and viva-voce examining techniques', *British Dental Journal*, vol. 123, pp. 227–32.

HUBBARD, J. P., LEVIT, E. J., SCHUMACHER, C. F., and SCHNABEL, T. G. (1965), 'An objective evaluation of clinical competence', *New England Journal of Medicine*, vol. 272, pp. 1321–8.

HUDSON, L. (1966), *Contrary Imaginations*, Methuen; Penguin, 1967.

HULL, C. L. (1933), *Hypnosis and Suggestibility: An Experimental Approach*, Appleton-Century-Crofts.

HUNTER, I. M. L. (1957), *Memory*, Penguin.

HUNTER, R. L. C. (1971), 'Some reflections on the relevance of educational thought for Scottish law teaching', *Juridical Review*, vol. 16, pp. 1–19.

ILLINGWORTH, C. (1963), 'The multiple choice or objective examination. A controlled trial', *Lancet*, vol. 2, pp. 1268–71.

INHELDER, B., and PIAGET, J. (1958), *The Growth of Logical Thinking*, Routledge & Kegan Paul.

JAHODA, M., and THOMAS, L. F. (1966), 'The mechanics of learning', *New Scientist*, vol. 30, pp. 114–17.

JAMES, D. E. (1967), *A Students' Guide to Efficient Study*, Pergamon.

JAMES, R. L. (1967), 'An investigation into the reading efficiency of students at a technical teaching training college', *Journal of Educational Psychology*, vol. 37, pp. 391–3.

JENKINS, D. E. P. (1968), 'The efficient use of laboratory time in the teaching of engineering', in *Innovations and Experiments in University Teaching Methods*, University Teaching Methods Research Unit, Dept Higher Education, University of London Institute of Education, pp. 25–9.

JEPSON, J. (1969), 'Some methods of teaching practical biochemistry', in E. D. Wills (ed.), *Practical Biochemistry in the Medical Course*, Federation of European Biochemical Societies.

JEPSON, R. W. (1936), *Clear Thinking*, Longman, reprinted 1965.

JEVONS, F. R. (1970), 'Liberal studies in science – a successful experiment', *Education in Chemistry*, vol. 7, pp. 98–9.

JOHNSON, P. C., and ABRAHAMSON, S. (1968), 'The effects of grades and examinations on self-directed learning', *Journal of Medical Education*, vol. 43, pp. 360–66.

JOHNSTON, R. F., and FIEL, N. J. (1967), *Structured Learning and Training Environments: A Preparation Laboratory for Advanced Mammalian Physiology*, Project Report no. 203, March, Michigan State University.

JOINT MATRICULATION BOARD (1968), *Engineering Science (Advanced). Notes for the Guidance of Schools. No. 1. Course Work Objectives*, Manchester.

JONES, G. (1965), 'Organic research projects in an undergraduate course', *Education in Chemistry*, vol. 2, pp. 238–40.

JONES, R. T. (1969), 'Multiform assessment: a York experiment', *Cambridge Review*, vol. 15, pp. 43–7.

JOYCE, C. R. B., and WEATHERALL, M. (1957), 'Controlled experiment in teaching', *Lancet*, vol. 2, pp. 402–7.

KALISH, R. (1958), 'An experimental evaluation of the open book examination', *Journal of Educational Psychology*, vol. 49, pp. 200–204.

KANDEL, I. (1936), *Examinations and their Substitutes in the United States*, Carnegie Foundation for the Advancement of Teaching, Bulletin 28, New York.

KING, B. T., and IRVING, T. L. (1956), 'Comparison of the effectiveness of improvised versus non-improvised role-playing in producing opinion changes', *Human Relations*, vol. 4, pp. 177–86.

KLEIN, J. (1965), *The Study of Groups*, Routledge & Kegan Paul.

KLINEBERG, O. (1938), 'The intelligent migrants', *American Sociology Review*, vol. 3, pp. 218–24.

KNOWLES, F. E., (1969), *Main Contrasts in Russian and Polish Morphology and Syntax*, presented at the Second International Congress of Applied Linguistics, Cambridge 1969.

KNUTSON, A. L. (1960), 'Quiet and vocal groups', *Sociometry*, vol. 23, pp. 36–40.

KÖHLER, W. (1925), *The Mentality of Apes*, Harcourt, Brace & World.

LAWRENCE, R. D. (1962), 'Learning anatomy by invention', *Lancet*, vol. 1, p. 156.

LEITH, G. O. M., and BUCKLE, G. F. (1966), *Mode of Response and Non-Specific Background Knowledge*, National Centre for Research and Documentation of Programmed Learning, University of Birmingham.

LENNOX, B., ANDERSON, J. R., and MOORHOUSE, P. (1957), 'Objective papers and essay papers in pathology and bacteriology class examinations', *Lancet*, vol. 2, pp. 396–402.

LEWIN, K. (1936), *Principles and Topological Psychology*, McGraw-Hill.

LEWIN, K. (1947), 'Group decision and social change', T. M. Newcomb and E. L. Hartley (eds.), *Readings in Social Psychology*, Holt, Rinehart & Winston.

LEWIS, B. N. (1971), Course Production at the Open University. (a) Some Basic Problems, *British Journal of Educational Technology*, vol. 2, pp. 4–13.
(b) Activities and Activity Networks, *British Journal of Educational Technology*, vol. 2, pp. 111–23.

LEWIS, B. N. (1972), 'Planning and scheduling', *British Journal of Educational Technology*, vol. 3, pp. 189–204.

LLOYD, D. H. (1968), 'A concept of improvement of learning response in the taught lesson', *Visual Education*, October, pp. 23–5.

LORGE, I. (1936), 'Prestige, suggestion and attitude', *Journal of Social Psychology*, vol. 7, pp. 386–402.

LOVELOCK, C. (undated), *A Bibliography and Analysis of Business Games*, London, BLITA.

McCARTHY, M. C. (1968), *The Employment of Highly Specialised Graduates: A Comparative Study in the United Kingdom and the United States (McCarthy Report)*, DES Science Policy Studies, no. 3, HMSO.

MACDONALD ROSS, M. (1971), *Practical work in science*, a talk given at the University of Birmingham, 24 November.

McGUIRE, C. (1963), 'A process approach to the construction and analysis of medical examinations', *Journal of Medical Education*, vol. 38, pp. 556–63.

McGUIRE, C. H. (1965), 'A process approach to the evaluation of medical curricula: theory and practice', in J. V. O. Reid and A. J. Wilmot (eds.), *Conference on Medical Education in South Africa*, July 1964, Natal University Press.

McGUIRE, C. H. (1963), 'A process approach to the construction and analysis of medical examinations', *Journal of Medical Education*, vol. 38, p. 556.

McLEISH, J. (1968), *The Lecture Method*, Cambridge Monographs on Teaching Methods no. 1, Cambridge Institute of Education.

McVEY, P. J. (1968), 'Student evaluation of lectures', in *Innovations and Experiments in University Teaching Methods*, University Teaching Research Unit, Dept Higher Education, University of London Institute of Education, pp. 170–73.

MACE, C. A. (1962), *The Psychology of Study*, Penguin.

MADDOX, H. (1963), *How to Study*, Pan.

MAIER, N. F., and SOLEM, A. R. (1952), 'The contribution of a discussion leader to the quality of group thinking', *Human Relations*, vol. 5, pp. 277–88.

MARKLE, S. M. (1964), *Good Frames and Bad*, Wiley.

MARRIS, P. (1964), *The Experience of Higher Education*, Routledge & Kegan Paul.

MARTIN, D. G., and LEWIS, J. C. (1968), 'Effective laboratory teaching', *Bulletin of Mechanical Engineering Education*, vol. 7, pp. 51–7.

MARWICK, A. (1970), *What History is and Why it is Important*, Humanities Foundation Course Unit 5, Open University.

MASLOW, A. H. (1954), *Motivation and Personality*, Harper & Row.

MASTIN, V. E. (1963), 'Teacher enthusiasm', *Journal of Educational Research*, vol. 56, pp. 385–6.

MILLER, G. (ed.) (1962), *Teaching and Learning in Medical School*, Harvard University Press.

MILLER, G. A. (1970), *The Psychology of Communication, Seven Essays*, Penguin.

MILLS, D. G. (1966), 'The use of closed-circuit television in teaching geography and in training teachers of geography', *Geography*, vol. 51, pp. 218–23.

MORRIS, F. C. (1950), *Effective Teaching: A Manual for Engineering Instructors*, McGraw-Hill.

MOSÉL, J. N. (1964), 'The learning process', *Journal of Medical Education*, vol. 39, pp. 485–96.

MOUNTFORD, J. (1966), *British Universities*, Oxford University Press.

MOWBRAY, R. M., and DAVIES, B. M. (1967), 'Short note and essay examinations compared', *British Journal of Medical Education*, vol. 1, pp. 356–8.

NATIONAL UNION OF STUDENTS (1969a), *Report of the Commission on Teaching in Higher Education, Presented to Liverpool Conference, April 1969*, NUS, London.

NATIONAL UNION OF STUDENTS (1969b), *NUS Executive Report on Examinations, Presented to Liverpool Conference, April 1969*, NUS, London.

NATKIN, E., and GUILD, R. E. (1967), 'Evaluation of preclinical laboratory performance', *Journal of Dental Education*, vol. 31, pp. 152–61.

NEDELSKY, L. (1949), 'Formulation of objectives of teaching in the physical sciences', *American Journal of Physics*, vol. 17, pp. 345–54.

NISBET, J., and WELSH, J. (1966), 'Predicting student performance', *Universities Quarterly*, vol. 20, pp. 468–80.

O'CONNELL, S., WILSON, A. W., and ELTON, L. R. B. (1969), 'A pre-knowledge survey for university science students', *Nature*, vol. 222, p. 526.

OWEN, S. G. (1966), *Electrocardiography*, English Universities Press.

OWEN, S. G., HALL, R., ANDERSON, J., and SMART, G. A. (1965), 'A comparison of programmed learning instruction and lectures in the teaching of electrocardiography', *Programmed Learning*, vol. 2, pp. 2–14.

PARLETT, M. R., and KING, JOHN G. (1971), *Concentrated Study: A Pedagogic Innovation Observed*, Society for Research into Higher Education.

PASSMORE, J. (1963), *Reading and Remembering*, 5th edn, Melbourne University Press.

PEMBERTON, C. (1952), 'The closure factors related to temperament', *Journal of Peronality*, vol. 21, pp. 159–75.

PERREN, G. E., and LUNT, HELEN N. (1971), *A Review of Current British Research on Language and Language Teaching*, Centre for Information on Language Teaching and Research, State House, 63 High Holborn, WC1.

PETERS, R. S. (1958), *The Concept of Motivation*, Routledge & Kegan Paul.

PIAGET, J. (1950), *The Psychology of Intelligence*, Routledge & Kegan Paul.

PIPE, P. (1966), *Practical Programming*, Holt, Rinehart & Winston.

PIPER, D. W. (1967), 'Strategies in course planning', *Design Education*, vol. 2, pp. 16–18, Horney College of Art, London.

POLE, K. (1972), *The Teaching of Physics*, in preparation.

POSTLETHWAIT, S. N., NOVAK, J., and MURRAY, H. (1964), *An Integrated Experience Approach to Learning*, Burgess Publishing Co.

POULTON, E. C. (1961), 'British courses for adults on effective reading', *British Journal of Educational Psychology*, vol. 31, pp. 128–37.

PRING, RICHARD (1971), 'Bloom's taxonomy: a philosophical critique (2)', *Cambridge Journal of Education*, vol. 2, pp. 83–91.

PROSSER, A. P. (1967), 'Oral reports on laboratory work', *Report of the Second Conference on Teaching for Efficient Learning*, University Teaching Methods Research Unit, University of London Institute of Education, p. 14.

RAE, J. (1971), 'Notes on the use of gaming simulation models in the education of architects – paper one – educational strategy', *Architectural Journal*, pp. 827–30.

READ, F. (1969), 'New techniques for the teaching of practical physics', *Physics Education*, vol. 4, pp. 77–81.

ROSS, M. G. (1966), *New Universities in the Modern World*, Macmillan Co.

RIECKEN, H. W. (1958), 'The effect of talkativeness on ability to influence group solutions of problems', *Sociometry*, vol. 21, pp. 309–21.

SALTZ, E., and NEWMAN, S. E. (1960), 'The effect of prior learning of symbols on performance in reasoning', *American Journal of Psychology*, vol. 73, pp. 91–9.

SCHONELL, J., ROE, E., and MIDDLETON, I. G. (1962), *Promise and Performance*, University of Queensland Press.

SCHONELL, F. J., et al. (1961), *University Teaching in Queensland: A Report of Conferences for Demonstrators and Lecturers*, University of Queensland, Brisbane.

SEYMOUR, W. D. (1966), *Industrial Skills*, Pitman.

SIMPSON, R. H. (1965), 'The use of self-evaluation procedures by lecturers in educational psychology', *Educational Review*, vol. 18, pp. 25–33.

SKINNER, B. F. (1953), *Science and Human Behaviour*, Macmillan Co.

SKINNER, B. F. (1958), 'Teaching machines', *Science*, vol. 128, pp. 969–77.

SMITH, P. B. (1969), *Improving Skills in Working with People: The T-group*, Dept Employment and Productivity, Training Information Paper 4, HMSO.

SOCKETT, H. (1971), 'Bloom's taxonomy: a philosophical critique (1)', *Cambridge Journal of Education*, vol. 1, pp. 16–25.

SPROTT, W. J. H. (1958), *Human Groups*, Penguin.

SPURGIN, C. G. (1967), 'What earns the marks?', *Physics Education*, vol. 2, pp. 306–70.

STAVERT, G. S., and WINGATE, T. H. (1966), 'Nelson's Navy needed none but . . .', *Tutor Age*, pp. 17–27.

STOLZ, C. J. S. (1970), *An investigation into the validity of various taxonomies of learning processes*, Unpublished M.Sc. Thesis. East Anglia University.

STONES, E. (1969), 'Students' attitudes to the size of teaching groups', *Educational Review*, vol. 21, pp. 98–108.

STUDENTS SOCIETY COMMITTEE OF ROYAL DENTAL HOSPITAL SCHOOL OF DENTAL SURGERY (1966), 'Report on opinion poll on the lecture "courses" ', supplement to *Extract*, vol. 33, part 1.

SWANN REPORT (1968), *The Flow into Employment of Scientists, Engineers and Technologists*, Committee on Manpower Resources for Science and Technology, Cmnd 3760, H M S O.

TANSEY, P. J. (1970), 'Simulation techniques in the training of teachers', *Simulation and Games*, vol. 1, pp. 281–303.

TAYLOR, J. L. (1971), *Instructional Planning Systems. A Gaming Simulation Approach to Urban Problems*, Cambridge University Press.

TAYLOR, J. L., and CARTER, K. R. (1969), *A Decade of Instructional Simulation Research in Urban Regional Studies*, Paper prepared for symposium on Instructional Simulation Systems in Higher Education, University of Birmingham.

TEATHER, D. C. B. (1968), 'Programmed learning in biology', *Journal of Biological Education*, vol. 2, pp. 119–35.

TERMAN, L. M., and MERRILL, M. A. (1937), *Measuring Intelligence*, Houghton Mifflin.

TERMAN, L. M., and ODEN, M. H. (1947), *The Gifted Child Grows Up*, Stanford University Press.

THODAY, D. (1957), 'How undergraduates work', *Universities Quarterly*, vol. 11, pp. 172–81.

THOMAS, W. I. (1937), *Primitive Behavior: An Introduction to the Social Sciences*, McGraw-Hill.

THURSTONE, L. L. (1944), *A Factorial Study of Perception*, University of Chicago Press.

TOLMAN, E. C. (1951), 'A psychological model', in T. Parsonss and E. A. Shils (eds.), *Toward a General Theory of Action*, Harvard University Press.

TREDGOLD, R. F., and SODDY, K. (1956), *A Textbook of Mental Deficiency*, 9th edn, Williams & Wilkins.

TRENAMAN, J. M. (1967), *Communication and Comprehension*, Longman.

TUBBS, M. R. (1968), 'Seminars in experimental physics', *Physics Education*, vol. 3, pp. 189–92.

UNIVERSITY GRANTS COMMITTEE (1964), *Report of the Committee on University Teaching Methods (Hale Report)*, H M S O.

UNIVERSITY GRANTS COMMITTEE (1965), *Report of the Committee on Audio-Visual Aids in Higher Scientific Education*, Dept Education and Science, Scottish Education Dept, HMSO.

UNIVERSITY TEACHING METHODS RESEARCH UNIT (1968), *Innovations and Experiments in University Teaching Methods*, report of the third conference organized by the Unit, Dept Higher Education, University of London Institute of Education, April.

UNIVERSITY TEACHING METHODS RESEARCH UNIT (1969), *Conference on Objectives in Higher Education*, report of the fourth conference organized by the Unit, Dept Higher Education, University of London Institute of Education, January.

UREN, O. (1968), 'The use of texts in language skill development – some problems', in *Innovations and Experiments in University Teaching Methods*, University Teaching Methods Research Unit, Dept Higher Education, University of London Institute of Education, pp. 50–55.

VAN DER WILL, W. (1968). 'The language laboratory in advanced language teaching: gimmick or challenge', in *Innovations and Experiments in University Teaching Methods*, University Teaching Methods Research Unit, Dept Higher Education, University of London Institute of Education, pp. 57–62.

VENESS, T. (1968), 'Developments in social psychology', *Penguin Social Science Survey*.

VERNON, M. D. (1962), *The Psychology of Perception*, Penguin.

VERNON, P. E. (1960), *Intelligence and Attainment Tests*, University of London Press.

WAKEFORD, J. (1968a), *The Teaching Methods and Techniques in Sociology*, paper read at British Sociological Association Teachers' Section Conference, Bedford College, January 1968.

WAKEFORD, J. (1968b), *The Strategy of Social Inquiry*, Macmillan.

242 References

WALLIS, D., DUNCAN, K. D., and KNIGHT, M. A. G. (1966), 'The Halton Experiment' and 'The Melksham Experiment' in *Programmed Instruction in the British Armed Forces*, H M S O.

WALTON, H., and DREWERY, J. (1964), 'Teaching psychiatry to undergraduate medical students', *Journal of Medical Education*, vol. 29, pp. 545–52.

WALTON, H., and DREWERY, J. (1967), 'The objective examination in the evaluation of medical students', *British Journal of Medical Education*, vol. 1, p. 225.

WATSON, J. B. (1914), *Psychology from the Standpoint of a Behaviorist*, Lippincott.

WERTHEIMER, M. (1912), *Productive Thinking*, Tavistock, 1961.

WHITELAND, J. W. R. (1966), 'The selection of research students', *Universities Quarterly*, vol. 21, pp. 44–7.

WILLIAM, P. (1967), 'The Northampton Study Composition Scale', in 'Examinations in higher education', *Universities Quarterly*, June.

WILLS, E. D. (ed.) (1969), *Practical Biochemistry in the Medical Course*, Federation of European Biochemical Societies.

WILSON, G. M., LEVER, R. McG., HARDEN, R., ROBERTSON, J. I. S., and MacRITCHIE, J. (1969), 'Examinations of clinical examinations', *Lancet*, vol. 1, pp. 37–40.

WITKIN, H. A., LEWIS, H. B., HERTSMAN, M., MACHOVER, K., MEISSVER, P. B., and WAPNER, S. (1954), *Personality through Perception*, Harper & Row.

WOOD, C. C., and HEDLEY, R. L. (1968), 'Student reaction to VTR in simulated classroom conditions', *Canadian Educational Research Digest*, vol. 8, pp. 46–59.

WOODING, E. R. (1968), 'Third year laboratory projects in physics', in *Innovations and Experiments in University Teaching Methods*, University Teaching Methods Research Unit, Dept Higher Education, University of London Institute of Education, pp. 75–7.

WOODING, E. R., and WILLIAMS, E. R. (1967), 'Planning a lecture course with the aid of network analysis', *Physics Education*, vol. 2, pp. 202–6.

WOODING, E. R., and WILLIAMS, E. R. (1968), 'The post-graduate education of physicists', *Physics Education*, vol. 3, pp. 152–6.

WOODWORTH, R. S. (1922), *Psychology*, 1st edn, Methuen.

WRIGHT, E. (1968), 'A research project for clinical medical students', in *Innovations and Experiments in University Teaching Methods*, University Teaching Methods Research Unit, Dept Higher Education, University of London Institute of Education, pp. 70–73.

WRIGHT, P. (1967), 'The use of questions in programmed learning', *Programmed Learning and Educational Technology*, vol. 4, pp. 103–7.

WRIGHT, P. (1968), 'Reading to learn', *Chemistry in Britain*, vol. 4, pp. 445–50.

Index

Adults Learning
Jennifer Rogers

There are more adults receiving part-time education than there are
people inside our school system. Every September millions enrol
for WEA or local education authority evening classes in subjects like
computer programming, languages or pottery. An increasing
number of industries run training courses for their employees, and
send their apprentices on day-release courses.

Yet there has been pitifully little research into the way that adults
actually learn; it is often assumed that the voluntary element in adult
learning makes the process effortless, and usually successful. *Adults
Learning* is the first book specially written for teachers of adults that
looks at the problems actually met by those who decide to continue
their education part time. It begins with a profile of adult students:
who they are, why they enrol for classes, how they react to different
styles of teaching. The second half is concerned with the practicalities
of adult classes, and with the relative merits of techniques like
discussion, simulation and project work. An appendix offers a
comprehensive account of the various outside agencies from which
the adult teacher can obtain help.

Adults Learning has been specifically written for the non-specialist,
and contains a large number of first-hand accounts by both teachers
and students of their experiences, the implications of which go
beyond the formal limit of the adult-education world. The book will
prove invaluable not only to adult-education teachers – many of
whom have had no professional training – but also to anyone who is
planning to enrol for a class, or who is simply interested in the
process of learning.

Patterns and Policies in Higher Education
George Brosan, Charles Carter, Richard Layard,
Peter Venables, Gareth Williams

The 1970s will be a decade of exceptional challenge and opportunity
in higher education. As talents that previously lay idle or wasted
knock at the doors of colleges and universities in unprecedented
numbers, the imagination and variety of courses, and the standards
and flexibility of institutes that offer them, will be tested to the full.
Decisions must be made now on how to provide an education that
can be judged – whatever its academic or vocational flavour – by its
contribution to the quality of the civilization we inherit and help
to shape, at a cost that allows the job to be properly done.

Many voices will contribute to the debate on choice and decision, but
few with the authority and realism that the authors of this book offer.
From different viewpoints they give alternative appreciations that
both clarify the wide range of issues involved, and face the reader
with the questions that, at a turning-point in the evolution of a
democratic society (for the opening up of education beyond school
is nothing less), every teacher, parent and student must confront
and resolve for himself.

George Brosan is Director of the North-East London Polytechnic, and
was formerly Principal of Enfield College of Technology
Charles Carter is Vice-Chancellor of the University of Lancaster
Richard Layard is Lecturer in Economics and Deputy Director of
the Higher Education Research Unit at the London School of
Economics
Sir Peter Venables was formerly Vice-Chancellor of the University
of Aston
Gareth Williams is Associate Director of the Higher Education
Research Unit at the London School of Economics